Frank Boyden Prints & Books

Frank Boyden Prints & Books

Prudence F. Roberts

Ian H. Boyden

Hallie Ford Museum of Art
Willamette University

Distributed by
University of Washington Press
Seattle and London

This book was published in connection with the exhibition *Frank Boyden: Prints and Books,* arranged by the Hallie Ford Museum of Art at Willamette University. The dates for the exhibition were June 10–August 5, 2006.

All works are from the collection of the Hallie Ford Museum of Art, Willamette University, Salem, Oregon, gift of Frank and Jane Boyden in honor of Maribeth Collins unless otherwise noted.

Designed by Phil Kovacevich

Copyedited by Laura Iwasaki

Printed and bound in China

Front cover and PLATE 110: *Phoenix for Gordon* (detail), 2001, ed. 60, drypoint, sugarlift, 14¾ x 10¾ in.

Back cover and PLATE 131: *Black Arc,* 2003, ed. 12; 4 artist's proofs, sugarlift, spitbite, 7½ x 17⅞ in.

Frontpiece and PLATE 118: *Crowning* (detail), 2002, ed. 10, line etching, spitbite, sugarlift; 2 plates, 4⅝ x 21 in.

Page 28 and PLATE 98: *Grass Dance* (detail), 2001, ed. 15, drypoint, spitbite, line etching, 4½ x 21½ in.

Photography by Anne Rybak except as noted. Pages 16, 19, 20, 22, 23, 24, 26, 63, 69, 72, 73, 92, 124, 125, 134, 135, 137, Ian Boyden; page 11, Colorado Springs Fine Arts Center; page 13, The J. Paul Getty Museum; pages 7, 8 (lower right), Dale Peterson; page 4, Jim Piper; page 8 (upper left), Portland Art Museum; pages 140, 145, 146, 152, William Stickney.

Library of Congress Control Number 2005938036
ISBN 1930957556

Distributed by
University of Washington Press
P.O. Box 50096
Seattle, Washington 98145-5096

Table of Contents

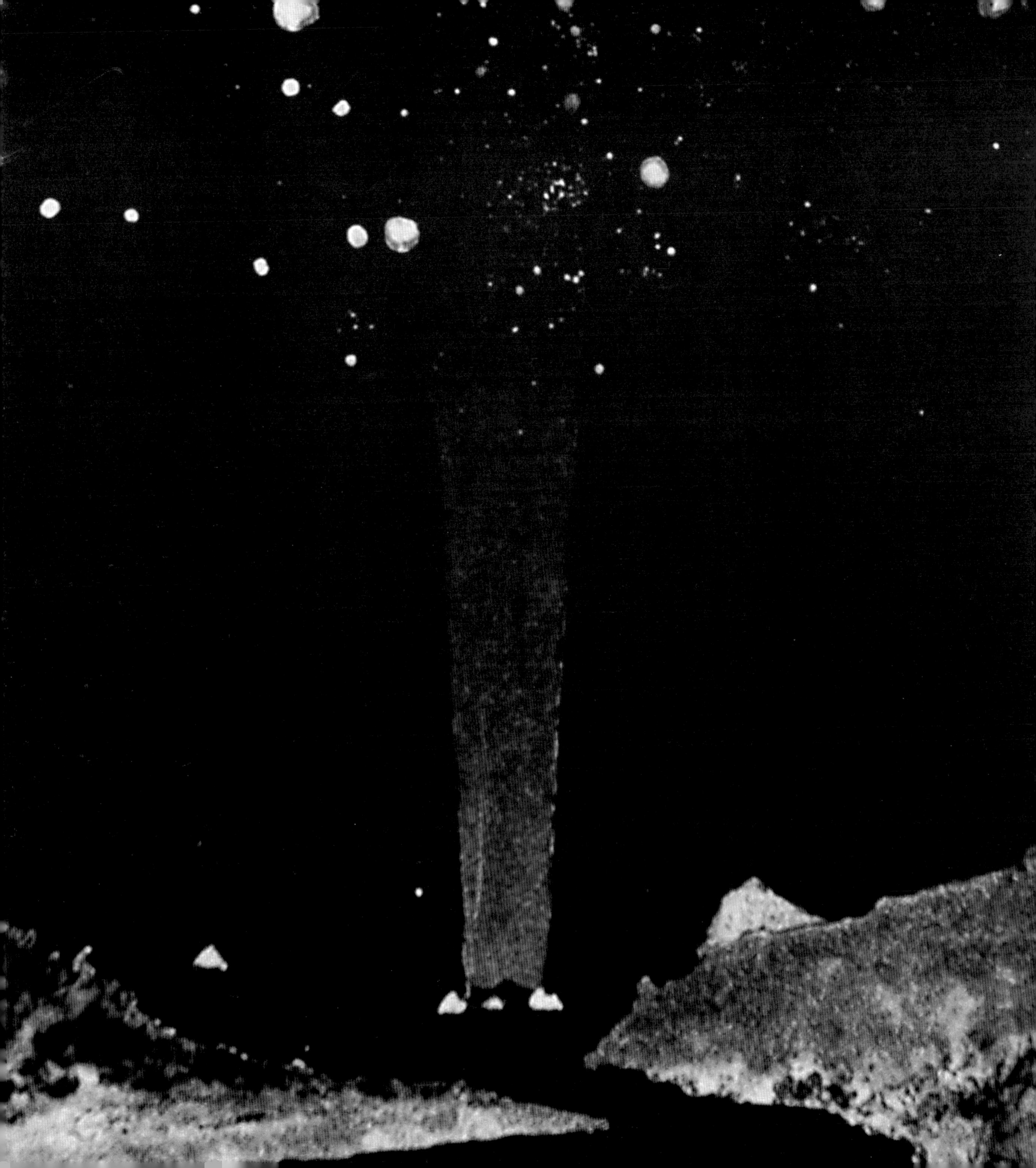

Preface

IN THE SUMMER OF 1998, I was invited to Frank Boyden's home near Otis, Oregon, to discuss a donation he wanted to make. Frank and Jane Boyden have created a wonderful home and studio, nestled in the hills below Cascade Head, with panoramic views of the coastal headland and the spectacular Pacific Ocean. They've lived in this location for more than thirty years, after returning to Oregon from New Mexico in 1971 to establish the nearby Sitka Center for Art and Ecology, a place that celebrates art, music, education, natural history, and creativity through classes, residencies, performances, and exhibitions.

Over lunch on that warm July day in 1998, Frank told me that he wanted to make a donation of prints to the Hallie Ford Museum of Art in honor of Maribeth Collins, a Portland philanthropist. In the early 1970s, Maribeth supported the Sitka Center for Art and Ecology through the Collins Foundation in Portland and has been an ardent supporter and champion ever since. Frank and I selected a range of work that he felt would provide a good survey of his prints over a ten- to fifteen-year period.

Gifts of the Sky #3 (detail)
1999
Ed. 15
Aquatint, drypoint, spitbite
6¾ x 4½ in.

Frank and I kept in contact, and in 2002, he invited me back to select a second batch of prints. As before, he wanted to honor Maribeth Collins with a donation of work. It was during this second visit that I approached him about the possibility of a major retrospective exhibition of his prints. While Frank was recognized throughout the United States as a ceramic artist and sculptor, his work as a printmaker and book artist was largely unknown.

Frank quickly embraced the idea of a retrospective exhibition of his prints and books, and we have been working on this project off and on for the past four years. Indeed, a project of this scope and magnitude does not happen overnight and would not have been possible without the help and support of a number of talented and gifted individuals.

I would like to express my sincere thanks and appreciation to Frank and Jane Boyden for their countless art donations over the past eight years. Thanks to their generosity and support, the Hallie Ford Museum of Art has one of the largest collections of Frank Boyden prints in the United States. They have been ardent supporters of the exhibition and publication from the get-go, and I am extremely grateful to them for their time, energy, enthusiasm, and help.

I am further indebted to Prudence Roberts, an independent art curator and faculty member at Portland Community College, who has written a thoughtful and insightful essay about the artist and his work, attempting to place Frank's graphic works within the broader context of modern and regional art. In addition, I want to thank Ian Boyden, owner of Crab Quill Press in Walla Walla, Washington, for his informative essay about his father as a book artist and collaborator. Both authors have contributed significantly to the final flavor of the book.

As always, a project of this magnitude would not have been possible without the support and help of a number of key individuals. I would like to thank graphic designer Phil Kovacevich, for his beautiful and spacious design of the book, and Laura Iwasaki for her careful proof editing of the Roberts and Boyden essays. I am further indebted to the Laura Russo Gallery and the Wyss Foundation in Portland, Oregon, and the Davidson Galleries in Seattle, Washington, for their generous contributions toward making this publication possible.

On the Hallie Ford Museum of Art staff, I would like to thank administrative assistant Carolyn Harcourt, education curator Elizabeth Garrison, exhibition designer/chief preparator Keith Lachowicz, front desk receptionists Lori Baldoni and Elizabeth Ebeling, safety officer Frank Simons, and custodian Dennis Leffler, for their help with various aspects of the project. I am indeed blessed to have such a professional and dedicated staff.

Finally, and by no means least, I would like to thank Maribeth Collins for her friendship and support over the years. A woman of grace, humility, warmth, and vision, it is because of her that the Boyden exhibition and accompanying publication have come to fruition, and it is to her that we lovingly dedicate this book.

JOHN OLBRANTZ
The Maribeth Collins Director
Hallie Ford Museum of Art,
Willamette University, Salem, Oregon

This book is lovingly dedicated to Maribeth Collins, philanthropist, visionary, friend, and patron of the arts.

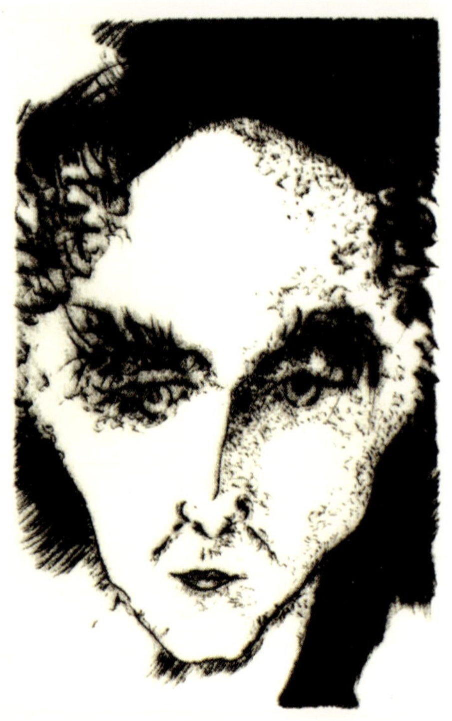

Frank Boyden: The Universal Carnival

PRUDENCE F. ROBERTS

A print is an impression on paper, an impression unique or multiplied, which requires of the image a human intermediary: the plate leaving all favorable liberty to the sensitivity of the person who prints.

From this, the diversity of proofs, which needs choice, and implies a small number, the rarity.

In former times, the connoisseur recognized the good proof.

—ODILON REDON

IN JANUARY 2005, Frank Boyden embarked on a horrific and treacherous journey: a journey that would take a year to complete and would result in a body of work unlike any he has done before. Along the way, he encountered such nightmarish anguish, cruelty, pain, and depravity that, more than once, he thought of abandoning his trip and had to set his eyes and mind elsewhere. But he persisted, adjusting his course to fit the ghastly terrain. For signposts, he consulted the images of some of the earlier travelers who had battled these wilds: Leonardo da Vinci, Rembrandt, Francisco Goya, Odilon Redon, James Ensor, and Pablo Picasso among them. And he read the coruscating prose of Cormac McCarthy, the midnight poetry of Gustave Flaubert's *Temptation of St. Anthony*, and the bleak power of Icelandic myths.

This was a journey begun in the grip of anger and disgust and concluded in humility and compassion. As such, it is a reflection of Boyden's career, which has seen its share of such opposing emotions and found its expression in paintings, sculpture, ceramics, and prints.

The ninety-six drypoint prints that Boyden carried home from his voyage make up *The Empathies*, undoubtedly the most difficult and powerful images he has ever made. The suite consists of forty-eight portraits of men and forty-eight of women. These haunted visages of misshapen, mutilated, and wounded human beings have a shocking and visceral power. In their perversions, their madness and their misery, Boyden has peeled off any remnant of veneer to show us the true tragedy of human existence. But once you begin looking at these faces, with each wart, twitch, and deformity so delicately and so tenderly rendered, repulsion fades before aesthetic appreciation, and that appreciation brings the sense of empathy to which Boyden alludes in his title. The beauty of these prints is indisputable: the nuances of tone, of depth, and of line that Boyden has coaxed from recalcitrant metal plates and nurtured through the process of inking

Empathies #45
2005
Ed. 12; 3 artist's proofs
Drypoint
3 x 2 in.
Collection of Frank and Jane Boyden, Otis, Oregon

and printing make each tiny image a tour de force of the drypoint technique. Both technically and intellectually, *The Empathies* suite moves Boyden's work into a new realm of potentialities, a place from which it is possible to look back over his twenty-plus years of printmaking and discern a connective line that traces back to its beginnings.

Boyden was born in Portland in 1942, the eldest of three boys. His parents nurtured his early talent for painting and drawing, and he encountered a few friendly and helpful teachers along the way, first in Oregon and then at The Taft School, a prep school in Watertown, Connecticut, which he attended for four years. While he is now a lover of poetry, he had trouble with writing and literature in school, although he loved anthropology, botany, anatomy and biology—anything to do with the natural world.[1] And he excelled in art classes.

Boyden came back to Portland and spent his senior year at Lincoln High School. He had a painting accepted for the Portland Art Museum's biennial that year and also became friendly with LaVerne Krause, the well-known painter, printmaker, and art teacher. Although he was still in his teens, Krause

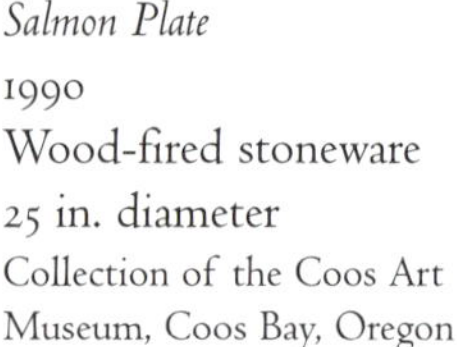

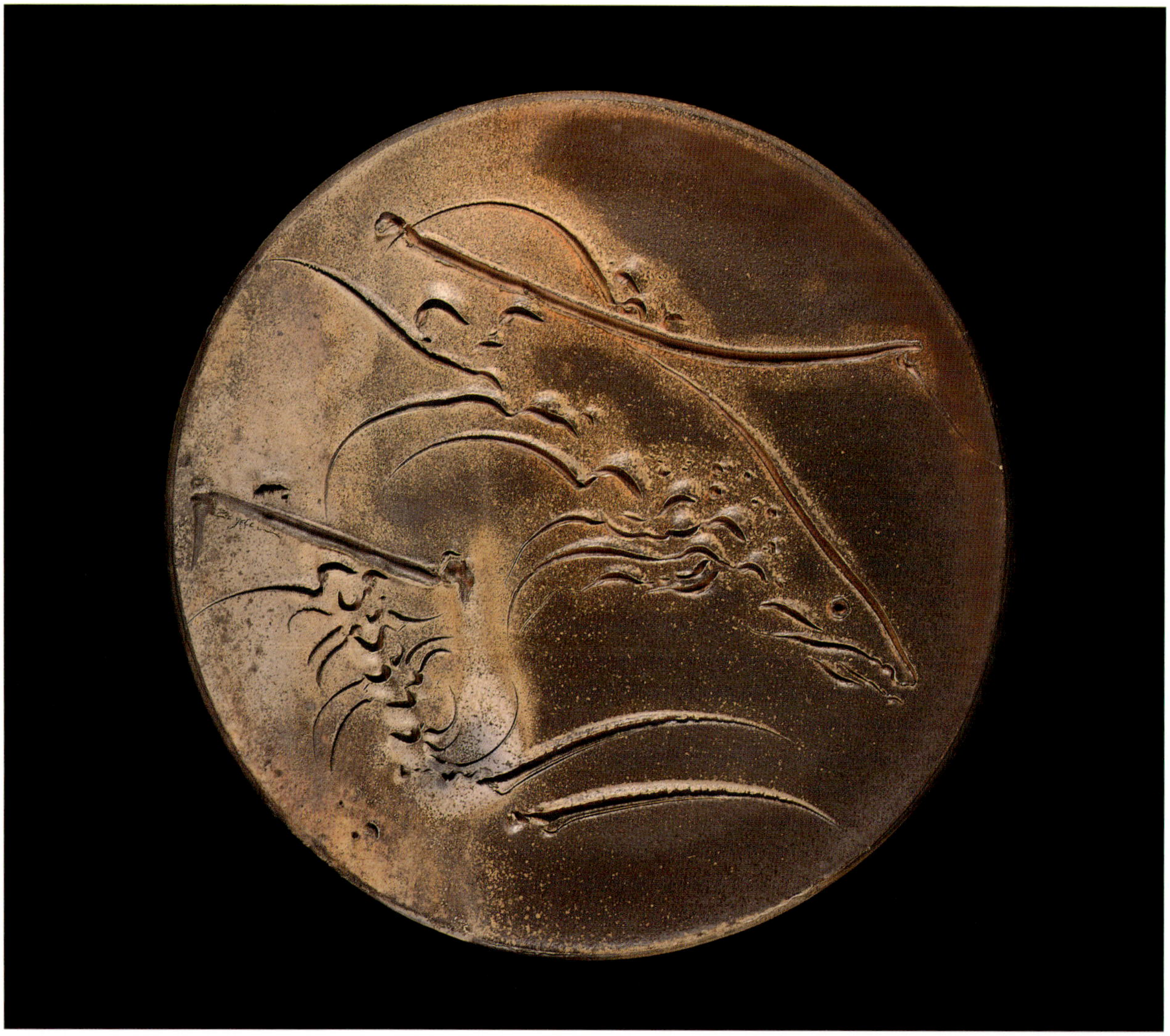

Salmon Plate
1990
Wood-fired stoneware
25 in. diameter
Collection of the Coos Art Museum, Coos Bay, Oregon

JENNY LIND
Running Horses
1989
Porcelain clay
21 in. high
Private collection

invited him to parties, where he met such Oregon luminaries as Louis Bunce and Bill Givler; she took him to Sauvie Island on painting trips and advised him on his art and education. Boyden credits her influence and also that of Carl and Hilda Morris: these were artists whose intellect and approach to materials and content he trusted.

Boyden spent four years at Colorado College, in Colorado Springs, where he took some printmaking classes and also painted. He went on to receive his MFA in 1968 from Yale University. He had intended to study printmaking with Gabor Peterdi, but finding Yale's printmaking facilities abysmal, he switched his major to painting and had classes with Buckminster Fuller and Jack Tworkov and seminars with the likes of Helen Frankenthaler, Clement Greenberg, and Robert Motherwell. The paintings he made were abstract, reflecting the art world of the times and the primacy of artists like Frankenthaler, Mark Rothko, and Morris Louis.

His Yale classmates were eager to break into the East Coast art scene, but it was clear from the start that Boyden was not cut out for city life or for the art world of the late 1960s and early 1970s, with its growing emphasis on Pop Art and the beginnings of Conceptualism. New York didn't beckon, but Oregon did. And, after a couple of years teaching at the University of New Mexico in Albuquerque, Boyden and his wife Jane, a musician, settled near Cascade Head on the Oregon coast, where they live today. It should be noted here that the two of them are responsible for bringing the Sitka Center for Art and Ecology, on Cascade Head Ranch, into existence in the early 1970s. It's a place that, with its workshops, residencies, and exhibitions, combines the Boydens' love of visual arts, music, education, natural history, and community. It is also testament to Boyden's fast-held belief that art can serve "as a baffle, as a foil against the present."

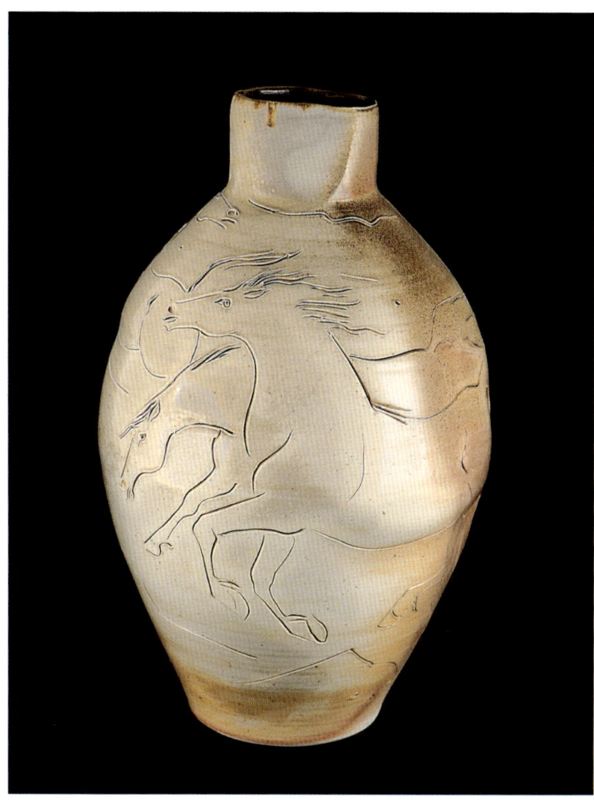

While he was teaching at the University of New Mexico, Boyden encountered Jenny Lind, a ceramic artist, who was, like him, a painter with an interest in printmaking. Boyden was unfamiliar with clay but was fascinated by Lind's approaches to a vessel. From her, he learned that he could make drawings in the round by incising lines on the bodies of pots, bowls, and plates: "It was a revelation to him that he could have the best of all worlds in this way: a plastic medium, a three-dimensional line, and unknown elements of texture, of burr, and the play of light providing a quality one cannot get from a straight ink or pencil line on paper."[2] It was precisely these qualities of texture, burr, and light that he would later seek in prints of ever-greater complexity and depth.

Once back in Oregon, Boyden gradually stopped painting and began to focus on learning more about clay. Over the course of the next fifteen years, he established his reputation as one of the finest and most innovative ceramic artists in the country. He is known in the art world not only for the virtuosity of his incised drawings but also for the beauty of his porcelain vessel forms and of his glazing effects, many of which are achieved through anagama wood-firing (he and fellow ceramist Tom Coleman built one of the first anagama kilns in this country in 1984.) Of the challenges and risks of Boyden's technique, Jack Troy has written,

> Very few artists with his drawing skills would risk firing their work in anagama kilns, because the power of fire can so easily bully that of the stylus, yet time and again he has shown us the adroitness of a runner at the beach, determined to keep one foot on dry sand and the other in the water—it's that difficult to merge drawing on clay with the method of firing he has chosen.[3]

On his plates, cups, bowls, and vases, Boyden inscribed the world he lived in: a world dominated by sea and sky, by the seasonal migrations of birds and fish, and by the teeming life nurtured by the rich moistness of the coast range. The unavoidable presence of nature in his imagery links him to the history of other artists of the Northwest, artists for whom the beauty and diversity of the natural world was unavoidable. One thinks here of the paintings of Louis Bunce, with their emphasis on Oregon landforms, of LaVerne Krause's luscious landscapes, of Charles Heaney's desert paintings and prints of fossils and sea forms. But Boyden himself points to the influence of Carl and Hilda Morris. In their command of processes and materials as much as in their imagery, and in their belief in the unquestionable importance of art as an endeavor, they made a deep impression on Boyden as a young man. In explaining his abstract paintings, Carl Morris alluded to their origins in the unique and young geology of Oregon's mountains and coastline. Like them, Boyden found it impossible not to be seduced by the beauty of a place he had known all his life. He was also drawn to its imperiled wildness and the ongoing fight for survival among any species. The inevitability of death is never far from the surface in Boyden's psyche and his art.

As his mastery of the vessel form progressed, Boyden became drawn to the idea of exploring the tension between interior and exterior spaces: one frequently intrudes on the other. Bird beaks, snouts, and feathers may break through the skin of his pots, and gashes and tears add to the plastic dynamics of form. Boyden has likened the vessel to a surrogate skull, in which the ideas and images roiling inside occasionally erupt in a meeting of conscious and subconscious states of mind.

By the early 1980s, Boyden was struggling to make enough ceramic pieces to meet the growing demand for his work in galleries and museums around the country.[4] Financially, he was on solid ground. But his restless intellect was not satisfied, and he worried that his commercial success might stifle his creativity: that he would give in to the temptation of repeating himself, and of taking an easy way out. It was at this point that his latent interest in printmaking reawakened. In 1984, he began working with Myrna Burks and Vicki Vanderslice at Northlight Editions in Portland.

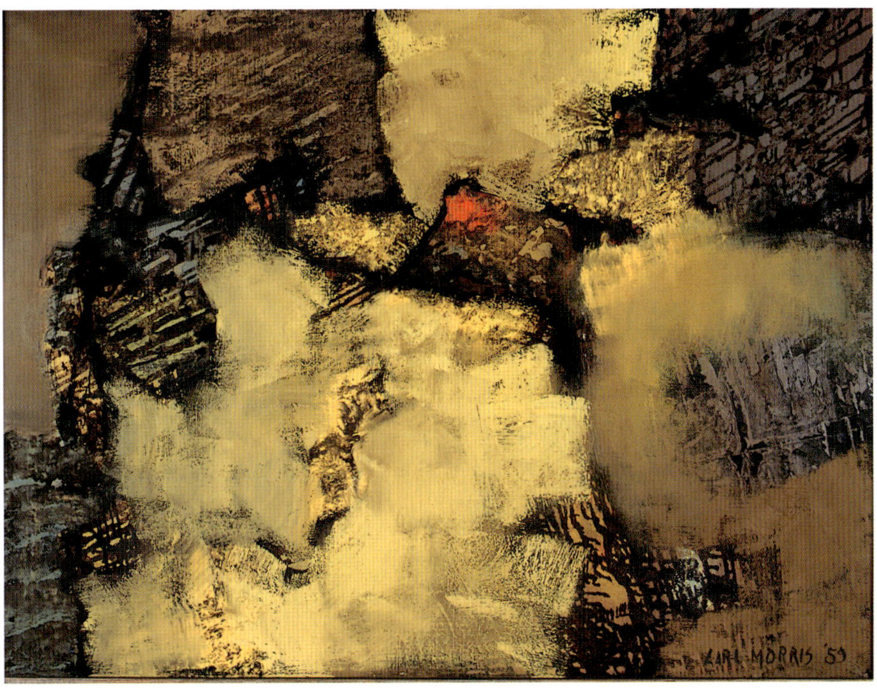

CARL MORRIS
Yellow Abyss
1959
Oil on canvas
41½ x 53¼ in.
Collection of the Hallie Ford Museum of Art, Willamette University, Salem, Oregon. Gift of Elizabeth Hoffman Dasch.

Burks and Vanderslice started Boyden's print education by introducing him to the lithographic process, which he found similar to the ink washes he had used over the years. *Changes 10* (1984–85; PLATE II) is the last image in an early two-color lithographic suite he made at North Light. As he has noted, his work in ceramics started him thinking about the implicit narrative to be found in a series of pots or plates, in which, despite slight differences in shape and imagery, each work is thematically related. He carried over his penchant for this subtle form of storytelling to the print medium. In its imagery, *Changes 10* and the other works in this suite are directly related to his ceramics: fish, birds, and bones allude to the processes of life and transformation through death and decay. Boyden's springy line animates the figures, and the richness of his restrained palette of blacks, grays, and whites adds a note of somber elegance to these simple compositions.

As Boyden immersed himself in making prints, he also began to study the history of the form, exploring the techniques, style, and imagery of other artists. In the mid-1980s, he also began to put together his own, still growing collection of prints. Given his love of the figure, it is not surprising that he is less interested in contemporary printmaking, with its penchant for abstraction and large-scale stand-alone pieces. Instead, he gravitates to the more intimate work of fifteenth-, eighteenth-, and nineteenth-century masters. He notes that in prints, more than in paintings, one comes closest to understanding the genius of these artists by looking at their extraordinary draftsmanship. While he frequently pays homage to Rembrandt, Boyden's own darker musings are closer in spirit and mood to the suites of Goya, whose *Los Caprichos* (published in 1799) chronicled the superstitions, vanity, and folly of Spanish culture of the late eighteenth century. The graphic works of artists associated with Symbolism—which emphasized the subjective, the unseen, the mystical, the otherworldly, and the erotic—also fascinates him, and he is particularly drawn to the lithographs of Redon and the etchings of Ensor.

Eventually, through his own prints and his growing immersion in the history of printmaking, Boyden would move beyond his regional focus on the landscape and animals of the Oregon coast and into a larger world of images and ideas. These are narratives that were always there and could occasionally be glimpsed in his ceramics, but as an element subsidiary to the more mainstream chronicles of nature that were, until recently, his mainstay and his signature.

In 1985, Boyden began a fifteen-year association with Martha Pfanschmidt and Tom Prochaska, who would go on to found Atelier Mars, in southeast Portland. With their help, he began to learn the myriad variations of the intaglio processes that have

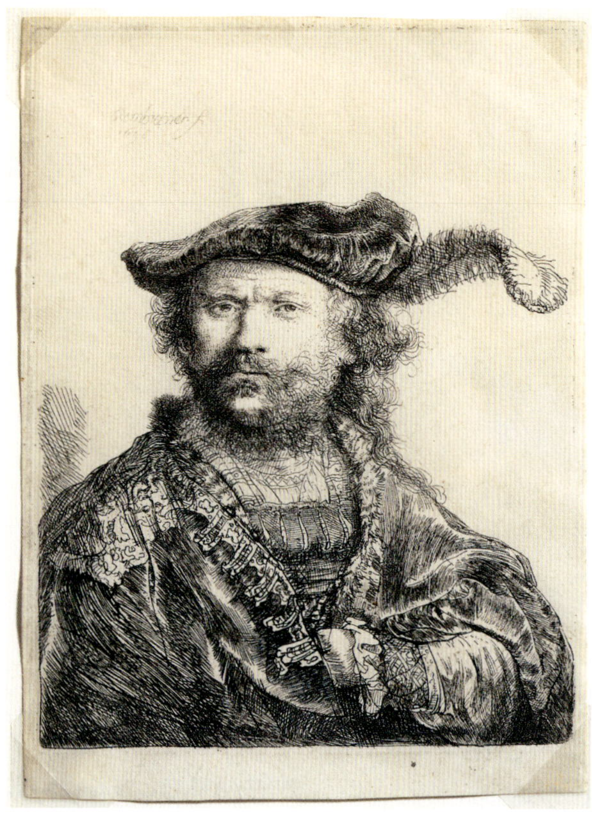

REMBRANDT VAN RIJN
Self-Portrait in a velvet cap with plume
1638
Etching
5¾ x 4 5/16 in.
Collection of the Portland Art Museum, Portland, Oregon. Gift of Ernest Swigert.

since become his primary focus. *Death Forming a Hummingbird Dream* (1986–87; PLATE 17) is an early example of his exploration of drypoint, a technique he favors because of its subtleties and velvety qualities of line: line that, as he puts it, "holds light." In its directness and simplicity as well as in its subject matter, this work still retains close ties to the incised drawings on his ceramics.

By 1994–95, when he made the *Traces* suite (PLATES 24–33), Boyden was moving beyond the stylized transcriptions of the natural world that had been at the core of his art for nearly twenty years. In *Traces*, Boyden isolates ideas of grace, rhythm, and motion through subtle depictions of a spider, seen in ten different poses. It is interesting to compare the pieces in *Traces* with the three works in *Dance* (PLATES 90–92), made about five years later. In their scale and complexity and in their mood of darkness, *Dance* signals Boyden's growing introspection. These spiders inhabit not only the space of a studio window, perhaps, or a corner of the ceiling but also the dark reaches of the inner mind. These are potent images of an encounter building up to the violent end that follows a spider's mating, when the female cannibalizes her partner. Technically, too, *Dance* is more complex. It was printed by Julia D'Amario at Boyden's studio. D'Amario's expertise in myriad techniques has furthered Boyden's understanding of aquatint, sugarlift, spitbite, and other methods.

Boyden's growing command of these processes is highlighted in a twelve-print suite from 1996, *Interstices, A Conversation with Alders* (PLATES 34–45), in which he uses line etching, drypoint, sugarlift, and aquatint to achieve an extraordinary variety of line,

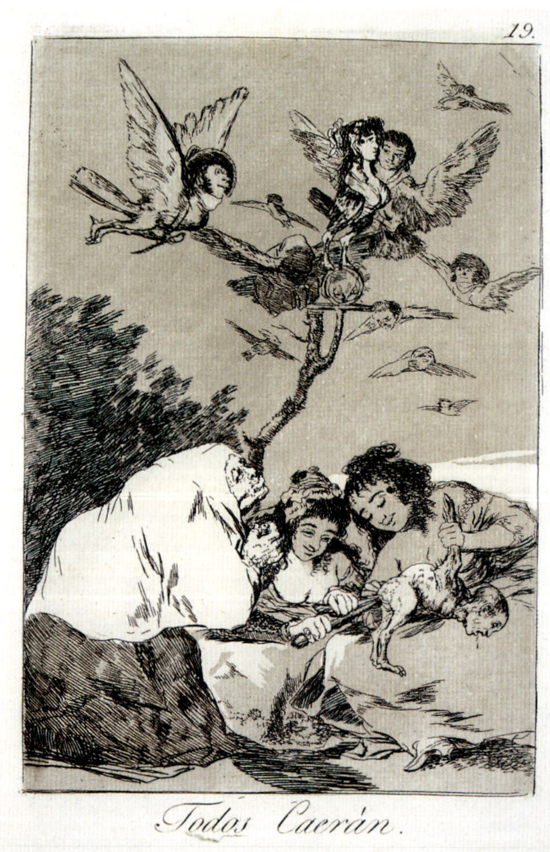

FRANCISCO GOYA
All Will Fall, from *Los Caprichos*
1799
Etching, burnished aquatint
12 7/16 x 8⅝ in.
Collection of the Hallie Ford Museum of Art, Willamette University, Salem, Oregon. Gift of Willamette University in honor of Henry and Sharon Hewitt, May 17, 2003.

volume, and mass. As the series progresses, Boyden moves from the pristine elegance of an alder's bare limbs as if seen in early morning light to the dark moodiness of a forest at night. In *Interstices 12* (PLATE 45), the Baroque masses of an old tree's gnarled form are rendered in white line, while behind the tree, undergrowth recedes into the darkness. The eloquence of these trees is reminiscent of the etchings and *cliché verre* prints of the mid-nineteenth-century painter and printmaker Jean-Baptiste-Camille Corot.

In the same year that he made the quiet images of *Interstices,* Boyden also created the raucous *Stances,* whose inspiration was not mediated by the history of printmaking but came directly from the garbage bin at a nearby Safeway. Boyden spent several days in the Safeway parking lot, making dozens of drawings and snapshots of the crows that congregated there as they bounced to the ground, hovered over chunks of stale bread, or simply stood, observing him and his camera. With the drawings and photos as visual notes, Boyden made nine drypoint prints that could be considered a dictionary of crow vocabulary: in their direct approach, they convey Boyden's respect for the buoyancy, grace, and noisy charm of these smart and sociable scavengers.[5]

The straightforward line and ebullience of *Stances* vanish in Boyden's moody *Dead Raven* (1996–97; PLATE 54), one of a series of prints he made with Julia D'Amario at Whitman College, in Walla Walla, Washington, where his son Ian is director of the Sheehan Gallery. The work, printed by Whitman students, is a masterpiece of drypoint technique. The broad tonal range and atmospheric effects give depth to this vertical composition, in which a raven plummets from life into instant death. As with *Stances* and *Interstices,* the depth and quality of direct observation distinguish this work from some of Boyden's earlier, more stylized drawings.

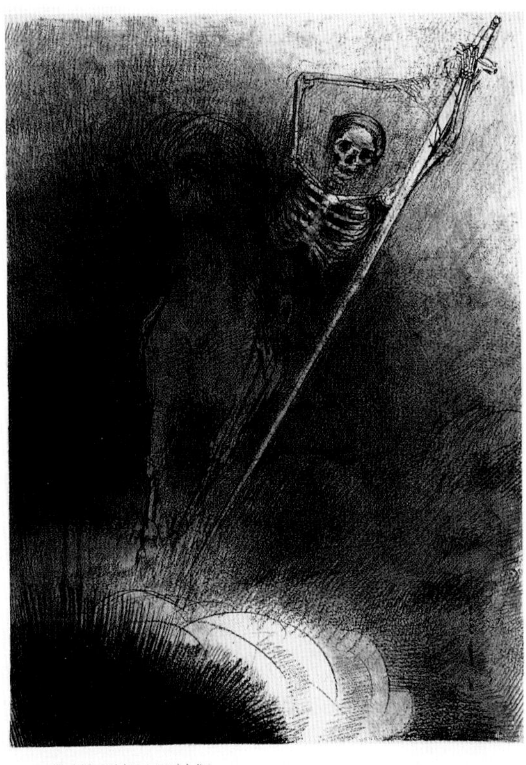

ODILON REDON
And I saw, and behold, a pale horse, and its rider's name was death, from *The Apocalypse of St. John*
1899
Lithograph
12⅛ x 8⅞ in.
Private collection

Among Boyden's pantheon of birds, owls occupy nearly as critical a position as ravens and crows. Boyden depicts them naturalistically, as in *Pajaro de Brujas* (PLATE 93), a drypoint from 1999–2000. Boyden's fishing guide in the Yucatan, where he spotted this owl, provided the title. But owls are also the fearful omens and harbingers of death that fly through the work of Goya, who associated them not with wisdom but with witchcraft and the treacheries and evildoing of darkness. Perhaps most famously, owls and bats are the creatures that hover around Goya's slumped shoulders and head in plate 43 of *Los Caprichos,* titled *The Sleep of Reason Produces Monsters.* Boyden's *Soft Owl Flying* (PLATE 79) heads straight out of Goya toward the viewer, its wings extending beyond the picture plane, silhouetted against a sky filled with sooty clouds. The work is one of a suite of *cliché verre* prints Boyden created with his son Ian, shortly after the two had collaborated for the first time on a book project, *A Carousel at Birth* (discussed in Ian Boyden's essay in this book). Boyden's *Mockery of the Black Angel and Three Spanish Owls* (2001; PLATE 94), from the *Black Angel Suite,* is similarly somber in mood. A dead raven falls from the sky, owls swoop out of the darkness, and the light is obscured by a single giant feather—fallen from the Black Angel's wing.

By the time he made *Mockery of the Black Angel and Three Spanish Owls,* Boyden had his own studio and etching press. He pulled his first prints there in 1999. The press was designed by the legendary Ray Trayle, eighty-plus years old, the retired machinist whose beautiful presses can be found in the studios of a select number of Northwest printmakers as well as in Oregon institutions such as Marylhurst University, Pacific Northwest College of Art, in Portland, and Crow's Shadow Institute of the Arts, in Pendleton.

As Boyden has noted, his knowledge of the fine subtleties of printmaking really developed after he set up his studio. Having his own press gave him the freedom to experiment with the processes he had been refining at Atelier Mars with Tom Prochaska. From printer Julia D'Amario, he learned the spitbite technique, which he uses frequently. He and artist Rick Bartow experimented with sugarlift, which he has continued to use, along with aquatint and line etching. He also has explored color and two- or three-plate processes as well as hand-coloring. And his production has soared: since 2001, he has made more than two hundred individual editions of prints. His shelves are stocked with the tools he values most, including Charbonnel inks from France, German Hahnemühle etching paper, which he favors for its rich surface and warm tones, and silk taffeta and organza for rubbing the copper plates.

While the majority of Boyden's prints rely on the strength of his line and his acute sensitivity to tonalities of blacks, grays, and whites, he has used color for its psychological and aesthetic effects rather than for any verisimilitudes to the natural world. Among his most beautiful works is a series of horizontal landscapes, in which the panorama of rock, water, and sky plays out in prints whose looseness might best be described as painterly. *Landscape with Densities* (2002; PLATE 119), rendered in deep blue-green, is as close to an abstract composition as one gets with Boyden. And yet, it is also based directly on the thing observed: on squalls of rain, brightening sky, and the boom of waves hitting the headlands. In its evocation of sound and light, this work is reminiscent of paintings such as Arthur Dove's 1929 *Fog Horns,* which captures the equivalencies between sounds and forms. In *Crowning* (2002; PLATE 118), Boyden used two plates to achieve the chromatic range of warm red-browns, blue-grays, and streaky yellows in the feathered sky and blowing grasses beneath.

These are scenes that Boyden observes daily from his studio windows, as he looks across meadows and forests toward the Pacific coast. It's a landscape he knows intimately, one that had been at the heart of nearly all his imagery—in ceramics, sculptures, and prints—since the 1970s. But by 2001, he knew that something was about to change. He was, as he puts it, "taking art away from a lot of things I'd held dear over the years. I was interested in more specific imagery."[6] There had been hints of this, even as early as the 1970s, when a human presence—a skull, a skeleton—occasionally made a startling appearance on a plate or a pot.

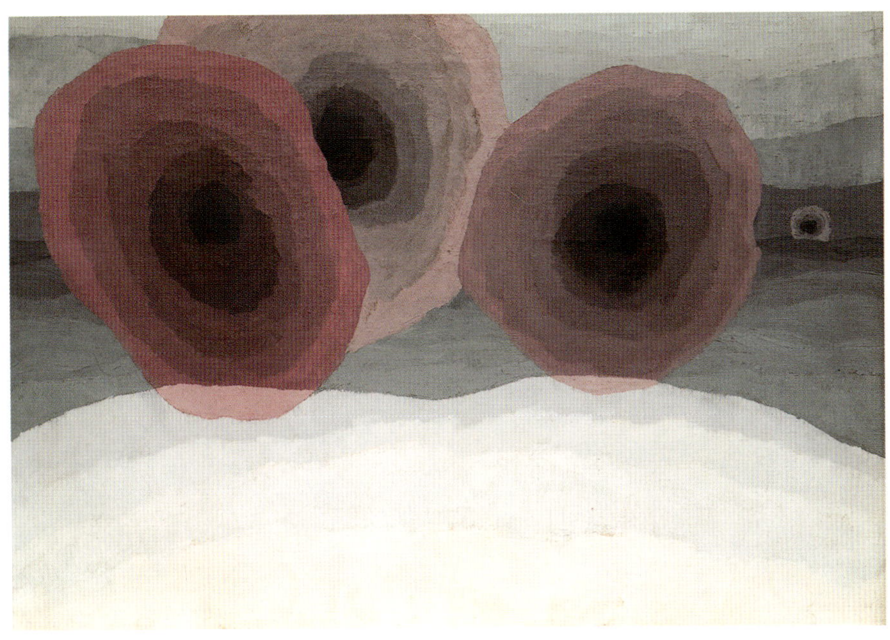

ARTHUR DOVE
Fog Horns
1929
Oil on canvas
18 x 26 in.
Collection of the Colorado Springs Fine Arts Center, Colorado Springs, Colorado

Phoenix Suite (2001; PLATES 105–109) is one of Boyden's most elegiac bodies of work and in many ways represents the start of his movement away from his earlier naturalism. Like the landscapes he would make in 2002, these two-color etchings are awash in vibrant hues. The brilliant red-oranges of fire and the blackest black of ashes and destruction are seen in *Burning Nest* (PLATE 106), in which flames surround the tragic figure of the mythical bird, the harbinger of new beginnings rising from the ashes of the old. *Last Flight* (PLATE 105) shows the still charred and bloodied bird awkwardly splayed against a tender pink dawn sky.[7]

By 2001, Boyden was also looking ever more closely at Redon's lithographs, in particular at his illustrations for Flaubert's *The Temptation of St. Anthony* (the forty-two lithographs in this series were published in three albums between 1888 and 1896).[8] Flaubert's trancelike prose along with the despair and horror of Redon's brooding prints of black angels, monsters, disembodied eyes, serpentine smoke, and bleak desert landforms resonated with Boyden's thoughts about the cruel contradictions of the human condition: "blind animals, disabilities, disastrous acts, tragedy."[9]

While his earlier *Black Angel Suite* alludes in many ways to Redon, Boyden really began to let his own demons emerge in *Lenses Suite* of 2002 (PLATES 121–129). In these prints, the skull functions as a lens in that it focuses attention on the thoughts and images projected on its surface or viewed inside its orifices. The references are as varied as a portrait of a wild-haired Rembrandt emblazoned on the skull's crown or a wide-eyed and malevolently whiskered small animal nesting inside an eye socket above a leering lipless grin. The latter image, in *Lens with Black Idea* (PLATE 127), is the seventh image of the suite. Owls and herons can also be found, along with such grotesque appendages as spines and tufts of hair. Clearly, these prints—which use a combination of spitbite, line etching, drypoint, aquatint, and sugarlift—are, in total, a self-portrait of the artist, an aperture through which a viewer may see his anger, his joys, and his gravest doubts.

If the *Lenses Suite* gives one a glimpse of Boyden's inner demons, he bares all in *The Irreverences, Provocations, & Connivances of Uncle Skulky* (2003; PLATES 134–143). This is Boyden's *Caprichos,* and Uncle Skulky is his irrepressible alter ego: a skeleton consumed by vanity, lechery, misgivings, and delusions—all the infinite vices and failings chronicled by Goya. *Uncle Skulky examines some fluff* (PLATE 138), the first image that appeared to Boyden, is the seventh in the suite. Skulky, with his constant bird attribute perched on his head and skin molting from his neck, holds before him the aforementioned fluff: "a metaphor for the amount of drivel we are asked to constantly and seriously examine," as Boyden writes.[10]

Uncle Skulky's appearance rattled more than a few cages and certainly took many of Boyden's longtime admirers by surprise, as it seemed an aberration and a somewhat violent departure from the vocabulary of imagery drawn from the natural world with which he had been associated. When the works were exhibited for the first time at Laura Russo Gallery, in Portland, in February 2004, Boyden's deliberately florid titles and his comments appeared in label form beside each print, not usual gallery practice. The labels were his way of easing people into the complexity of the compositions, with their layers of art-historical and personal references and their relationship to contemporary events: a post-9/11 world, the start of the war in Iraq, and the growth of conservatism. Boyden speculates that Uncle Skulky's emergence may have been hastened by "a period of what I consider to be the greatest debauchery and selfishness of American government in my lifetime."[11] Although Boyden has never considered himself a political artist, Uncle Skulky is permitted to indulge in a trumpet-blowing "convulsion of patriotism" and to become the fifty-sixth in the deck of fifty-five cards, issued after the invasion of Iraq, bearing images of the United States'most-wanted members of Saddam Hussein's regime.

But, more than anything, and in spite of the mordant wit of these frequently ribald images, the majority of the drypoints and etchings in the Uncle Skulky suite convey Boyden's deepening understanding and appreciation of the history of printmaking as well as his expanding vocabulary of techniques. Many of the prints are indebted to the imagery not only of Leonardo, Rembrandt, and Redon but also of James Ensor, the late-nineteenth-century Belgian artist whose paintings and prints are populated with jousting skeletons, masked figures, and grotesque satires of rectitude and religiosity. Like Boyden, Ensor was impatient with pomposity, and, like Boyden, he was acutely aware of life's brevity and folly. In writing of Ensor's art, Paul Haesaerts might well be describing Boyden's: "The idea of death consummating the absurdity of life is always present in Ensor. It is rarely macabre; it merely climaxes the strangeness of the universal carnival."[12]

In *Uncle Skulky appears to James Ensor and mocks him with a fake nose* (PLATE 137), Boyden builds on one of Ensor's satirical self-portraits. In his etching, Ensor transformed himself into a skeleton and replaced the face of a woman peering at him through a window with a skull. In Boyden's work, Uncle Skulky is the skull, leering at Ensor. Uncle Skulky's fake nose may refer to Ensor's own, prominent nose and to the masks that are such an important part of his iconography.[13]

Boyden's growing sense of self-examination and his movement away from the images and ideas that had been his mainstay for so many years are illustrated in the hilarious *The pompous, arrogant, copycat Uncle Skulky sells out another exhibition* (PLATE 140). As the title suggests, Boyden throws his art open to parody by depicting a gallery filled with crudely rendered caricatures of his own production—bronze sculpture, ceramic pieces, and prints. Skulky himself exults pridefully over the sea of red "sold" dots.

Two works in the Uncle Skulky series really presage the difficult explorations that lay ahead for Boyden with *The Empathies* (2005; PLATES 147–150). They are *The Possession of Uncle Skulky* (PLATE 135) and *The resplendent Uncle Skulky leers from behind his curtain of stars as his dolled-up and pompous detractors, like fetid bits of odium, gather to mock him* (PLATE 141). Both images deal with the presence of demons and of horrors that come, unbidden, to

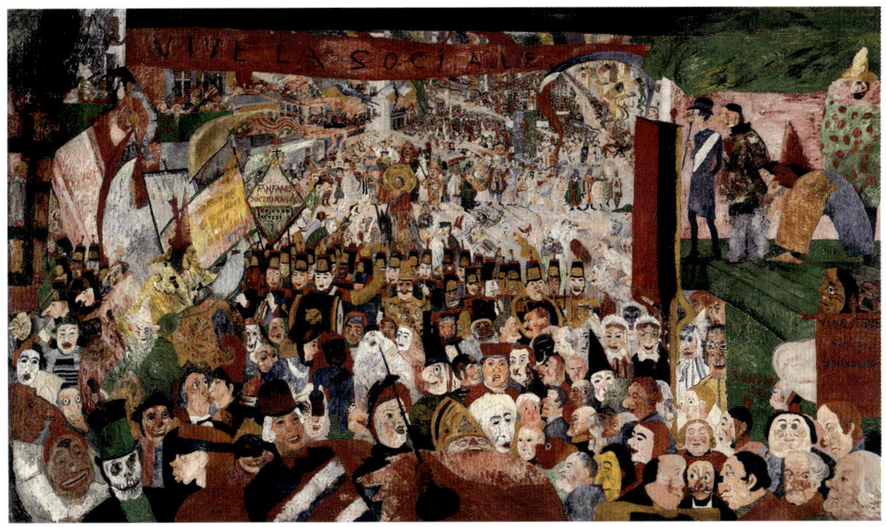

JAMES ENSOR
Christ's Entry into Brussels in 1889
1888
Oil on canvas
99½ x 169½ in.
Collection of The J. Paul Getty Museum, Los Angeles, California

haunt the mind. As Boyden explains, the dreadful chimeras and bestial creatures that inhabit Uncle Skulky's head in *The Possession* are loosely derived from Leonardo da Vinci's "drawings of grotesques, the most unfortunate and hideous-looking people."[14] Grotesques also surround Uncle Skulky in *The resplendent Uncle Skulky*. The beautiful hand-coloring, rendered in tender hues of lavender, mauve, pink, and green watercolor and colored pencil, is at odds with the hideousness of its inhabitants: an audience of vile human creatures who spew forth their venom at Uncle Skulky, floating imperviously amidst them in a red cocoon spangled with gold stars.

Who are these creatures and how did Boyden come to be possessed by them? In answer, Boyden might respond by referring the questioner to the images of grotesque, hideous, pathetic, and death-ridden visages that appear throughout the history of art, sometimes with comic, often with tragic, overtones. He might also cite literary sources, such as Cormac McCarthy, an author whose books have become a touchstone for him as he has read and reread them for the last twenty years. In particular, Boyden has been affected by *Blood Meridian,* a novel set in the American West of the early nineteenth century. In rich and elaborate prose, McCarthy writes of a physical and emotional frontier: a place of unspeakable brutality. The beauty and perfection of his language are the written equivalent of Leonardo's exquisite line or Redon's smoky transfigurations. Here is an excerpt from a passage recounting the attack of a Comanche war party that could serve as an initial reaction to the creatures Boyden summons forth in *The Empathies*:

> A legion of horribles, hundreds in number, half naked or clad in costumes attic or biblical or wardrobed out of a fevered dream. . .all howling in a barbarous tongue and riding down upon them like a horde from a hell more horrible yet than the brimstone land of Christian reckoning, screeching and yammering and clothed in smoke like those vaporous beings in regions beyond right knowing where the eye wanders and the lip jerks and drools.[15]

As noted earlier, arriving at *The Empathies* was exceedingly difficult for Boyden. Making these prints required him to venture further into "regions beyond right knowing." His early title for the series was *A Chronicle of God's Love,* and he found his immersion painful. In the early days of the project, he went to a piano recital:

> It turned out to be a terrifying evening, because as I looked at that horde of people surrounded by the beauty of the music, I realized I was still in my studio. Everyone was flawed, and the flaws were exaggerated by the work I was doing and the way I had set myself to see. It scared me. Work stopped and did not commence until I

> changed the title of the suite to 'A mirror of our reflections or a chronicle of God's love.' This change allowed me to think about the imagery more from a point of reverence and kindness....

Eventually, the working title became *Reflections,* as Boyden "dropped the sarcastic ugliness of a creator's misguided control."[16]

When Boyden showed friends and family the first forty-eight drypoints, they all had one major question: Why were there no women? Boyden had to do some soul-searching to come up with the answer to that query and to realize that he could not treat one gender differently from the other in his imagery. He commenced the making of his second forty-eight prints in May and finished them by the end of October. Now came the next challenge. As Boyden placed his latest work against the earlier pieces, he was astonished by their differences, by the greater complexity and emotional depth of the women, in terms both of their imagery and of his own more nuanced use of drypoint: the subtlety of his line, the richness of the tonalities, and the resolution of his imagery. The comparison made him feel that his men were more like caricatures—some of them were reminiscent of R. Crumb's bestial creatures—while his women, in their sadness and wretchedness, were more tragic than melodramatic, with no trace of the irony and occasional ribaldry with which he had begun the project. The contrasts also came because of what he had learned technically in the months since he had begun the suite. "I had made large numbers of drypoints in my life, but what I had done here was to stretch the possibilities of drypoint beyond anything I had ever done. I had learned a great deal. Etching allows very fine nuance, and attempting to have that with drypoint is extremely difficult. Much relies in degrees of subjective printing...."[17]

As he reworked the images of the men and made his final prints of the women, Boyden arrived at the epiphanies that gave him his final title:

> I slowly came to realize that what had started out seven months before as anger had metamorphosed into empathy. It is interesting to look now at all the prints and see how that is reflected. I ended the suite with a manipulation of Rembrandt's "The Jewish Bride," which I find to be an unbelievably sad image cloaked in a dark stoicism which is hardly bearable.
>
> I finally decided to title the suite *The Empathies.*[18]

The title is a measure of Boyden's journey, of his restlessness and his constant striving to move into new realms of aesthetic, intellectual, and emotional complexity. By letting go of the serenity of things familiar and comfortable, he has propelled himself into a deeper and truer engagement with the materials and ideas he loves. He illuminates the darkness of our times with beauty and compassion. ❧

Prudence Roberts is an independent art curator and faculty member at Portland Community College.

ENDNOTES

1 Boyden is a fisherman, former whitewater guide, and hiker.

2 Pamela Morris, Frank Boyden notes, April 30–May 1, 2005.

3 Jack Troy, "No ideas but in things," in *American Woodfire '91* (Iowa City: University of Iowa Museum of Art, 1991), pg. 13. Quoted in *The Soul of a Bowl* (Portland, Ore.: Contemporary Crafts Museum & Gallery, 2003).

4 Boyden estimates that he had twenty galleries across the nation and as many as five to seven one-person shows per year.

5 Boyden later translated the forms of the crows into a series of bronze sculptures.

6 Conversation with Frank Boyden, March 26, 2005.

7 Along with his suite of *Phoenix* prints, Boyden also made an individual *Phoenix for Gordon,* a tribute to Gordon Gilkey, the legendary printmaker, collector, and curator emeritus at the Portland Art Museum, who had died in November 2000.

8 Odilon Redon, the French painter and printmaker, found a wellspring of inspiration in Gustave Flaubert's *The Temptation of St. Anthony,* published in 1872, Flaubert's account of the night during which the hermit Anthony is ceaselessly tormented by devils and demons.

9 Conversation with Frank Boyden, March 26, 2005.

10 Pamela A. Morris and Frank Boyden, *The Irreverences, Provocations & Connivances of Uncle Skulky* (Portland, Ore.: Portland Art Museum, 2004), p. 32.

11 Ibid., p. 52.

12 Paul Haesaerts, *James Ensor* (New York: Harry N. Abrams, 1959), p. 167.

13 The Oostende museum in Belgium, which holds much of Ensor's work, happily accepted Boyden's gift of this print.

14 Morris and Boyden, *The Irreverences,* p. 22.

15 Cormac McCarthy, *Blood Meridian, or, The Evening Redness in the West* (New York: Vintage Books, 1992), pp. 52–53.

16 Frank Boyden, "*The Empathies*: A suite of 96 drypoints," September 9, 2005.

17 Ibid.

18 Ibid.

My deepest gratitude to Frank Boyden, first for inviting me to work on this project and then for his unfailing generosity and good humor. Thanks also to Jane and Ian Boyden. Pamela Morris provided lots of insights and shared her copious notes, and J. C. Schlecter of the Portland Art Museum's Vivian and Gordon Gilkey Center for Graphic Arts educated me on printmaking techniques. Finally, I am grateful to John Olbrantz, for his vision and commitment to the art and artists of the Northwest.

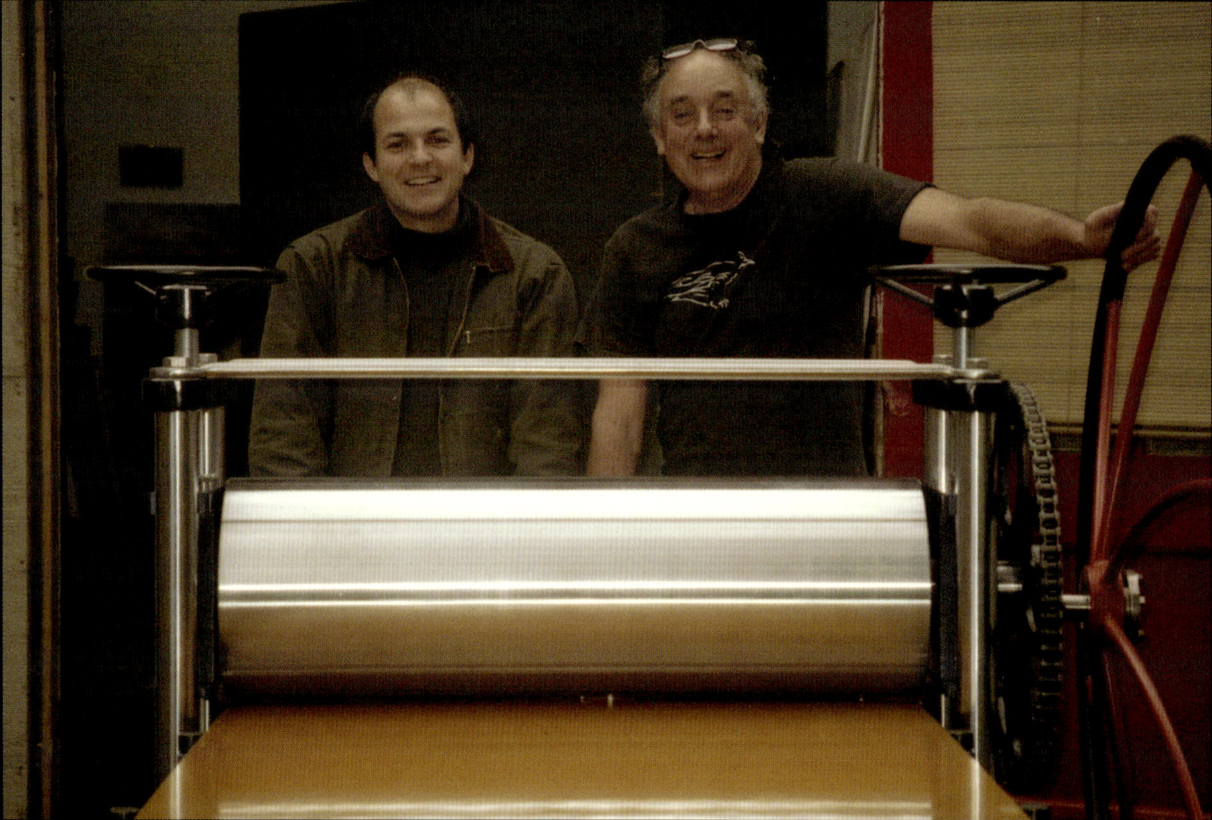

Some Observations about Frank Boyden as Collaborator and Accounts of His Book Projects at Crab Quill Press

IAN H. BOYDEN

Ian Boyden and Frank Boyden stand triumphantly by the side of a Ray Trayle etching press that they built during the spring and summer of 2003.

BEGINNINGS

There is a decisive beginning to my book collaborations with my father, Frank Boyden, the circumstances of which feel more literary to me than real. On Sunday, May 28, 1996, we were traveling by train to Wuwei, an ancient oasis town at the edge of the Gobi Desert in Gansu province, People's Republic of China. It was nighttime, and our train car, called a "hard sleeper," was pulling slowly through smoky air; the floor of the car was strewn with fruit rinds and Styrofoam noodle bowls. We had just been visited by the train's conductor, who, hearing there were foreigners on board, had come back to welcome us and regale us with amusing stories about learning English during the Cultural Revolution. As the rest of the passengers fell asleep, Frank and I sat at a small table lit by the dull glow of the running lights and talked for hours about the variety of systems the Chinese had used over the past three millennia to track time, astral cycles, and the evocative Chinese zodiac. While at the time we did not know it, our conversation that evening triggered a series of thoughts and events that significantly changed both of our lives and our artistic development; it led to our first collaborative book, *A Carousel at Birth* (1997; PLATES 68–69), published by Kathy Kuehn of Salient Seedling Press, joining my poetry and Frank's prints, which was then followed by six more book projects to date.

FRANK BOYDEN AS A COLLABORATOR

Over the past four decades, Frank has worked with a remarkable variety of materials, including ceramics, fabricated and cast metal sculpture, painting, drawing, prints, and, most recently, books. Scholarly discussions of his work tend either to be technical in nature (these being mainly about his ceramics) or to reflect on Frank as an idiosyncratic individual devoted to the estuarine ecology of the Oregon coast (these being primarily about his images of fish, birds, and coastal landscapes). An aspect of his work and personality that has been overlooked thus far is the extent to which Frank and his work in all of these media have been, and continue to be, shaped by collaboration.

In fact, collaborative projects have been a fundamental part of Frank's relationship with many of his closest friends and associates as well as members of his own family. And it can be argued that collaboration has been one of his primary vehicles not only for experimenting with new materials and learning new technologies but also for exploring and promoting the ideas and personalities of others. A narrow list includes other sculptors, potters, and printmakers; poets, writers, and composers; and a host of other artists and technicians such as woodworkers, stone carvers, calligraphers, and bookmakers. His relationships with his collaborators are filled with delight and magic and are often fraught with a sense of immediacy and consequence.

Frank sees each material as a separate language for expression. Because different materials are capable of conveying aesthetic thought in different ways, the very process of learning to work with them brings added richness and depth to his ideas. And because many of the materials he works with entail complex sets of processes and techniques, it is often necessary for him to find an individual (or team of people) to teach him how to work with the given material. In this process, Frank is drawn toward those who will not simply provide technical support or teach him the desired techniques but with whom he can collaborate creatively as well. It comes as little surprise that many of the major developments of his artistic career are the direct result of collaboration. Among the most prominent of his collaborative endeavors are the founding, with his wife, Jane Boyden, of Sitka Center for Art and Ecology (1970); the building of an anagama kiln with Tom Coleman and Katsuyuki Sakazumi (1983–85); his sculptural work with the technicians at Walla Walla Foundry (especially in the early 1990s); his large-scale public art installation at Doernbecher Children's Hospital with Brad Rude (1997–98); his experiences making prints with master printmakers Myrna Burks, Tom Prochaska, Martha Pfanschmidt, and Julia D'Amario (1984–present); and, since 1997, the making of limited-edition books at Crab Quill Press.

The word *collaboration*, meaning literally "to suffer (work) together," is commonly applied when describing prints and books that are the product of two or more persons. For good or bad, the use of this term is now so ubiquitous that it has become something of a nebulous signifier. The general fact of collaboration is less interesting than the quality of a given collaborative relationship. Frank and I have worked together across multiple disciplines, on multiple cognitive levels (including that time-honored state of suffering), and with a number of other individuals. While some aspects of these collaborations conform neatly to established practices and divisions of labor (like that of the artist and the publisher/bookmaker, or the artist and the technician), others are more unwieldy and unique to our own relationship, humor, and shared aesthetic space. These latter aspects inform much of the technological, material, and conceptual elements of each one of the books we have made together.

TECHNICAL AND MATERIAL EXPLORATIONS— ENCOUNTERS BY THE HAND AND THE EYE

Frank has taken distinct delight in exploring with me some of the technologies and materials of book production. Together we have constructed a variety of tools for making our books, including etching presses, spray booths, and ball mills; we have located and processed woods for book covers and papers to carry etchings and type; and we have experimented with a variety of wood finishes and printing inks. Our projects attend with great care to essential aesthetic and material experiences of the book—especially those of the hand and the eye.

Because of his background in clay—especially the production of hand-held drinking vessels—Frank has been unusually receptive to my own attention to the haptic and kinetic experiences of the book. Unlike large sculptures or framed prints, books are generally meant to be held in the hand, cradled in the hand, operated by the hand. How the book does this is extremely important, and I have attempted to include Frank in as many of these decisions as I can. The most conspicuous element of the book's encounter with the hand is, of course, the cover. And of all of our books, our two lacquer-covered books—*Bird Spirits* (Crab Quill Press, 2000; PLATES 52–53) and *The Irreverences, Provocations, and Connivances of Uncle Skulky* (Crab Quill Press, 2003; PLATES 144–145)—are the most successful from a collaborative standpoint.

Bird Spirits is a book that celebrates the crow through a series of nine piano compositions by American composer and pianist William Bolcom (b. 1938), written in response to a portfolio of drypoint prints by Frank titled *Stances* (1996; PLATES 46–51). In the book, the original handwritten musical scores appear alongside the original intaglio prints. The book invites multiple forms of readings and viewings: the music can be read in response to the images, the images can be understood through the medium of music, the handwriting of the original autographs can be compared with the lines of the drypoints, and

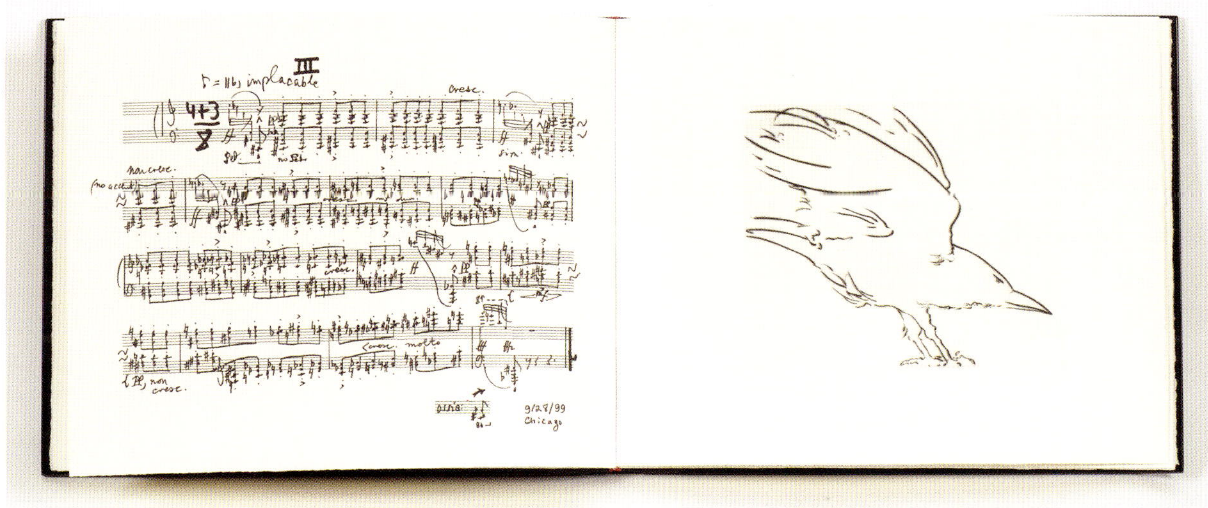

Bird Spirits: Nine Piano Pieces for Jane Boyden
Piano pieces by William Bolcom, prints by Frank Boyden
2000
Published by Crab Quill Press, Walla Walla, Washington
Ed. 15
Handmade book with lacquer cover
11¼ x 14⅜ x 1 in.
Collection of Frank and Jane Boyden, Otis, Oregon

Cover of *Bird Spirits: Nine Piano Pieces for Jane Boyden*

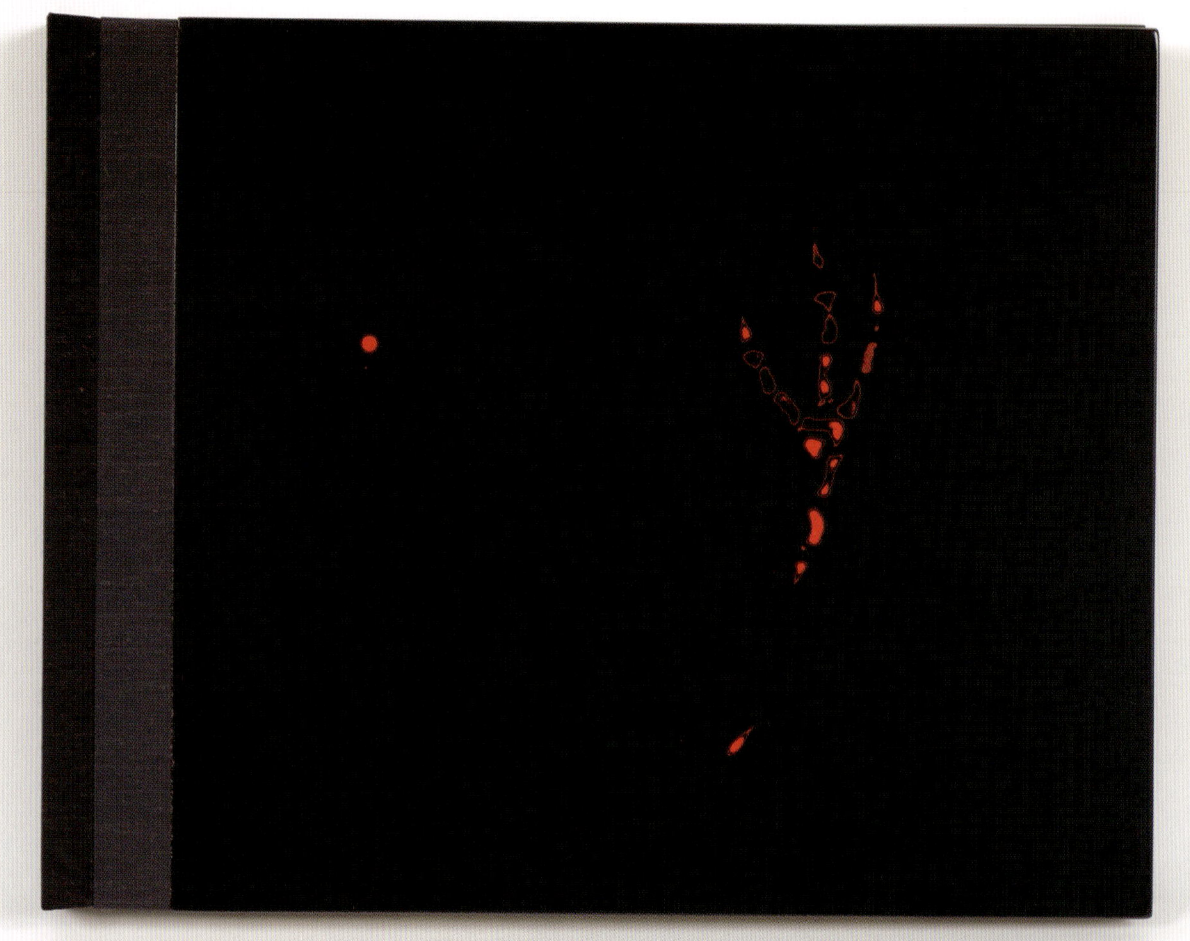

so forth. It is a book that Frank and I produced in honor of Jane Boyden (Frank's wife, my mother) on the occasion of her retirement after thirty years of teaching.

As the producer and designer, I wanted the book itself to pay homage to both the crow and the piano. And so we decided that the book should sport black lacquer covers, specifically the black lacquer used on Steinway pianos, and that I would paint the footprint of a crow on each cover employing a Ming dynasty (1368–1644) lacquer technique found mainly on musical instruments. In my search for Steinway's lacquer, I ended up having the opportunity to speak with John Herkaler, one of the primary technicians who developed lacquers for Steinway pianos. Not only did he supply me with the lacquer and colorants; he enthusiastically led me through the process of their application.

One obstacle in using wood for a book cover is the material's tendency to warp due to both moisture and the pressures exerted by a given finish. Our intended edition size for the book was ninety copies, which meant locating a minimum of 180 pieces of wood measuring 11.5 x 14.5 inches. Because of the difficulty of finding stable, quarter-sawn material of that width, we decided to use plywood and ultimately chose a type of Finnish aviation-grade plywood that, despite being extremely thin and lightweight, was *virtually* guaranteed not to warp.

Bird Spirits has a sewn-boards binding with a drop-away spine. This means that we not only needed to cut the plywood to size but also needed to machine the spine edge of each piece to accept the text block and sewing stations. Finally, everything was ready, and I carefully wrapped up and stored the text blocks of the entire edition, cleaned out my studio, built a spray booth, and turned the space into a lacquer finishing shop. We donned masks and other protective gear and proceeded to finish the covers with a vinyl sealer and then sand them in preparation for the lacquer. We drew images of crow footprints with lacquer on the front side of half of the pieces of wood. All was well. We then sprayed our first coat of lacquer. To our utter surprise, about half of the covers warped after the first coat, —and the edition changed from ninety to forty-five. With the second coat, another portion of covers warped, and this was the case for each subsequent coat until, at the end of the process (approximately ten coats of lacquer), we had enough covers to make twenty books. We absorbed the blow.

SYSTEMIC EXPLORATIONS—REMARKS ON THE DESIGN OF *EVIDENCE OF NIGHT*

It is important to remember that books are not just structures for storing information; they are also sophisticated systems for shaping and delivering information. How a given bit of information resides in us is shaped by how we initially encounter it. With the book, we encounter the information with our hands and with our eyes, not to mention with our hearts and minds. There are two types of books: those whose design remains relatively indifferent to the content and to the reader (the standard trade novel is an excellent example), and those whose design informs and is informed by the content and that present the reader with an overtly aestheticized experience. When these two types are laid side by side, one realizes how broad the term *book* really is.

It has taken me many books to begin to appreciate how a book shapes information; however, beginning with our first book, the exploration of this idea has been a central part of my collaborations with Frank. I search for ideas that have the capacity to take full advantage of the form of a book, ideas that require or employ many of the features unique to the book, such as sequence, pacing, and intimacy. There are some basic technical aspects of book construction that lead to (or impose) a certain consistency of geometry and meter to these systems. Books are composed of folded pages, each with a front and a back, a right and a left. This tends to lead to bilateral spatial considerations and information that is sequenced in powers of two: two, four, eight, and sixteen. Most books also have a beginning and an ending, and a specific sequence of pages that the reader/viewer is expected to follow. This consistency presents some very significant obstacles. For instance, the rigidity of the sequence easily leads to soporific monotony—how does one maintain the interest of the reader/viewer over the course of the book? Or how does the designer cope with ideas that are not necessarily so strict and/or severe, ideas that have a more organic shape?

After making several books, I began to consider the book in terms of music. The first four books I made with my father are dominated by rhythms inherent to

Lip bird, from *Evidence of Night*

Jennifer Boyden painting her lips with a lift-ground solution of ink and sugar in preparation to gently kiss the copper plate for an image in *Evidence of Night*. Otis, Oregon, Summer 2002.

the book: one-two, one-two, or one-two-three-four, one-two-three-four. These rhythms began to feel tyrannical, and I started to puzzle over how to create a book that would not fall prey to this monotony and would instead generate a more organic sequence. The eureka moment came while listening to one of Beethoven's late piano sonatas. I suddenly saw a book unfold as a sequence of three parts, with poems, prints, drawings, and blank paper functioning like voices that would rise and subsequently be subsumed by one another. Their duration would be marked not just by pages but by density as well. The result was *Evidence of Night*, a book that presents a sequence of ten poems by my wife, Jennifer Boyden, and a sequence of original intaglio prints and drawings by Frank.

Evidence of Night (2003; PLATES 132–133) is the only one of Frank's collaborative books in which the specter of the book's form, rather than text or images, came first. The next step was to select the poems. To do this, Jennifer gave Frank a manuscript of her poems and asked him to identify ones he felt he could respond to visually. Out of the twenty or so poems he chose, she then selected ten that she felt made a coherent group. And out of this selection emerged the theme of night. Jennifer and I put those poems in a sequence composed of three parts. I typeset the poems and determined the size of the book based on the dimensions of her typographically largest poem. I then made a dummy book and placed the poems, leaving space for prints, drawings, and blank pages. Jennifer and I presented this dummy to Frank, and he set about making the prints with the dimensions and sequence in mind. Once the prints were finished, I retypeset the poems, this time in response to the prints. After the books were printed and bound, I delivered them to Frank, who finished each book with three original drawings, which, of course, responded to the poems, the type, and the other prints.

I am tempted, in the case of *Evidence of Night*, to consider the book from the perspective of a collaborator as well. For the object itself exerted an unusually significant influence on the content, to such an extent that the line between content and carrier is blurred—every material in the book, with the exception of the binding thread and glue, was selected to augment the book's argument.

THE BOOK AS A TRANSLATION—*THE FIELD OF AKI*

Like *Evidence of Night*, Frank's sixth collaborative book, *The Field of Aki* (2004; PLATE 146), also presents an excellent example of how a book insinuates its structure, material, and system into the information it carries. *The Field of Aki* challenges some of the usual expectations of a book. It is quite large, measuring

10.75 x 29 x 1.25 inches, and heavy (book, box, and corbel weigh more than twenty-eight pounds). Rather than being held in the hand, it is meant to be presented on a wall; and while most books are viewed at arm's length, this one is designed to be viewed from much greater distances. Most books close when the reader's attention drifts away, but this book is designed to remain open. And while most books of poetry present a set of poems, this one presents a single poem in multiple manifestations—including material, visual, haptic, and polylingual expressions.

The Field of Aki, like *A Carousel at Birth*, began with a memorable conversation, this time on a rooftop in Manhattan. On a clear evening in October 2002, my close friend Edward Morris and I were discussing book design, when I voiced the desire to make a book that would present not a series of poems (as books of poetry generally do) but a single poem. I wanted to isolate a single poem so that the reader and the poem might have a chance to allow the text full sway over their shared space. Edward then made the incisive observation that such a book as a whole could be understood as a form of translation, and that the book itself would be understood to be part of that poem. This observation became the kernel from which *The Field of Aki* took shape: a book that would simultaneously house a set of translations of a single poem and be a translation itself.

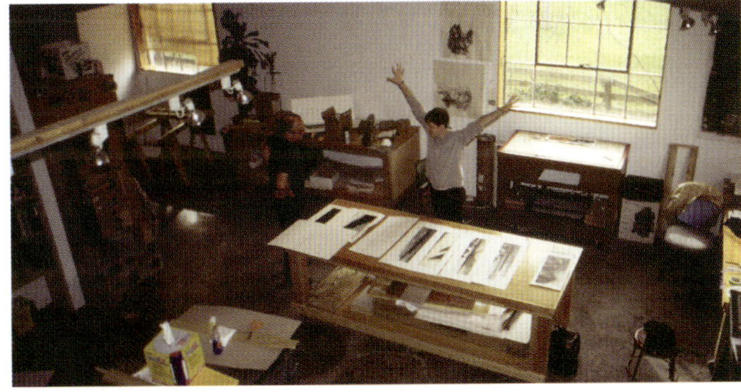

Edward Morris and Frank Boyden discussing the sequence of images in *The Field of Aki* at Crab Quill Press, Summer 2003.

Edward had spent several years studying and translating poems from an early collection of Japanese poetry, the *Man'yōshū* (Collection of ten thousand leaves). While doing this, he translated several poems thought to be written in the voices of the dead or that dealt with ceremonies for the dead. Among these poems was an unusual text (perhaps a linked sequence of five poems) titled "The Field of Aki," by Kakinomoto no Hitomaro. It describes events surrounding a ritual that took place on the winter solstice in the year 698 and begins with the journey of a young prince to an alpine meadow. Once he arrives, a ritual takes place throughout the course of the night to conjure the spirit of his dead grandfather. In the early light of morning, as the full moon sets and the sun rises, the grandfather's spirit appears, and the imperial soul is transferred to the prince.

One salient quality of the poem is the transformation of landscape and the line of the horizon. Edward saw this landscape as strikingly similar to some of Frank's landscape prints and suggested that we invite him to translate the poem through the medium of prints. Edward sent Frank the poem, and a few months later the three of us were in Frank's studio discussing the poem, his prints, and the book. Among Frank's prints was a recently completed series of fourteen images, variously drypoint, aquatint, and spitbite. These were long, horizontal prints of brooding landscapes, and to our astonishment, one image juxtaposing the sun and the moon seemed to precisely describe the climax of the poem. In that portfolio, we also found six prints that seemed to be worthy analogues to the sequence. Over the next few months, Frank produced an additional seven prints to complete the translation. And so it was that part of a preexisting portfolio

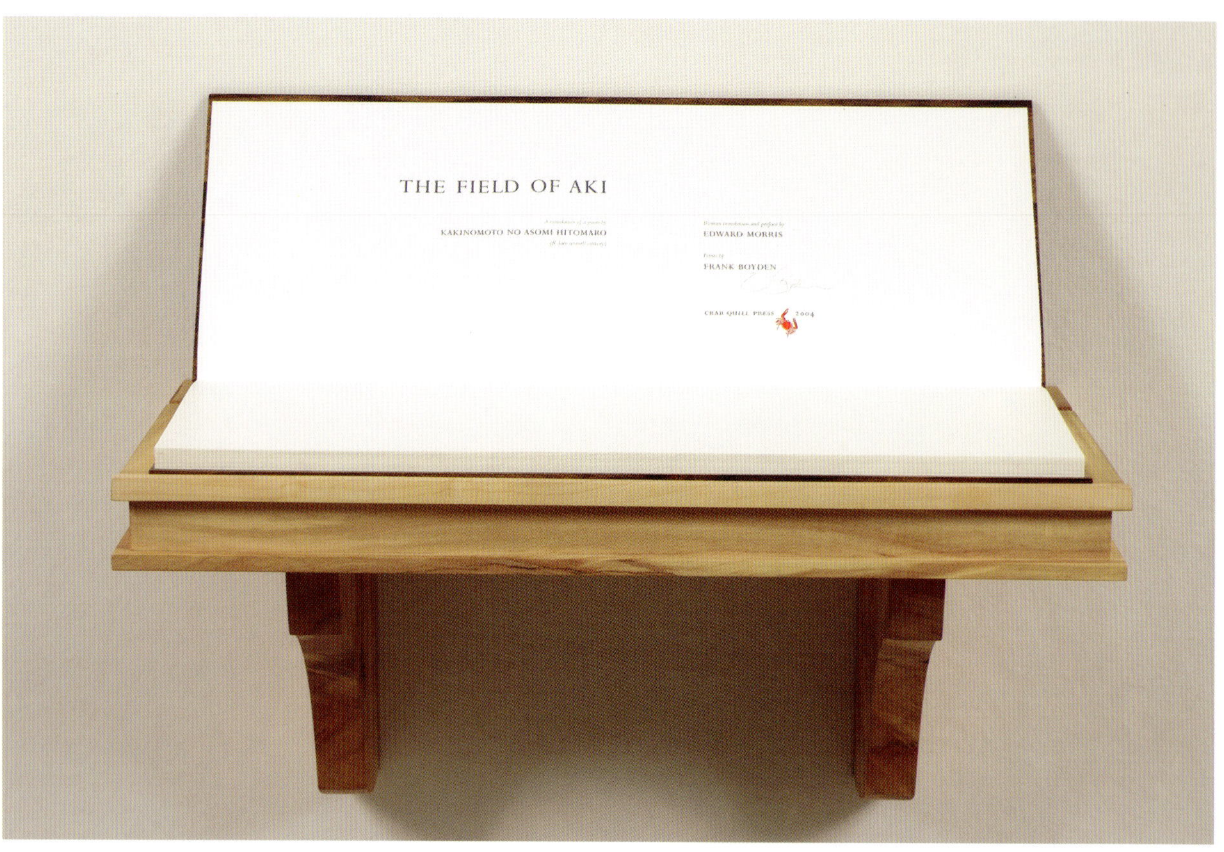

The Field of Aki: A Translation of a Poem by Kakinomoto no Asomi Hitomaro
Translation by Edward Morris, prints by Frank Boyden
2004
Published by Crab Quill Press, Walla Walla, Washington
Ed. 6
Handmade book
10¾ x 29 x 1½ in.
Collection of Frank and Jane Boyden, Otis, Oregon

was reshaped to become a component of a larger narrative.

The book took the form of a very long, horizontal structure. The wood for the box and the covers was chosen for its capacity to inform the sense of landscape and horizon. The spine of the book augmented this sense of horizontality, running along the back so that opening the book created not a right and a left but a top and a bottom. It is thought that the poem was chanted much like a Noh performance, so I decided to have each element of the book appear isolated on the upper half of the page, with the turning of each page evocative of the slow drumbeat of a performance. The reader encounters the poem in multiple manifestations: the original Chinese characters (the style of the calligraphy was chosen to reflect the written language of seventh-century Japan); a romanized version that would allow the English-speaking reader to pronounce the sounds of the original poem; Edward's English translation; Frank's translation of the poem into images; and, finally, Edward's translation once again.

The production of this book was informed by the otherworldliness of its content. Our collective effort to make a 1400-year-old poem—its logic, magic, and imagination—come to life in the present moment made the poem a visceral entity. And from a collaborative standpoint, it felt at times that the three-year collaboration was extending beyond the three of us to include the poem itself.

FROM PORTFOLIO TO BOOK— CHARTING A SHIFT FROM LYRIC TO NARRATIVE IMAGES

When we stop to consider the sequence of materials with which Frank has worked over the past forty years (canvas to clay, to metal and stone, to paper, to books), it becomes clear how the logic of one has informed the next, re-informed the previous, and so on. Frank's two- and three-dimensional objects are predominantly fixed or stationary carriers of images and textures. In these objects, we witness an artist obsessed with lyric images—mostly solitary images of extraordinary beauty and technical virtuosity that present aesthetic arguments that are primarily formal in nature. However, not long after he began to work with books, a notable change occurred in his imagery—he began to introduce significant narrative qualities to his work. For instance, Frank now often creates images that present one or more characters engaged in some activity. He also frequently creates *sequenced* series of images, which take into account complicated issues of pacing, rhythm, and shifts in tone. I ascribe this shift in large part to the tremendous conceptual impact that the structure, system, and history of the book have had on how he considers images and their functions; another obvious source is his involvement with the history of prints (see Prudence Roberts's essay in this book).

Our most recent books—*The Irreverences, Provocations, and Connivances of Uncle Skulky* and *The Field of Aki*—evidence the extent and depth of this change. It is interesting to note that both books began as portfolios of prints. Here, it is important to describe a manic aspect of Frank's image making. He will virtually disappear into his studio for weeks and months at a time. When he reappears, he will have magically produced a new set of images/objects, which he then presents to the larger world. Because of my proximity, as his son, I often have a chance to see and respond to these projects as they unfold in his studio. Some clearly have the capacity to become books, and when this occurs, we are able to take that possibility into account early in the process of making the prints so that they will be "book-friendly."

The portfolio titled *The Irreverences, Provocations, and Connivances of Uncle Skulky* (2004; PLATES 144–145) is the product of one such highly productive six-month period. It began as a portfolio of etchings and drypoints in which Frank used the figure of a skeleton named Uncle Skulky to address a multitude of individuals and issues: from the work of printmakers such as Rembrandt (Dutch, 1606–1669), Franscisco Goya (Spanish, 1746–1828), Katsushika Hokusai (Japanese, 1798–1861), Odilon Redon (French, 1840–1916), and José Posada (Mexican, 1852–1913); to his relationships with fellow artists, galleries, and museum curators; to the vicissitudes of current politics and the foibles of the human spirit; to contemplations of his own mortality. And this set of prints, like its protagonist Uncle Skulky, has appeared in several manifestations. The prints and the portfolio as a whole are a tour de force, and the Portland Art Museum subsequently decided to publish the portfolio as an offset catalogue, with an essay by Pamela Morris and extensive commentary by Frank. But that was not enough; the portfolio begged to be reinvented as a Crab Quill Press book. The question was: What could a fine-press book accomplish that the portfolio and catalogue had not?

I happen to be fond of evocative book dedications, dedications that set the tone of the book. For instance, *Twenty Views of Cascade Head* (2001; PLATES

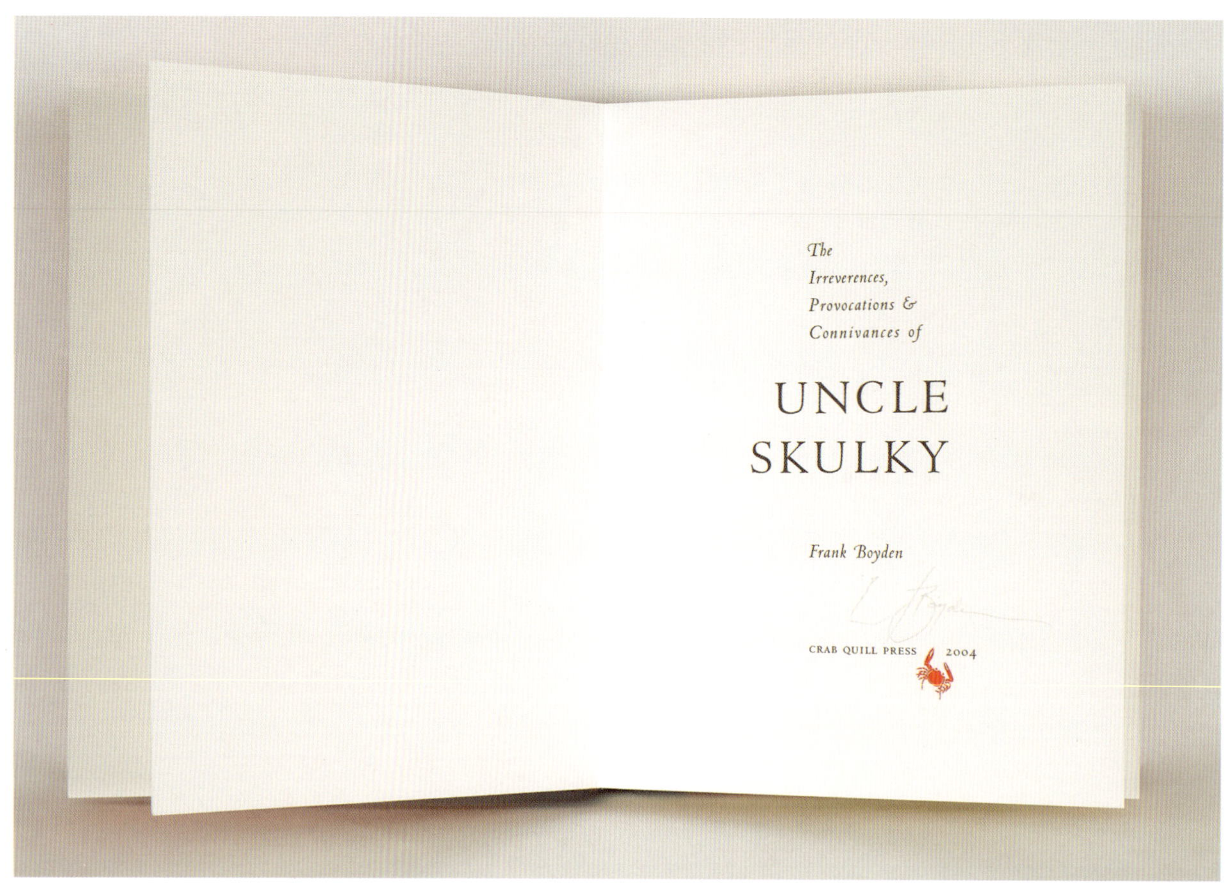

Uncle Skulky
2004
Published by Crab Quill Press, Walla Walla, Washington
Ed. 6
Handmade book with lacquer cover
14⅜ x 11⅝ x 1⅞ in.
Collection of Frank and Jane Boyden, Otis, Oregon

75–76) is "dedicated to the margins of place," and *Evidence of Night* is "dedicated to dreams too far from shore." After I looked through the Uncle Skulky series, my thoughts turned to the history of skeletons and eventually to a wily tenth-century Viking poet named Egil Skallagrimmson (ca. 910–990), the hero of the great Norse epic *Egil's Saga*. Why not see what happened if we dedicated the book to him?

The name Skallagrimsson means "Bald Head." But Egil was not just bald; he had a skull that has become legendary for its size, resilience, and hideousness. It is speculated that he suffered from osteitis deformans, or Paget's disease, in which bones keep growing excessively throughout one's life. In the case of Egil, his skull enlarged until his brow grew over his eyes and he became blind. His skull and skeleton seemed a worthy match for Uncle Skulky, and, like Uncle Skulky, Egil's poetry is full of trickery, invective, and blood. So it was that Frank and I presented his prints as a book dedicated to Egil that paired Frank's images with Egil's verse. Short of a séance, it is impossible to truly collaborate with the dead; however, as in *The Field of Aki*, Frank seemed to channel the inanimate, so that the book becomes informed by a logic of a spirit from the distant past.

HOMO COLLABORATUS—A MODEST PROPOSAL

Earlier I remarked that the word *collaboration* is a fairly nebulous signifier. The prevailing definition seems to be that it means a defined group of people working in concert toward some end. Some believe it essential that all of the collaborators share authorship of the end product; others consider it enough to recognize that several individuals shaped the final product. But where does one draw the line? In this essay, I have gone so far as to suggest collaborating with the inanimate: for instance, a book, a poem, and even a dead Viking.

Frank is keenly aware of our species' collaborative spirit. In fact, he points it out with such regularity that it has become something of a mantra. He has delivered several lectures on the vast industrial web that is required to produce simple objects such as a spoon or a cup. And in the production of our own books, he has often stopped to consider what it took for a tool to arrive at its given form. For Frank, these are moments of reverie. It seems important therefore to acknowledge that the very book you are holding is the product of collaboration—and a vast one at that. From Frank to the contributing writers; to the editors, designers, and photographers; to the team of workers at the print shop; to the team at the bindery. But the list does not stop there, for none of us could have done a single thing without the involvement of a host of others, most of whom remain totally anonymous. A few examples will suffice. Who designed the computers? Who built the cameras? Who harvested the wood for the paper? Who designed the shapes of these letters?

Collective suffering is certainly not a newly articulated concept. The first of Buddhism's Four Noble Truths, stated more than 2000 years ago, is that life and suffering are inseparable. Species names often indicate an essential trait of a given animal. In our case, *Homo sapiens,* the species indicator would indicate that we are "of knowledge." But really, the case can be made that the state of collaboration is far more noteworthy in our species than that of knowledge. So here is a modest proposal: change our species' name to *Homo collaboratus.* ❧

Ian Boyden is proprietor of Crab Quill Press and the director of the Sheehan Gallery at Whitman College in Walla Walla, Washington.

Plates

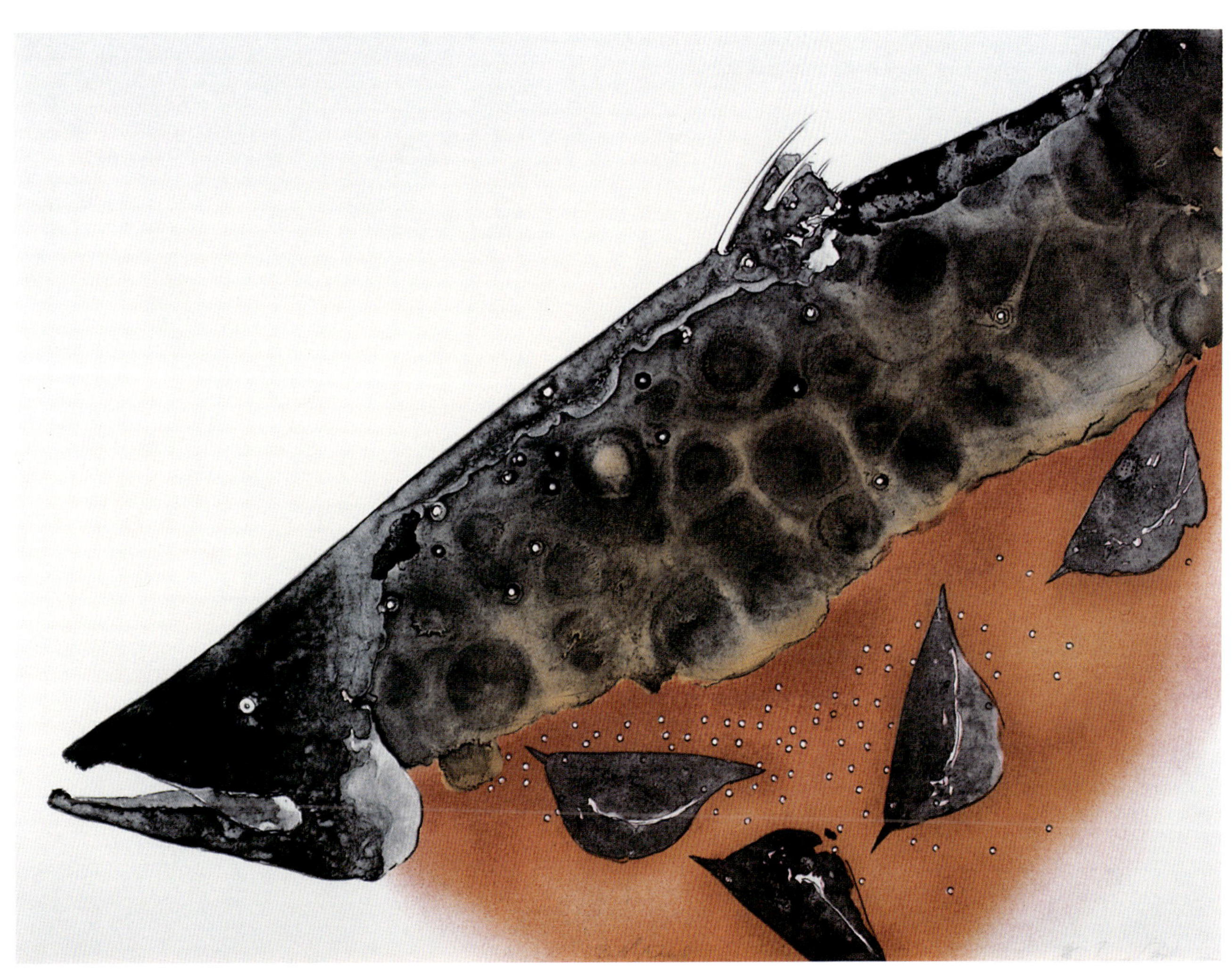

PLATE I
Birth of Fossils
1984–85
Ed. 40
3-color lithograph
22½ x 30 in.

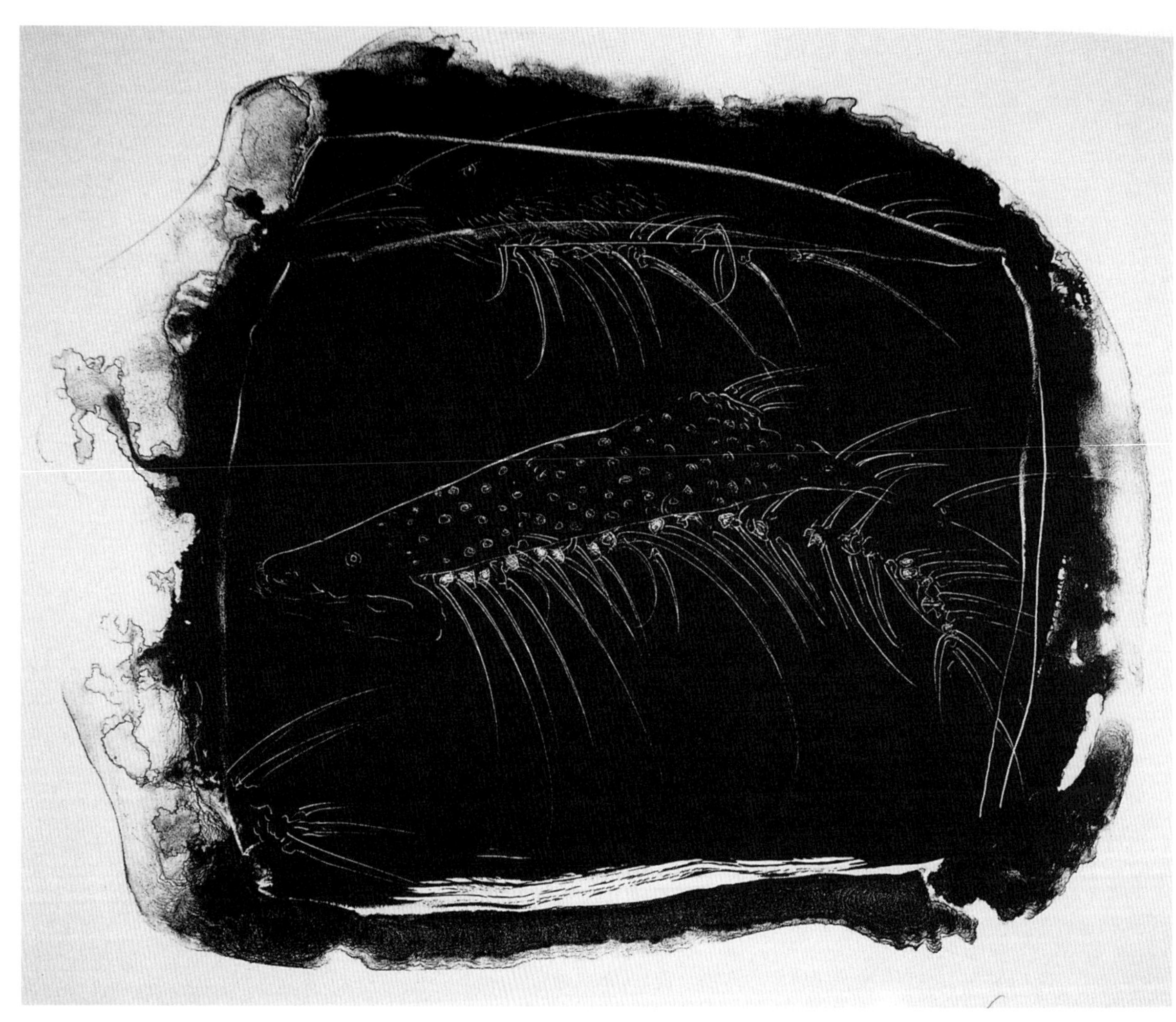

PLATE 2
Changes 1
1984–85
Ed. 40
2-color lithograph
8⅛ x 9⅞ in.

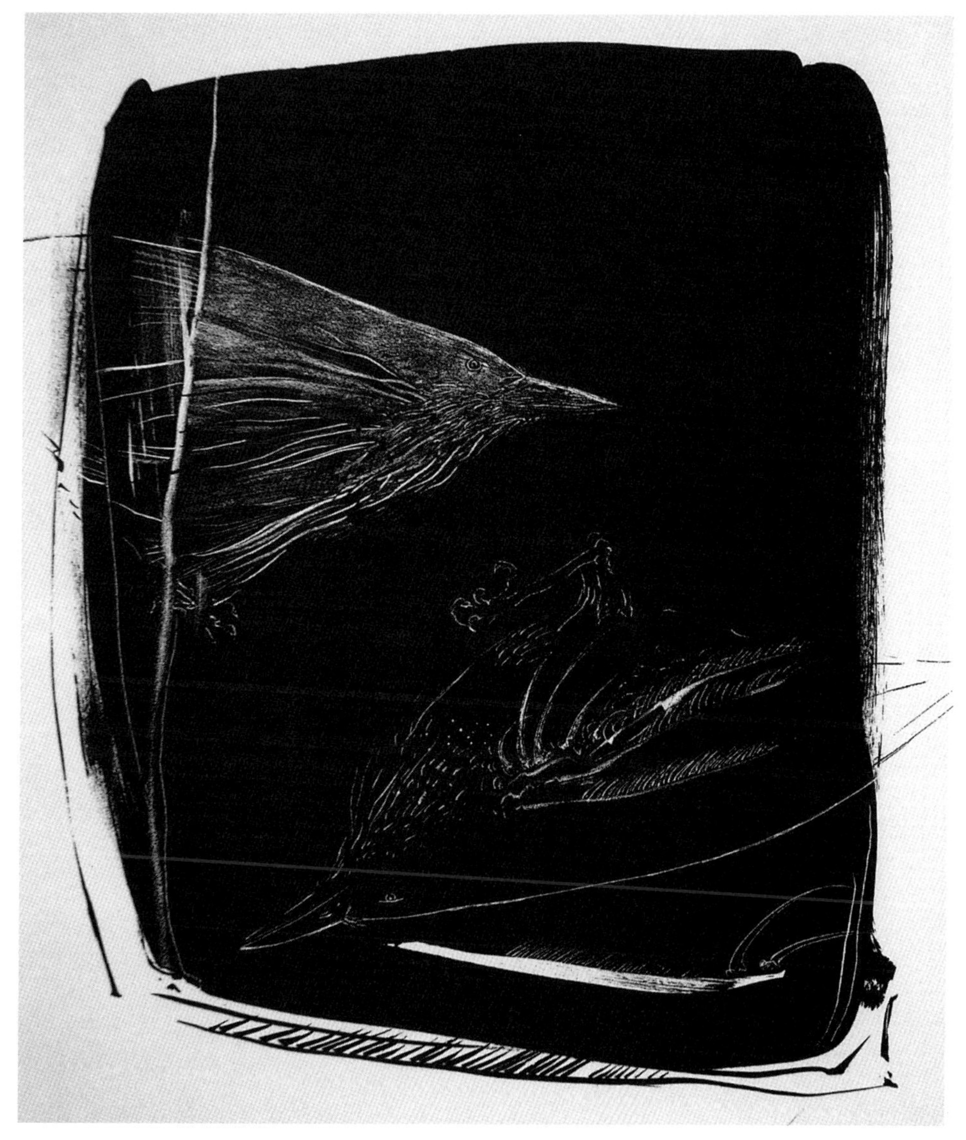

PLATE 3
Changes 2
1984–85
Ed. 40
2-color lithograph
9¼ x 8⅛ in.

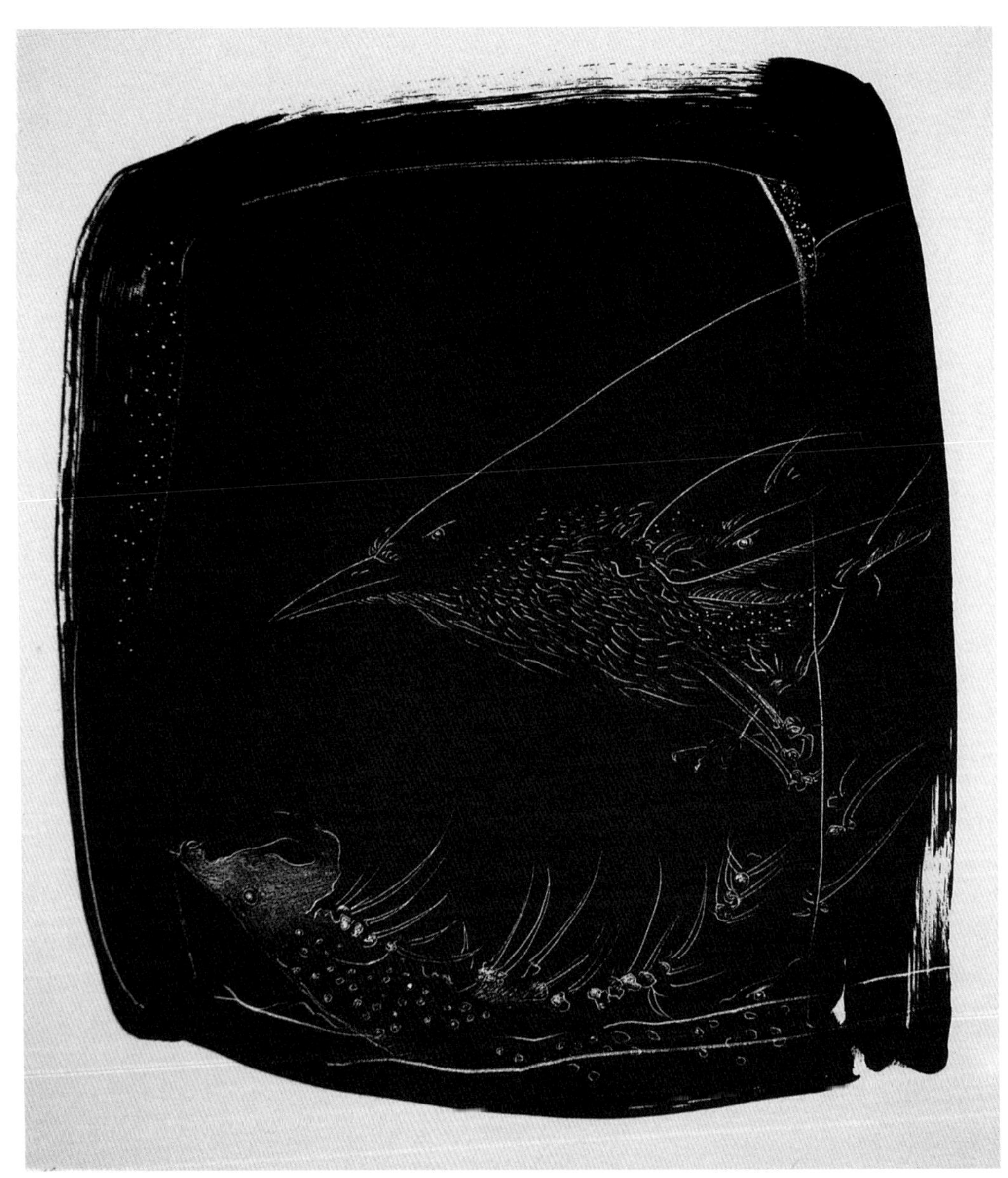

PLATE 4
Changes 3
1984–85
Ed. 30
2-color lithograph
9 x 7¾ in.

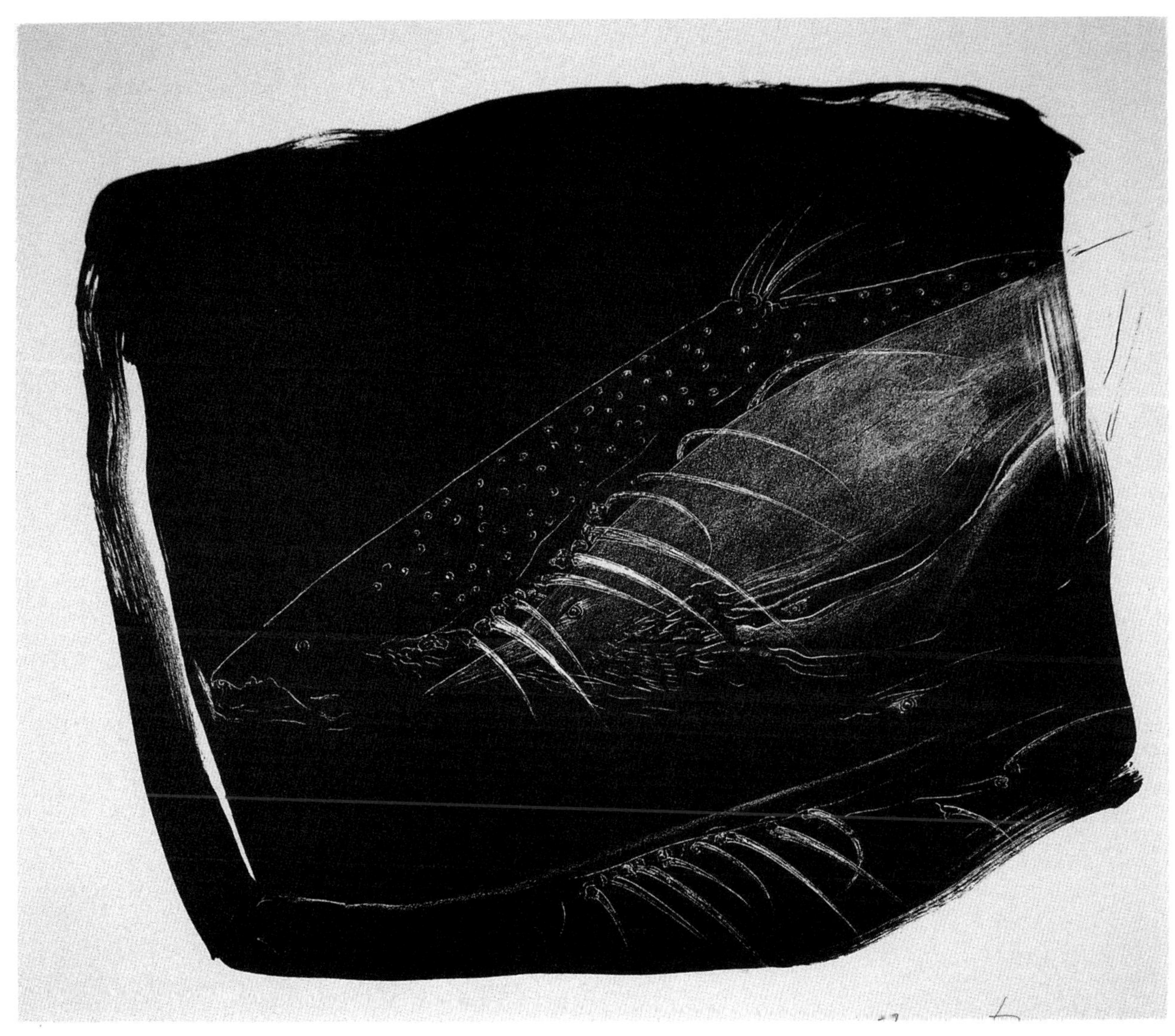

PLATE 5
Changes 4
1984–85
Ed. 30
2-color lithograph
9 x 7¾ in.

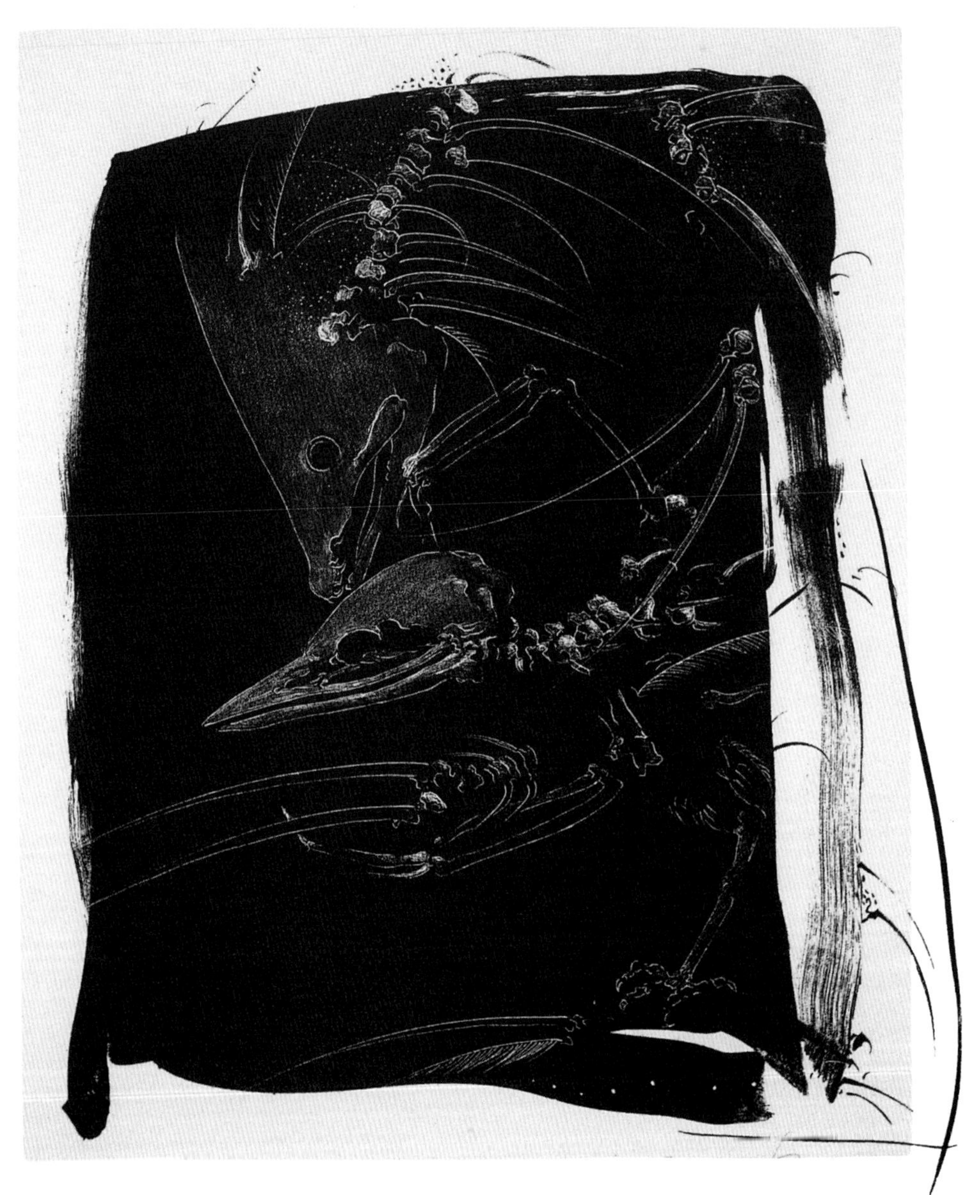

PLATE 6
Changes 5
1984–85
Ed. 45
2-color lithograph
9⅛ x 7⅜ in.

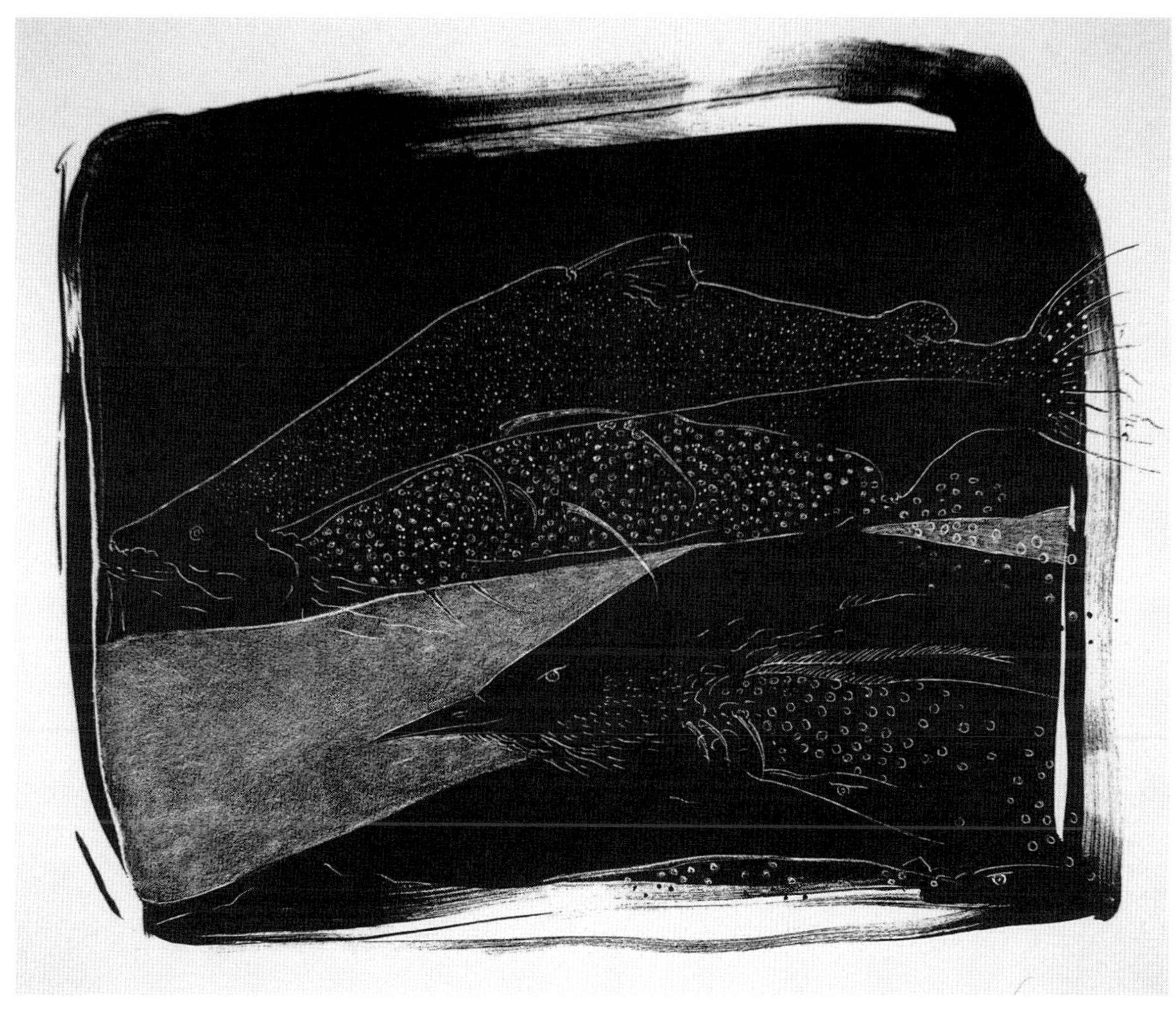

PLATE 7
Changes 6
1984–85
Ed. 45
2-color lithograph
8 x 9¾ in.

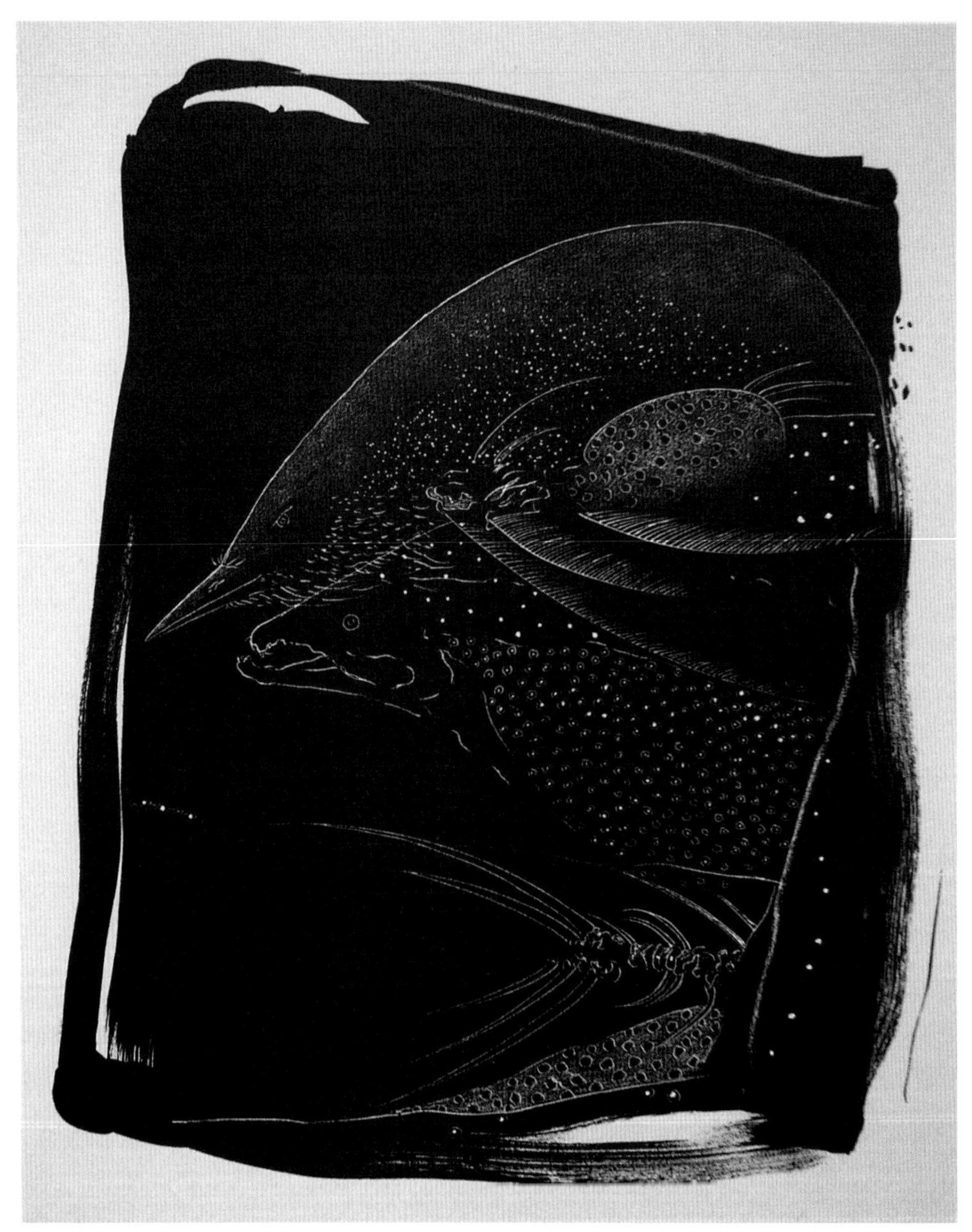

PLATE 8
Changes 7
1984–85
Ed. 45
2-color lithograph
9½ x 7⅝ in.

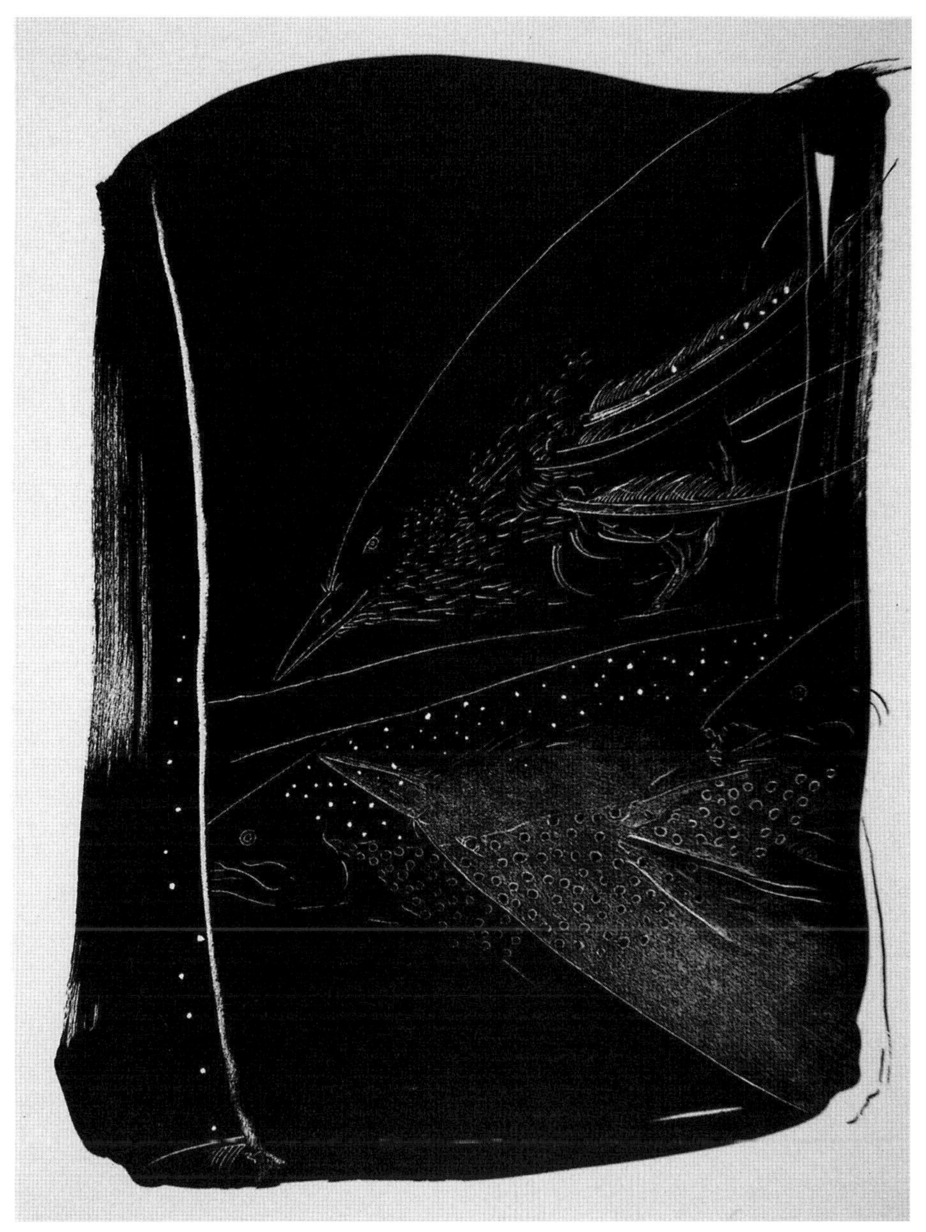

PLATE 9
Changes 8
1984–85
Ed. 45
2-color lithograph
9⅝ x 7⅜ in.

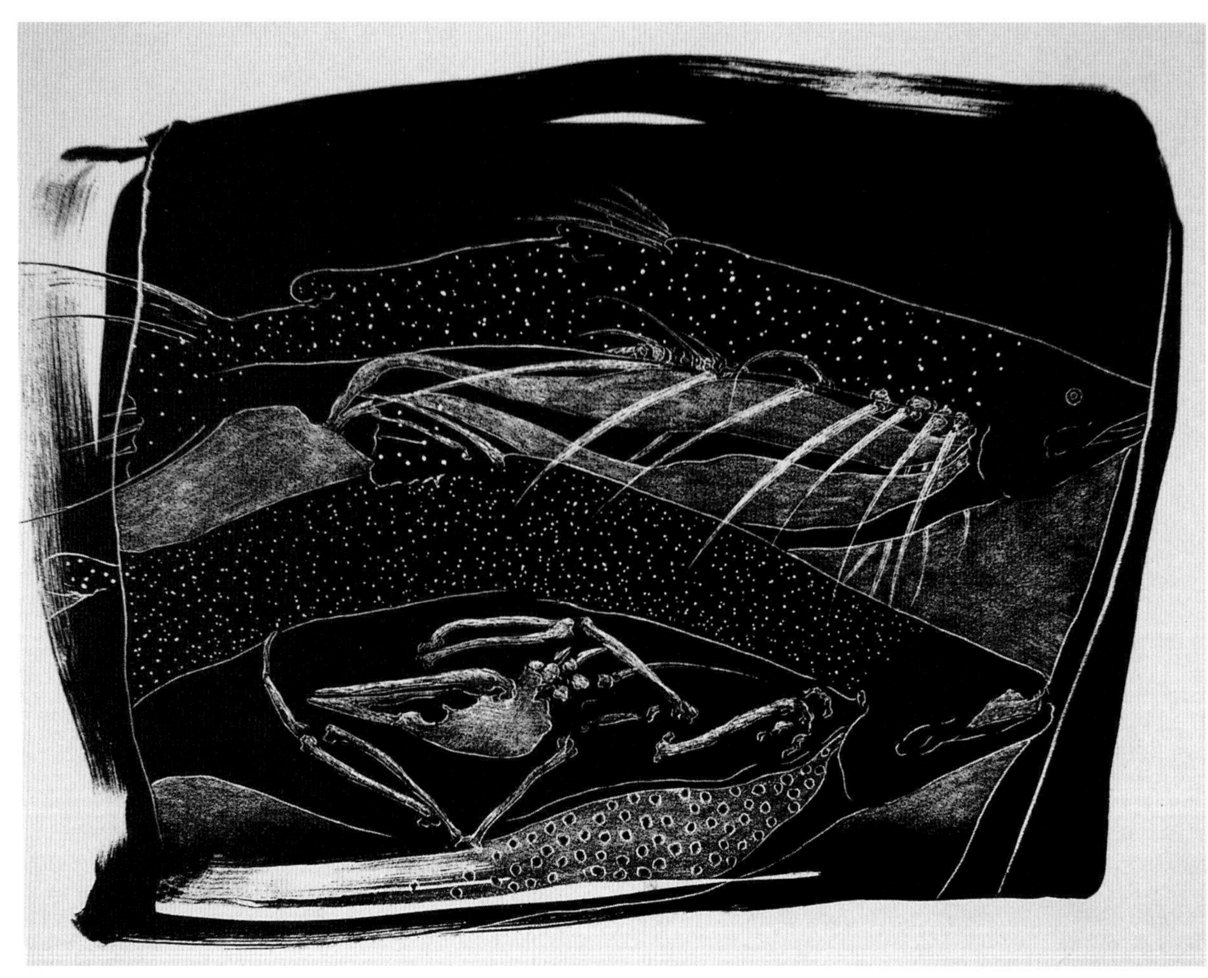

PLATE 10
Changes 9
1984–85
Ed. 40
2-color lithograph
7½ x 9⅝ in.

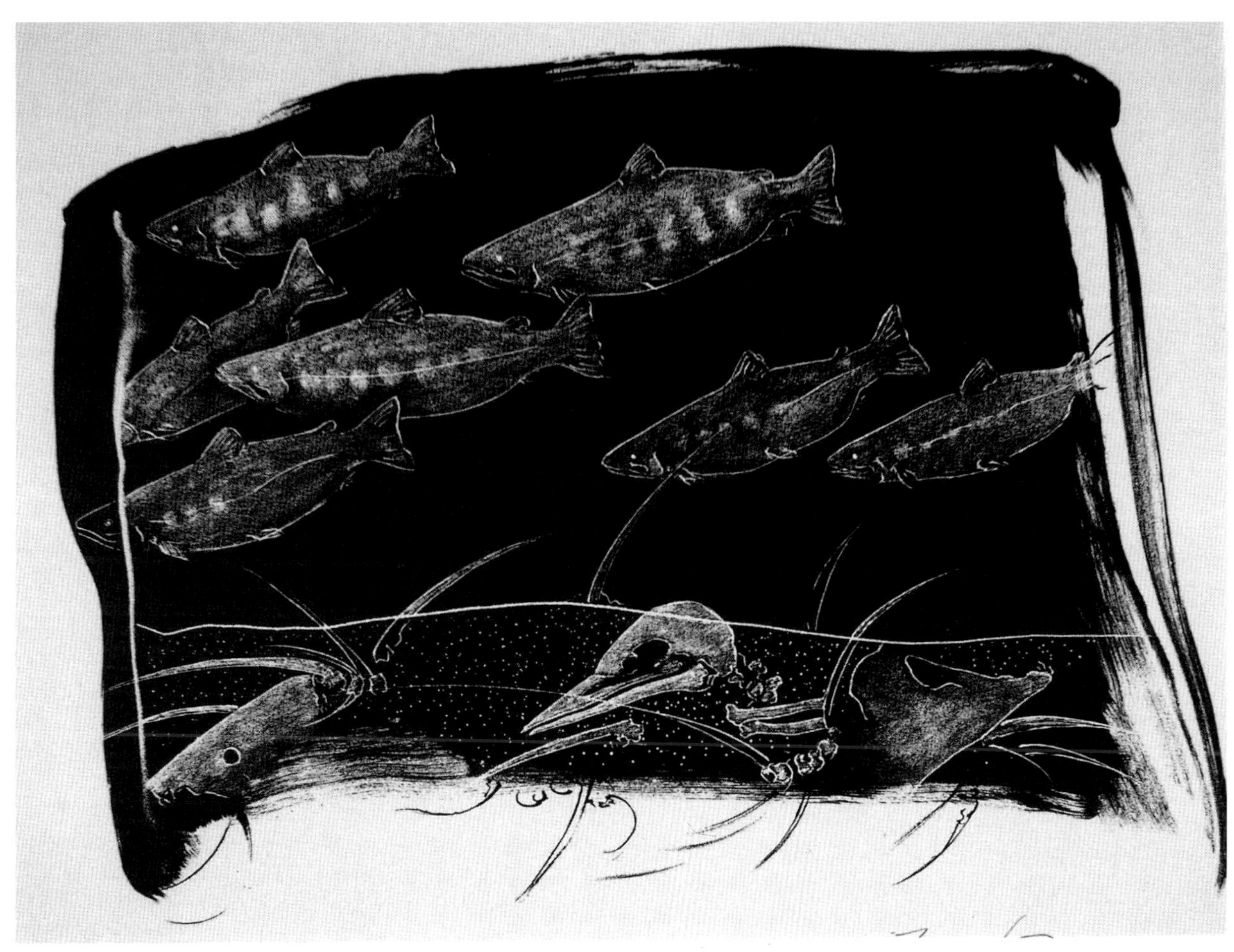

PLATE 11
Changes 10
1984–85
Ed. 40
2-color lithograph
7 x 9¼ in.

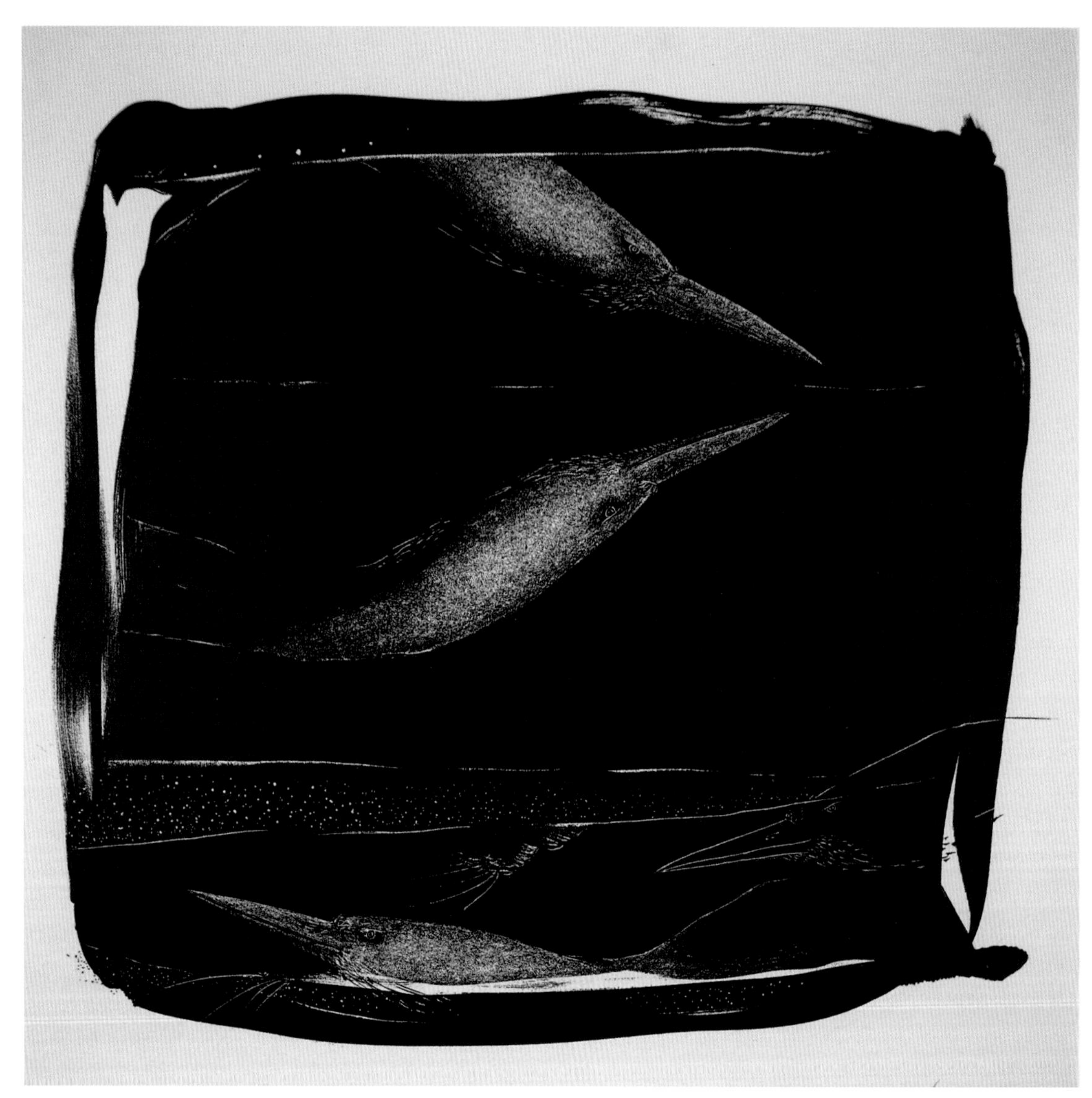

PLATE 12
Heron Reflections 1
1984–85
Ed. 19
2-color lithograph
11¼ x 11⅝ in.

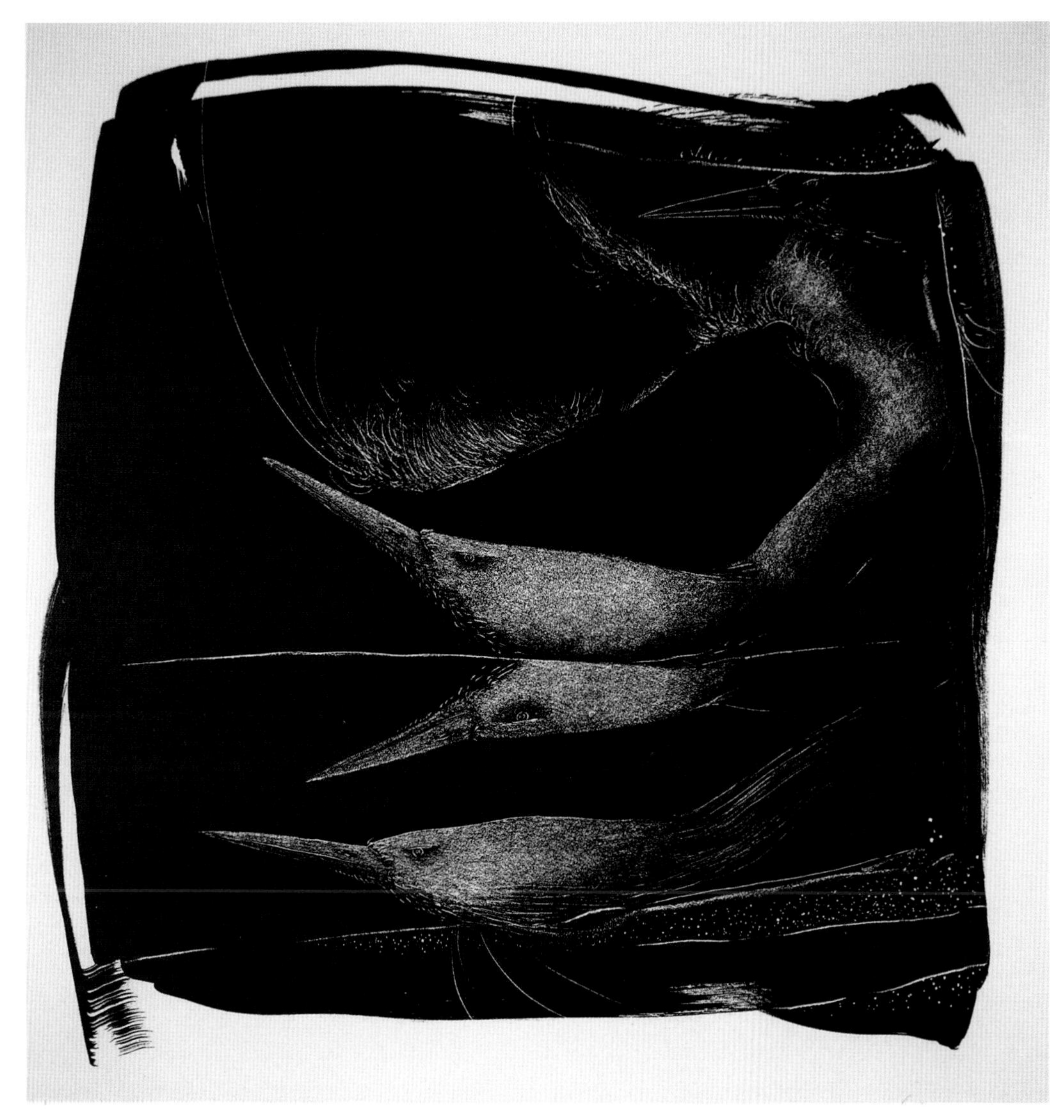

PLATE 13
Heron Reflections 2
1984–85
Ed. 24
2-color lithograph
11½ x 11 in.

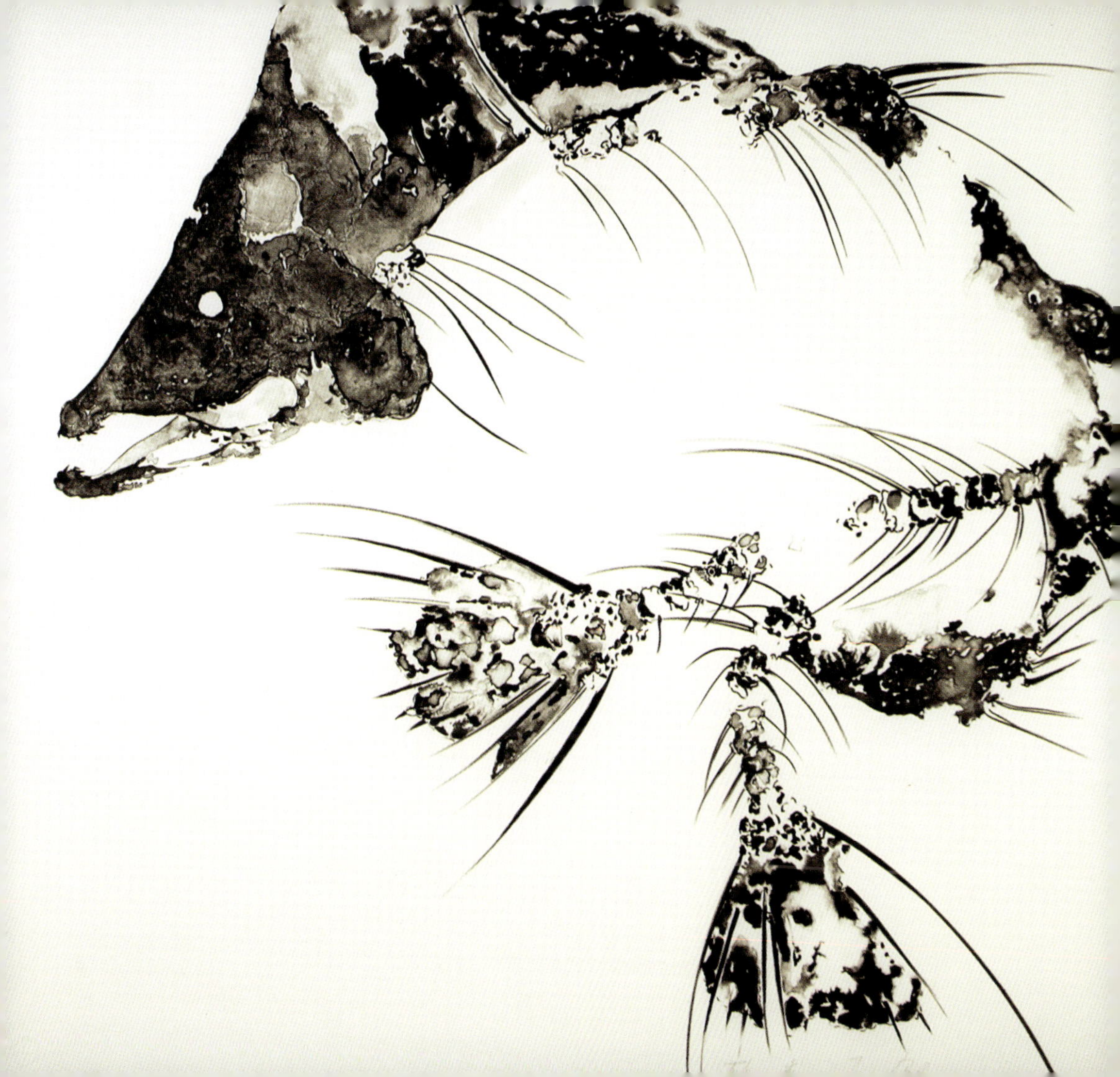

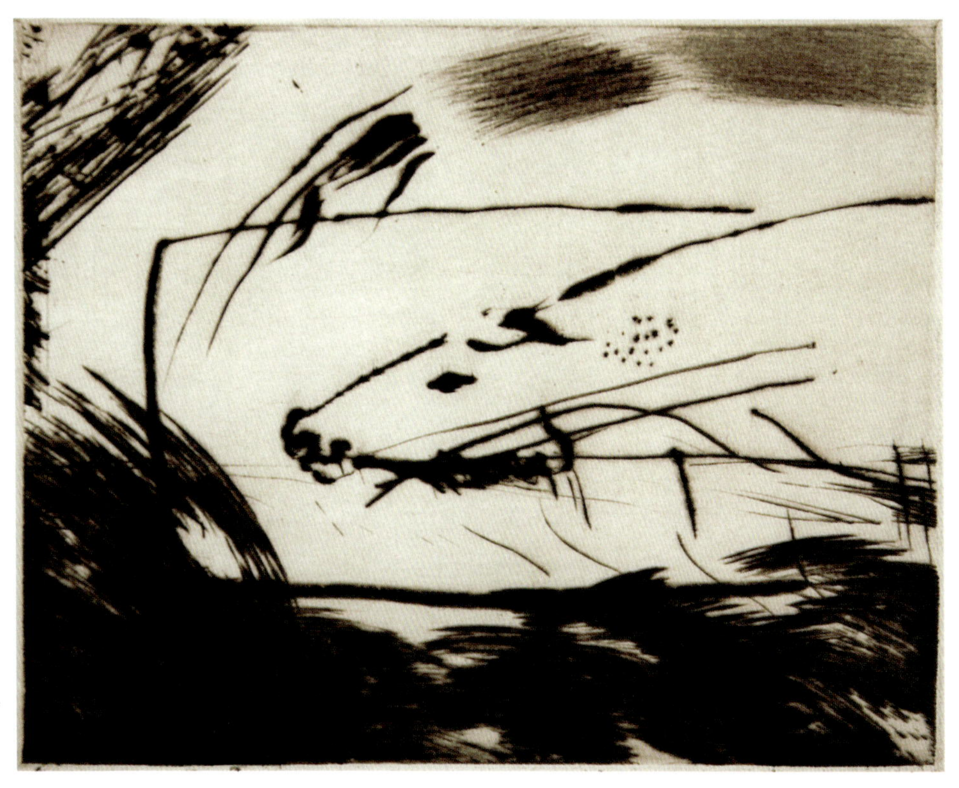

PLATE 16
Dream Lightning
1985
Ed. 40
Drypoint
4¼ x 5½ in.

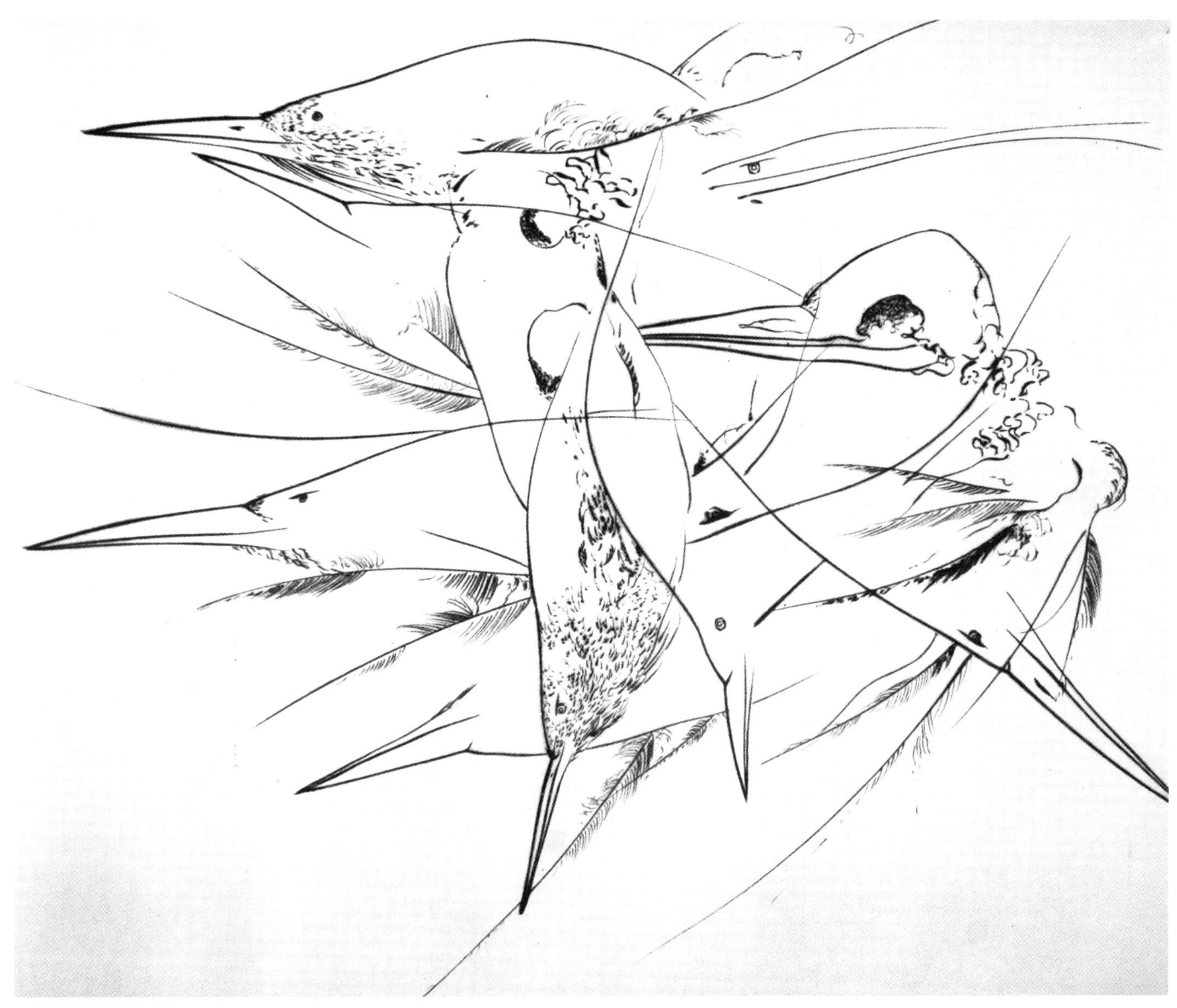

PLATE 17
Death Forming a Hummingbird Dream
1986–87
Ed. 40
Drypoint
9¾ x 11¾ in.

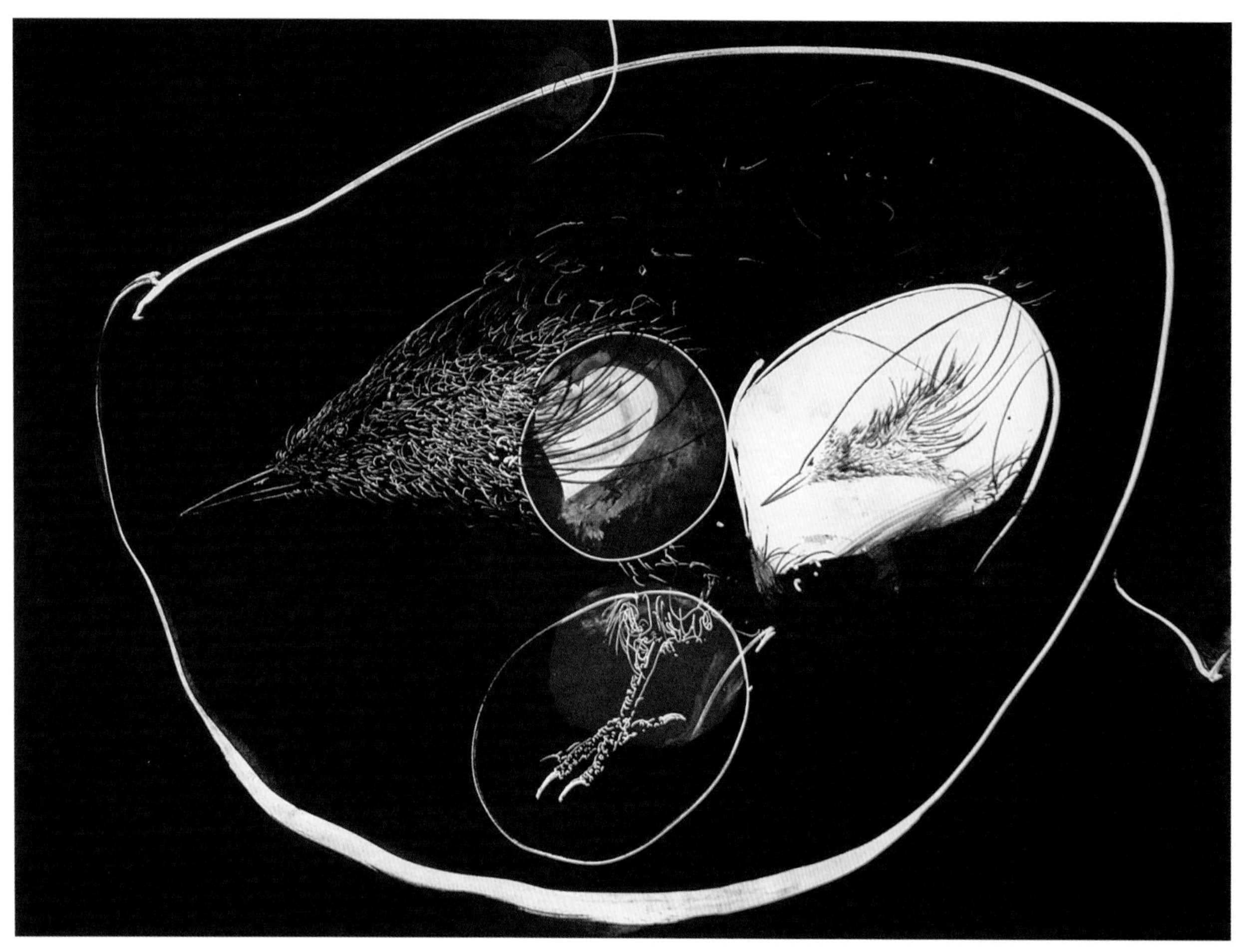

PLATE 18
Crow Foot
1991
Ed. 30
Drypoint, aquatint
17½ x 23½ in.

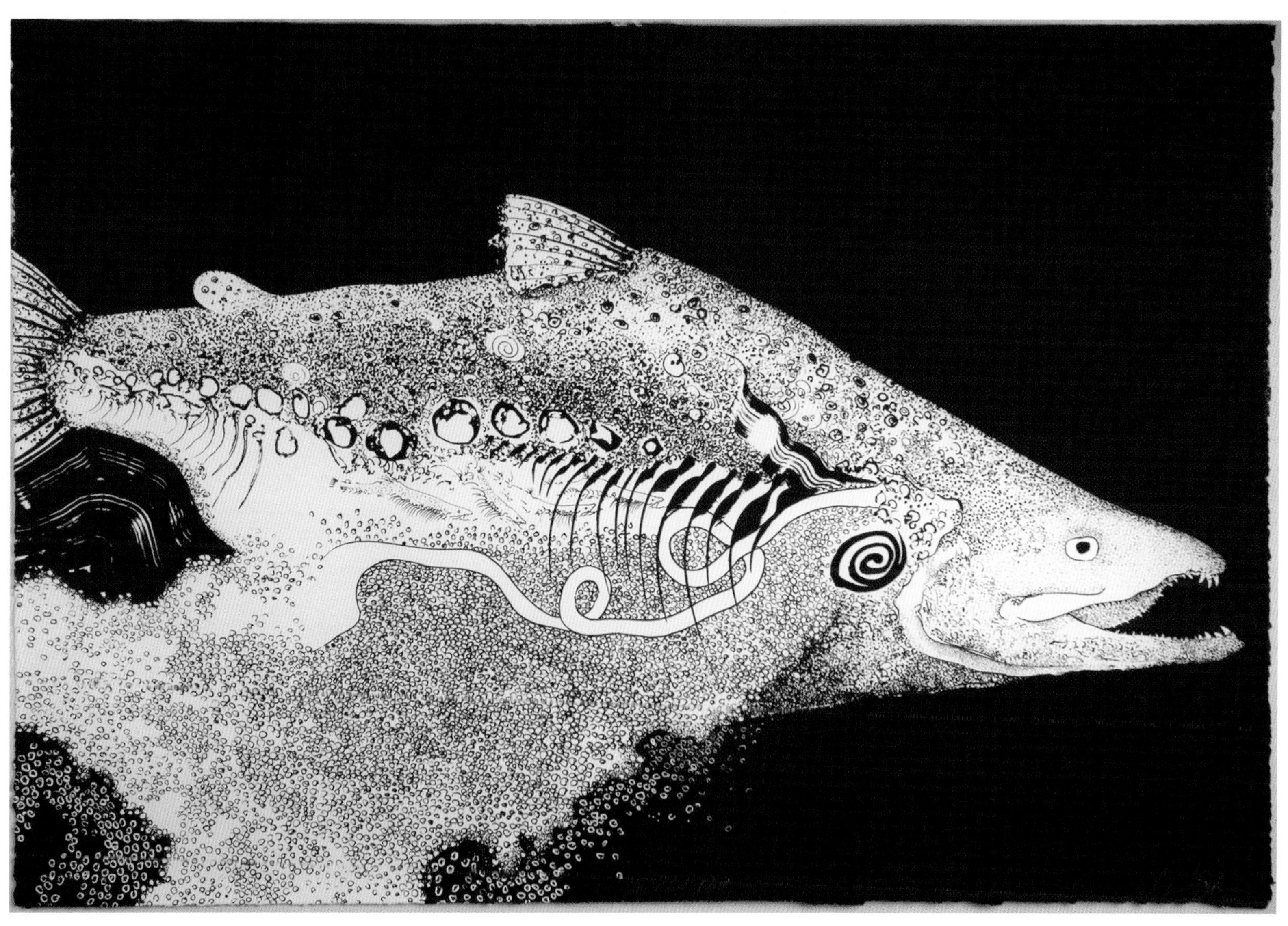

PLATE 19
Clock of Fall
1993–94
Ed. 45
Silkscreen
29½ x 42 in.

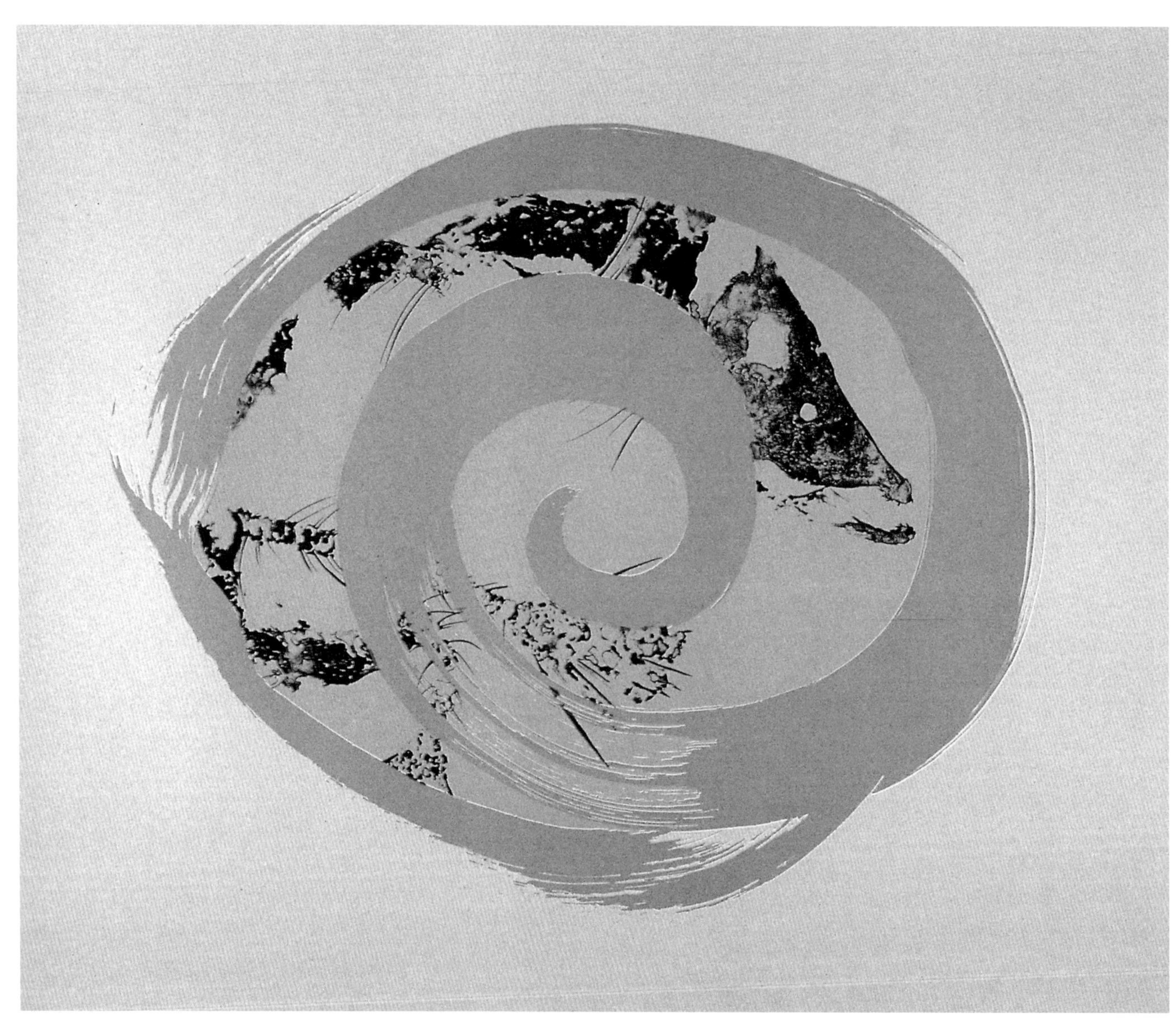

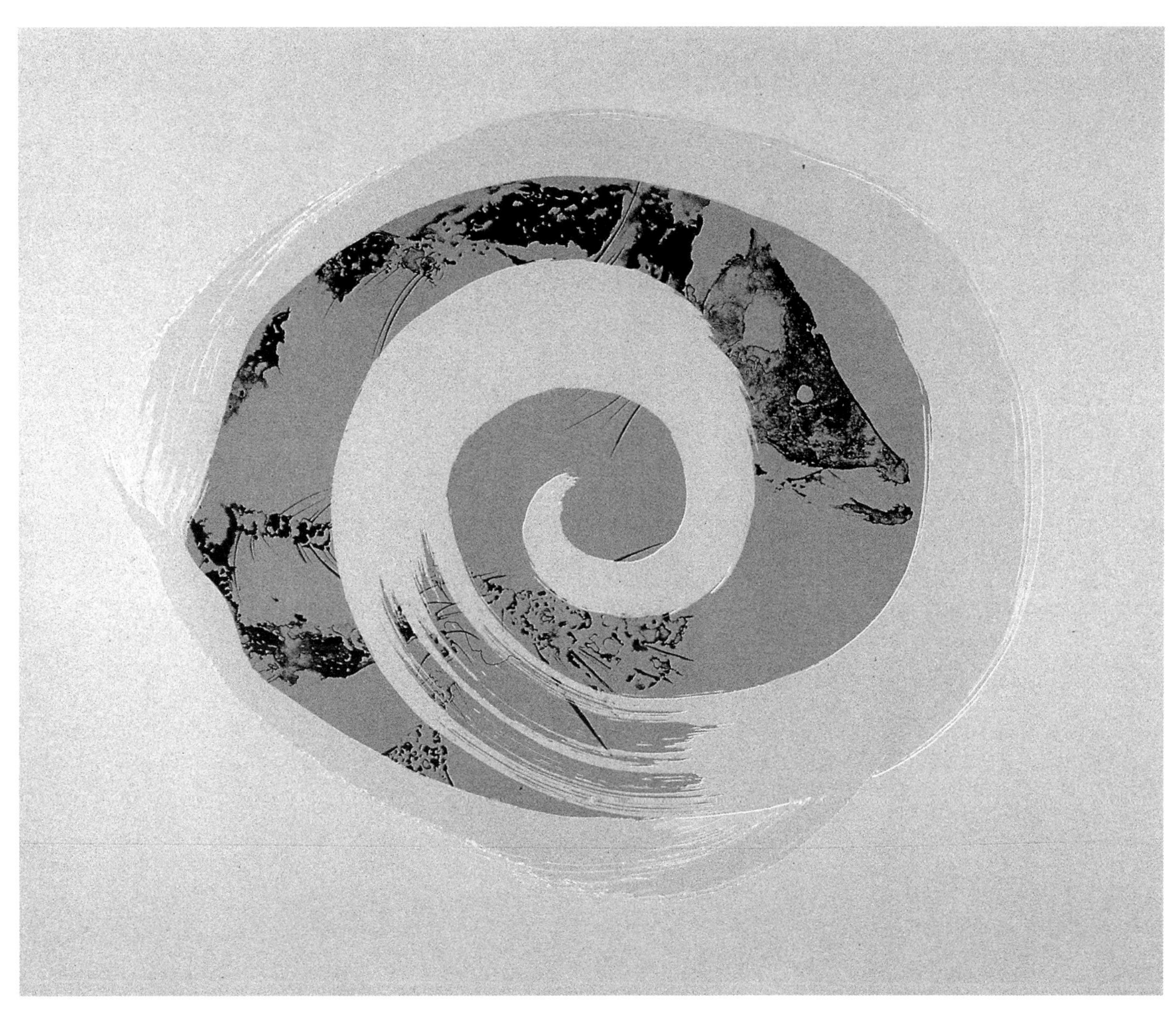

PLATES 20–21
Maelstrom for Shimmering Spines
1993–94
Ed. 14/State 1, 14/State 2
Silkscreen
32 x 38 in. each

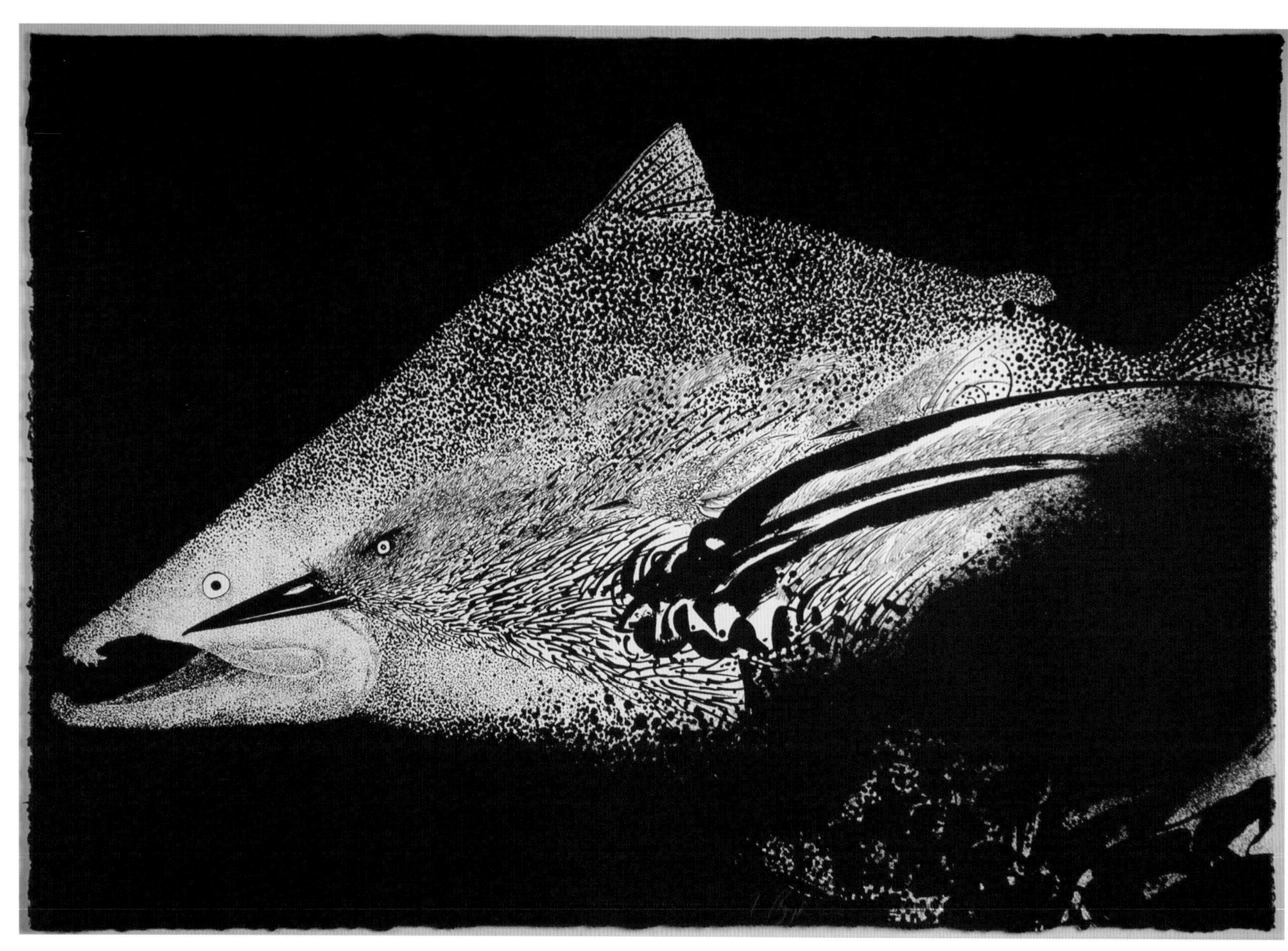

PLATE 22
Much of What Is Seen Is Not
1993–94
Ed. 45
Silkscreen
29½ x 42 in.

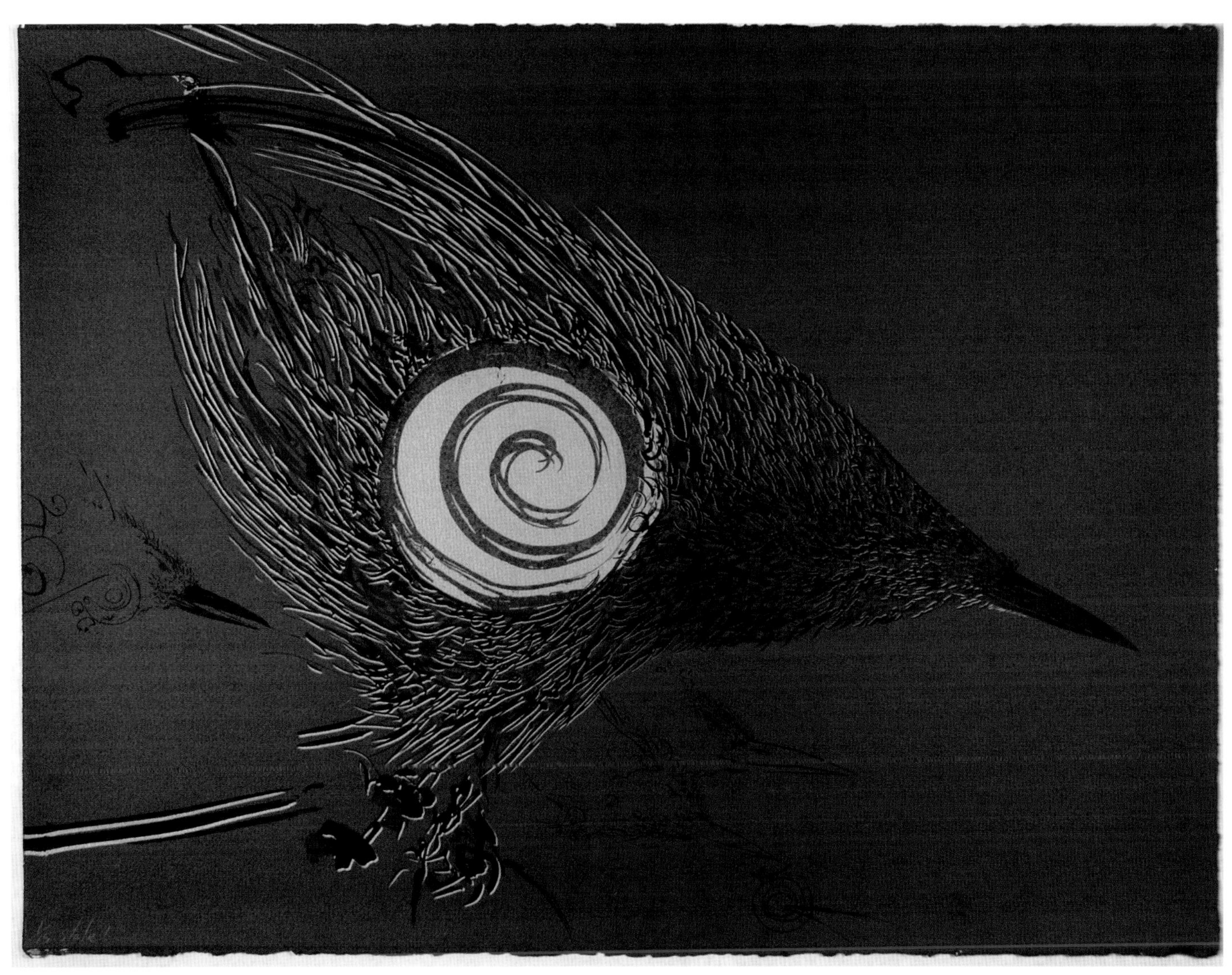

PLATE 23
Raven Coil
1993–1994
Ed. 15 of State 1, 8 of State 2, 6 of State 3
Silkscreen
30 x 22½ in.

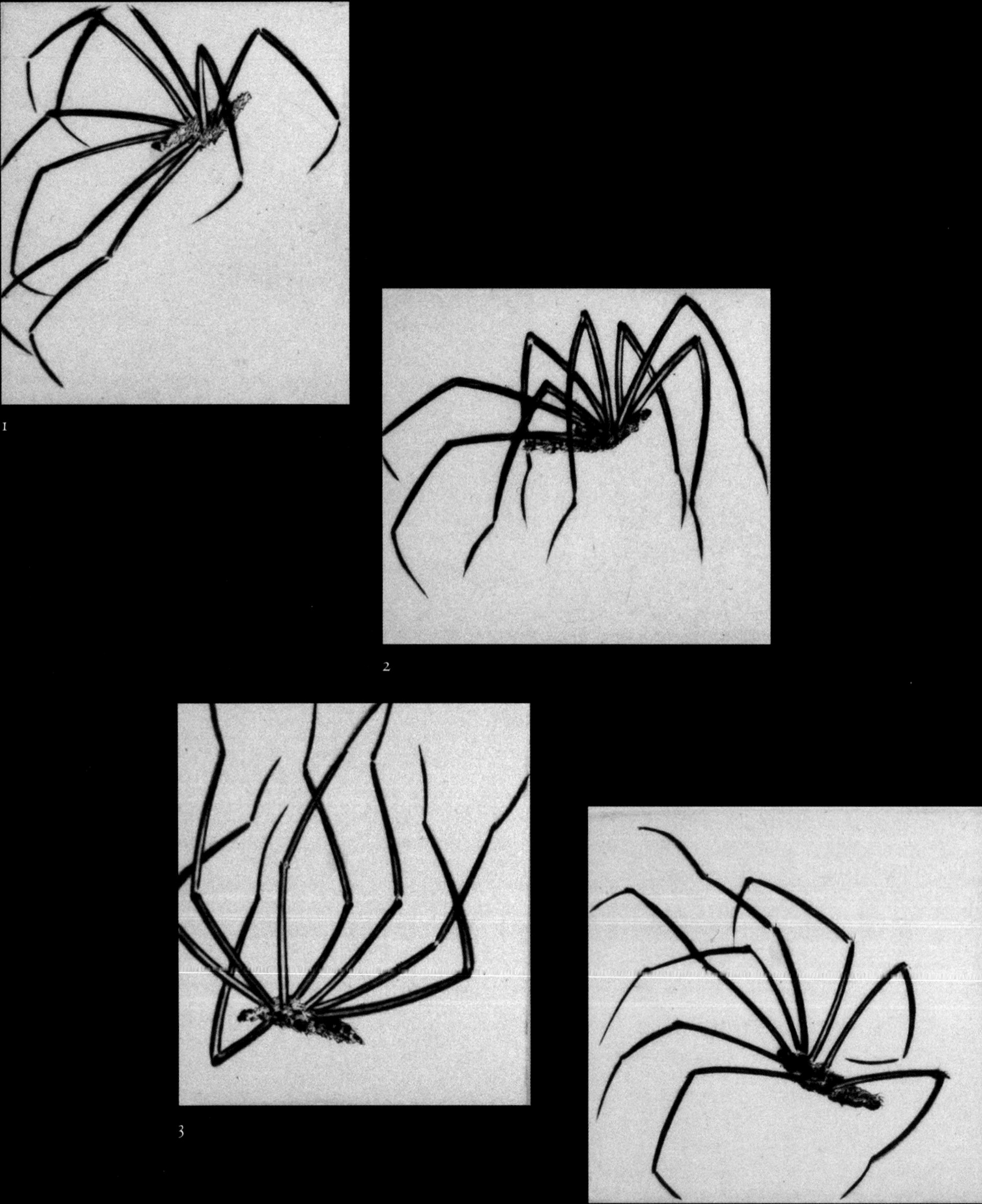

1

2

3

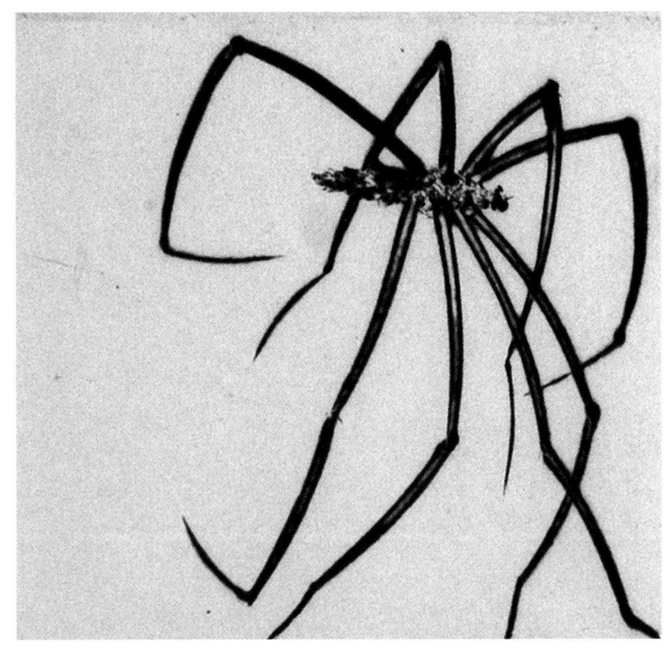

5

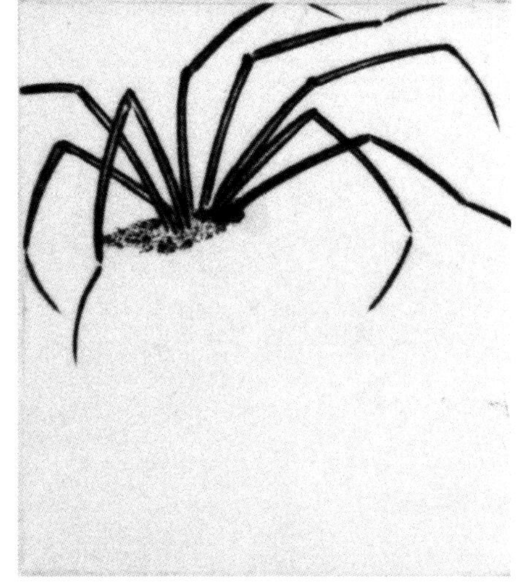

6

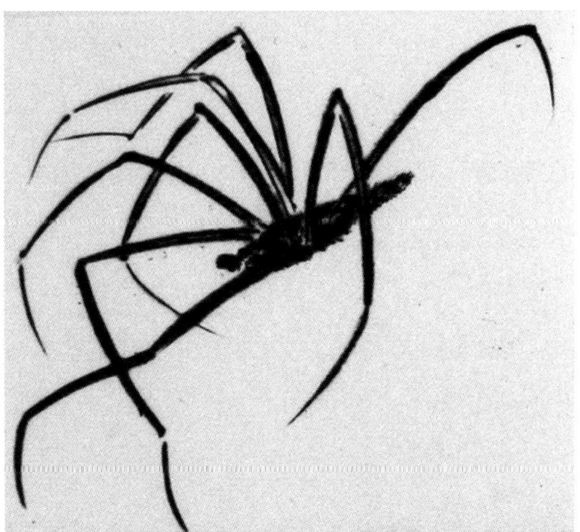

7

PLATES 24–30
Traces 1–7
1994–95
Ed. 22
Drypoint
3¾ x 3¼ in. each

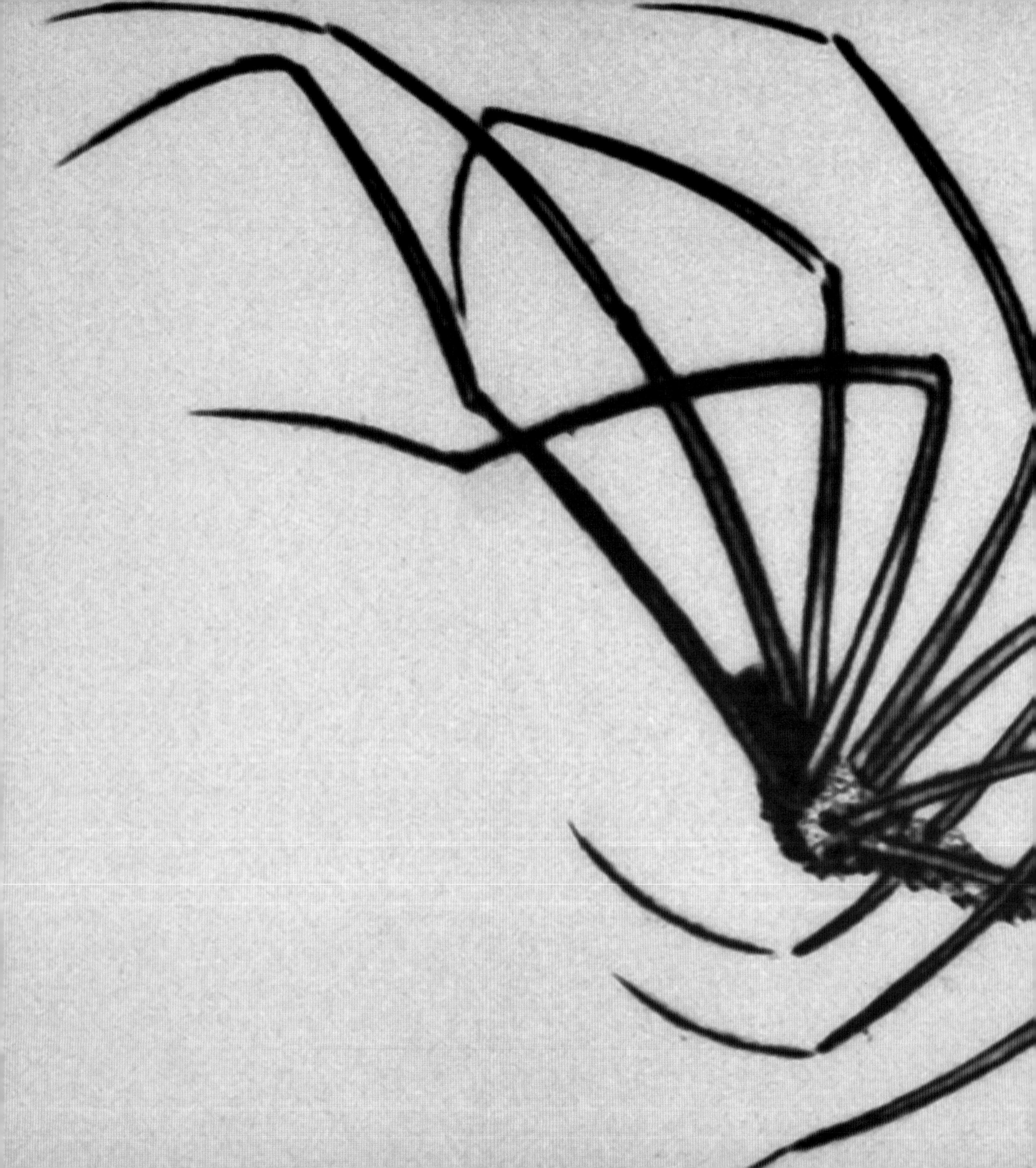

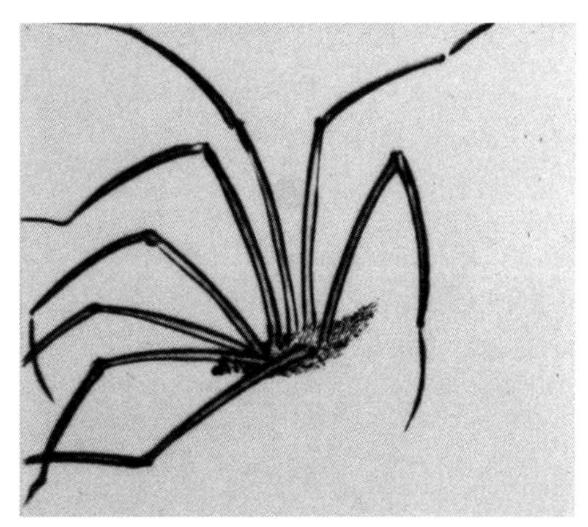

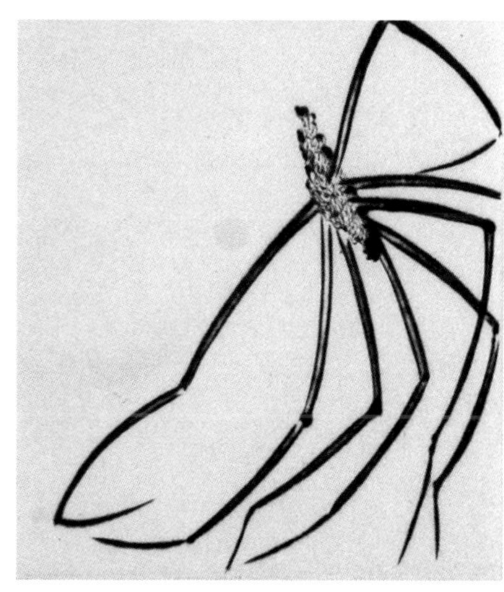

PLATES 31–33

(left) *Traces* 8 (detail)
1994–95
Ed. 22
Drypoint
3¾ x 3¼ in.

(above) *Traces* 9
1994–95
Ed. 22
Drypoint
3¼ x 3¾ in.

(right) *Traces* 10
1994–95
Ed. 22
Drypoint
3¾ x 3¼ in.

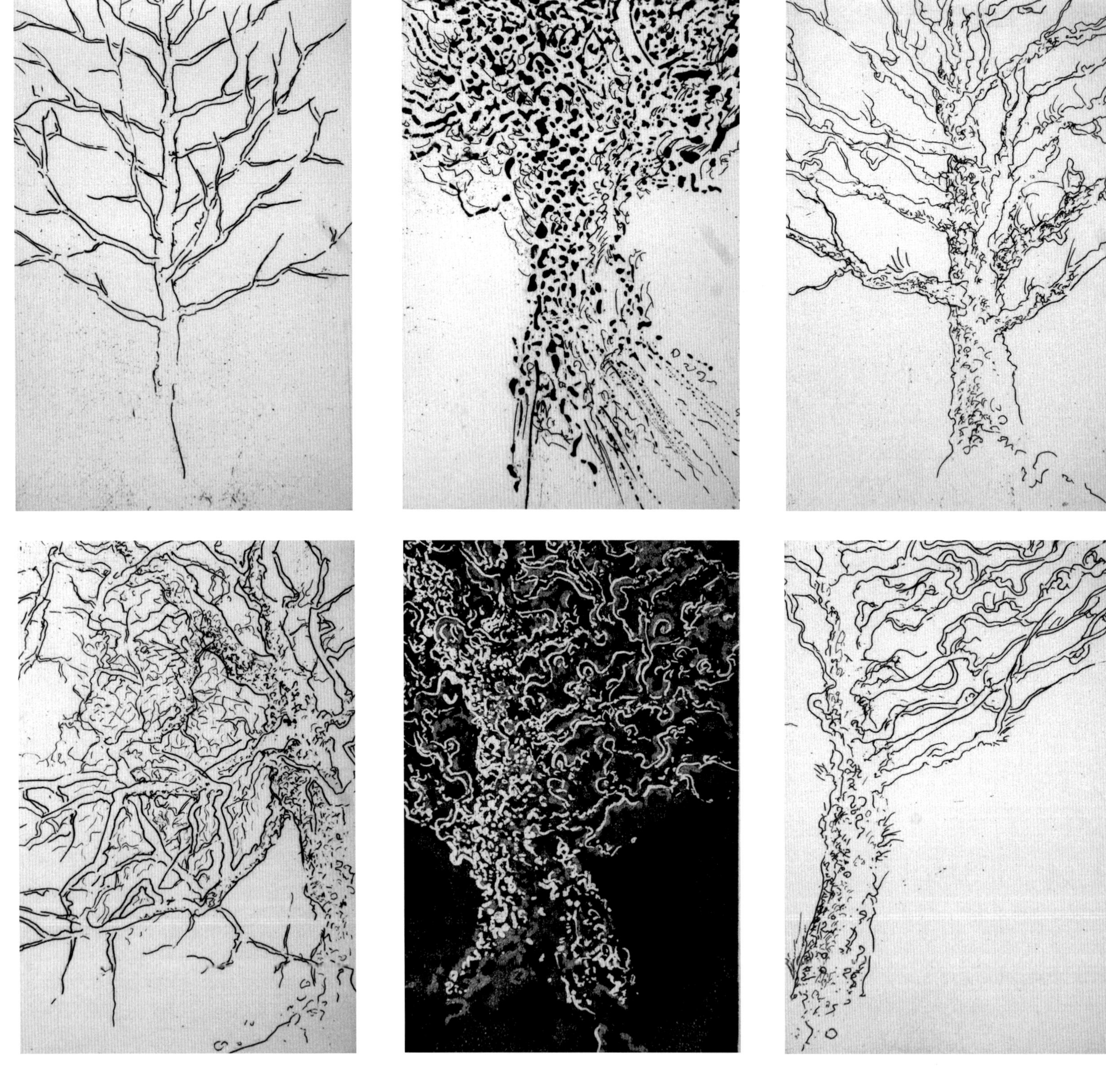

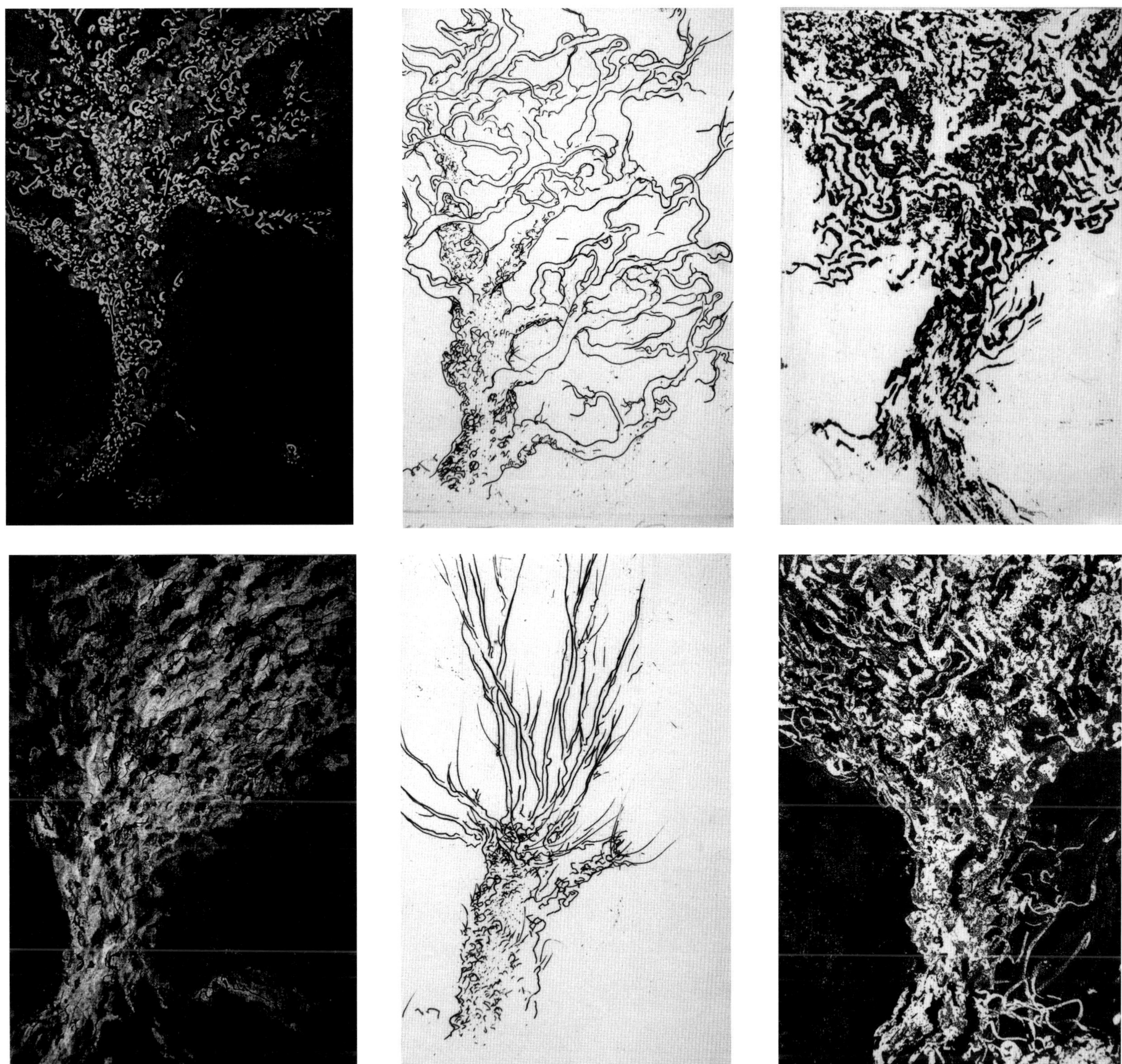

PLATES 34–45

(from left to right, top to bottom)

Interstices, A Conversation with Alders 1–12

1996

Ed. 10

Line etching, aquatint, sugarlift

5¼ x 3½ in. each

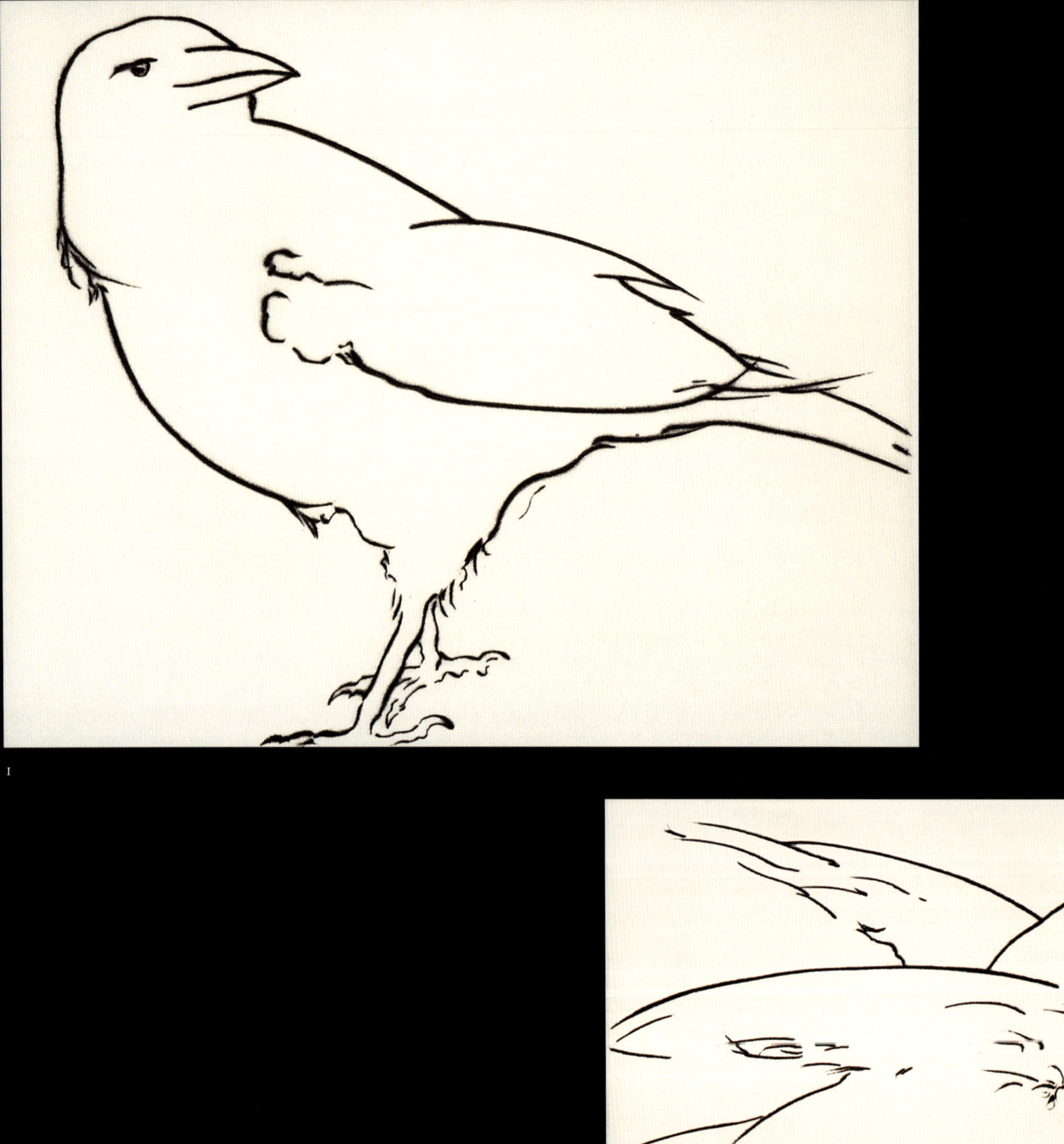

1

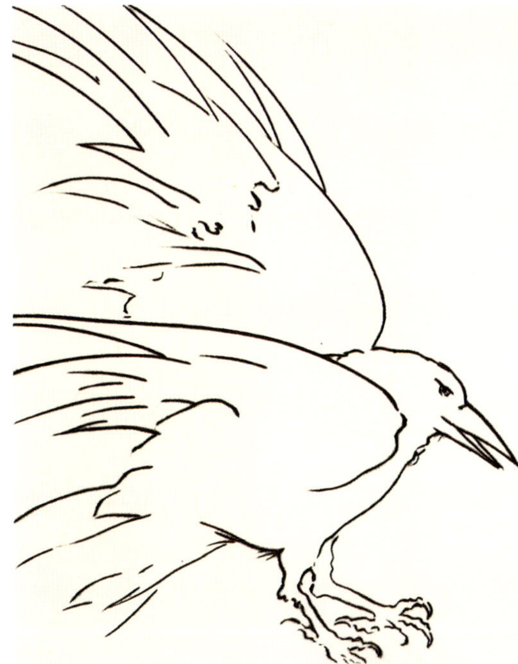

4

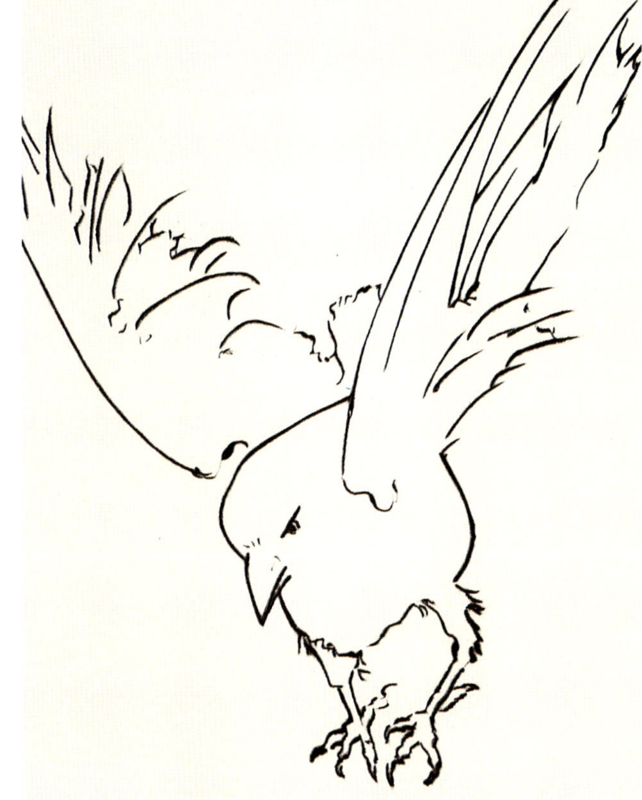

5

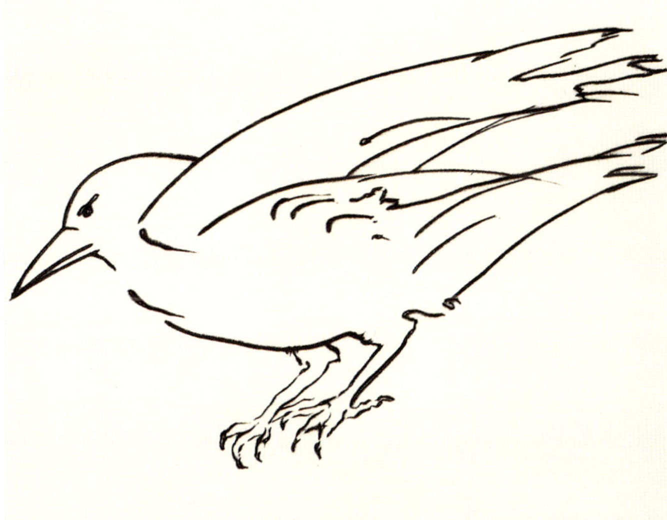

8

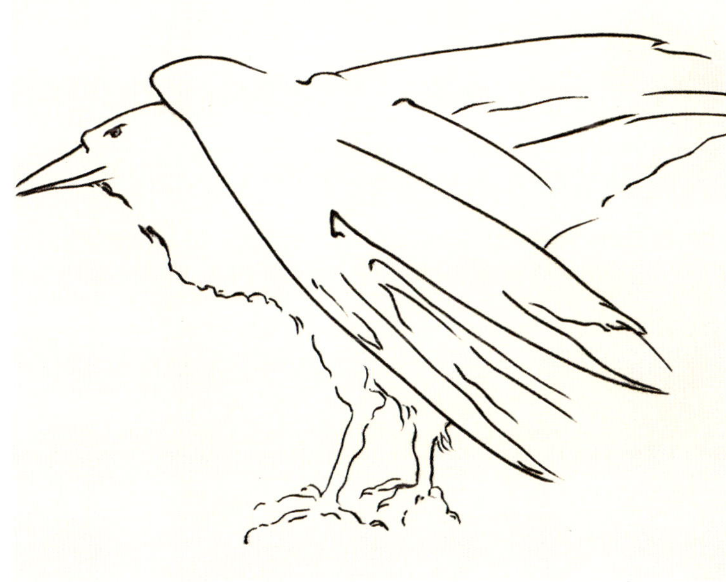

9

PLATES 46–51
Stances 1, 2, 4, 5, 8, 9
1996
Ed. 30
Drypoint printed on tan flat
6⅜ x 8 in. each

PLATES 52–53

Bird Spirits: Nine Piano Pieces for Jane Boyden
Piano pieces by William Bolcom, prints by Frank Boyden
2000
Published by Crab Quill Press, Walla Walla, Washington
Ed. 15
Handmade book with lacquer cover
11¼ x 14⅜ x 1 in.
Collection of Frank and Jane Boyden, Otis, Oregon

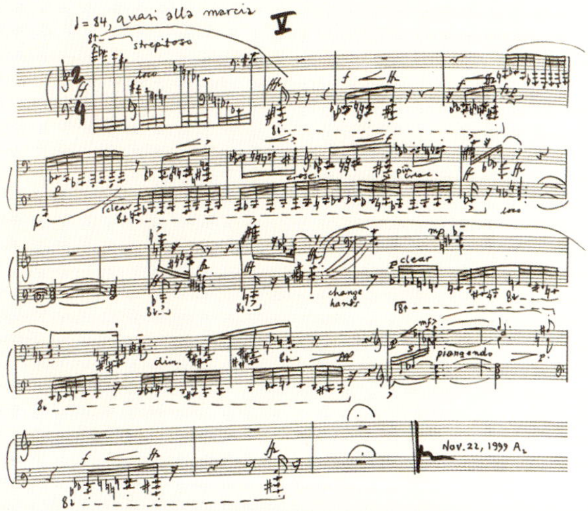

♩ = 84, quasi alla marcia

V

strepitoso

loco

cresc.

più cresc.

loco

clear

clear

change hands

dim.

piangendo

Nov. 22, 1999 A.

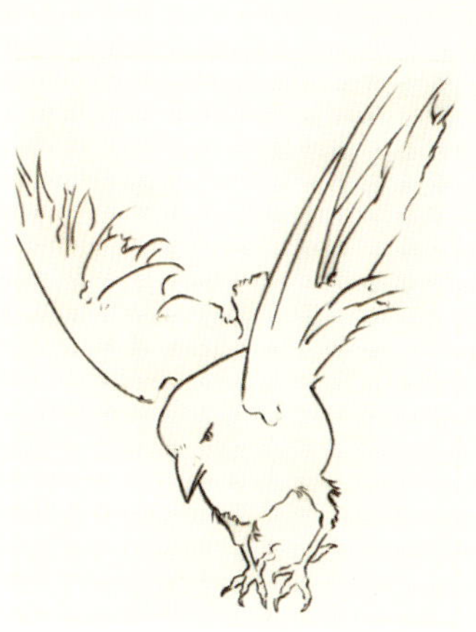

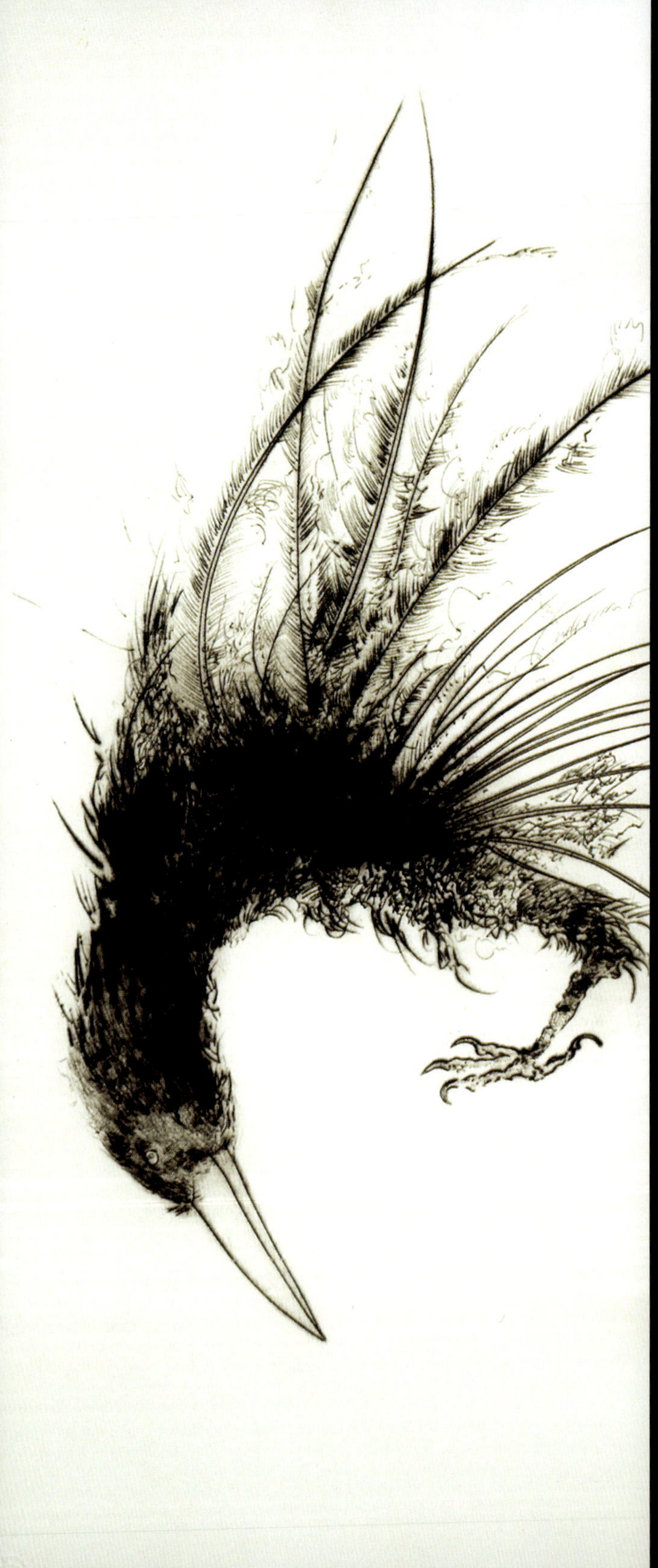

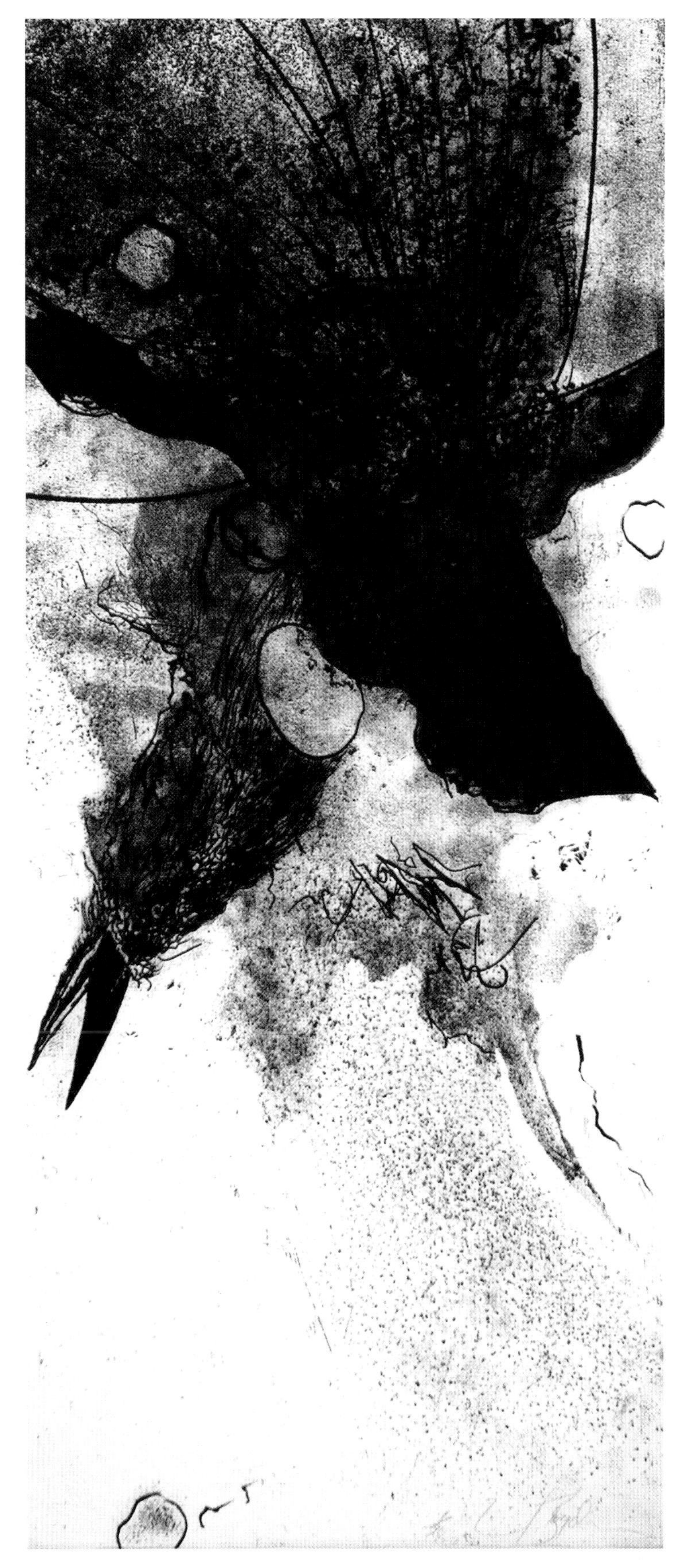

PLATE 55
Disintegrating Raven 3
1996–97
Ed. 20
Soft ground, drypoint, sandblasting
10 x 22¼ in.

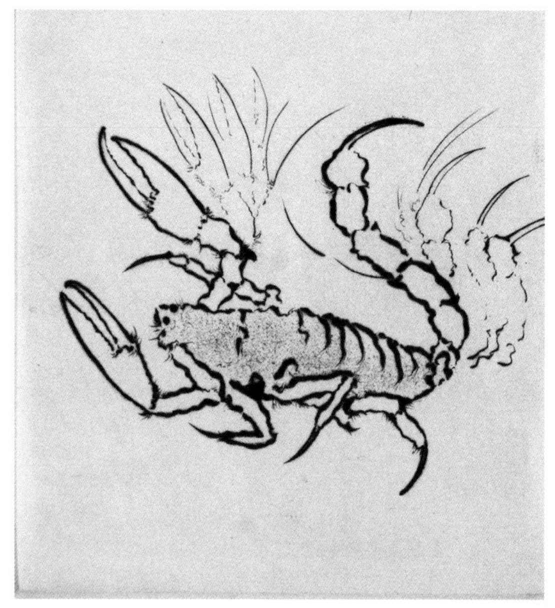

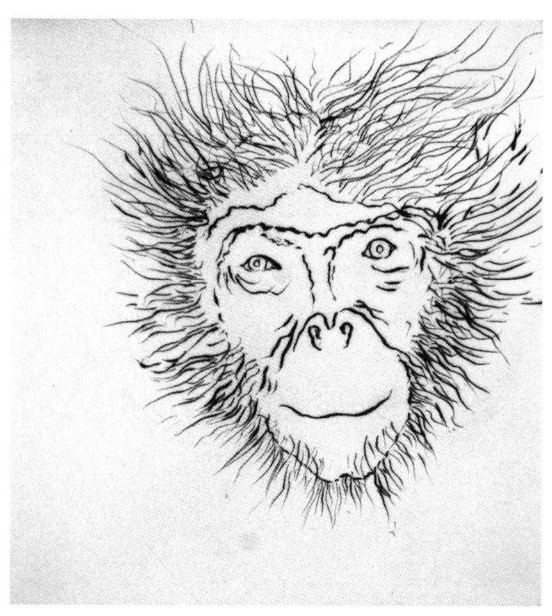

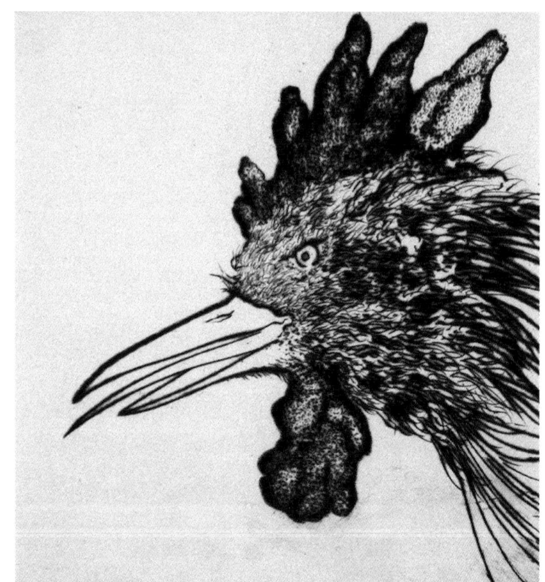

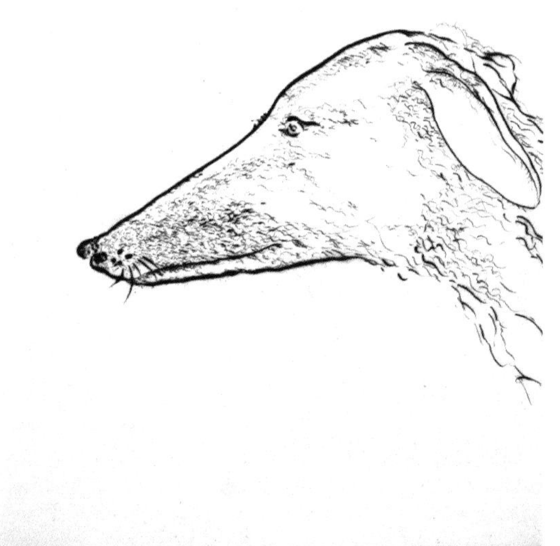

PLATES 56–59
(from left to right, top to bottom)
Scorpion, Monkey, Rooster, and *Dog,* from *A Carousel at Birth*
1997
Drypoint
6¼ x 5¾ in. each

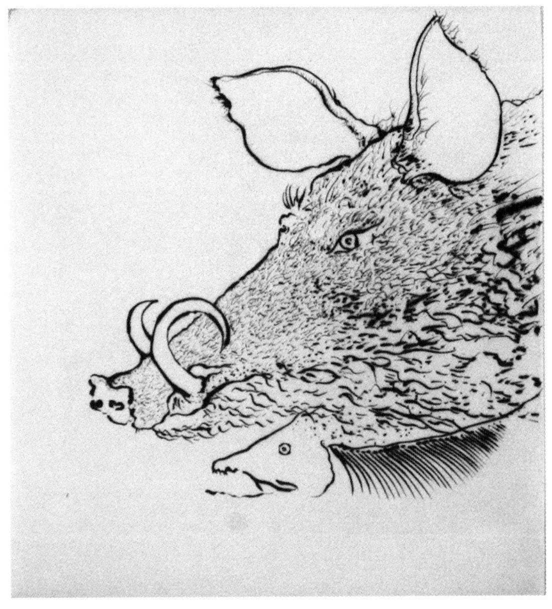
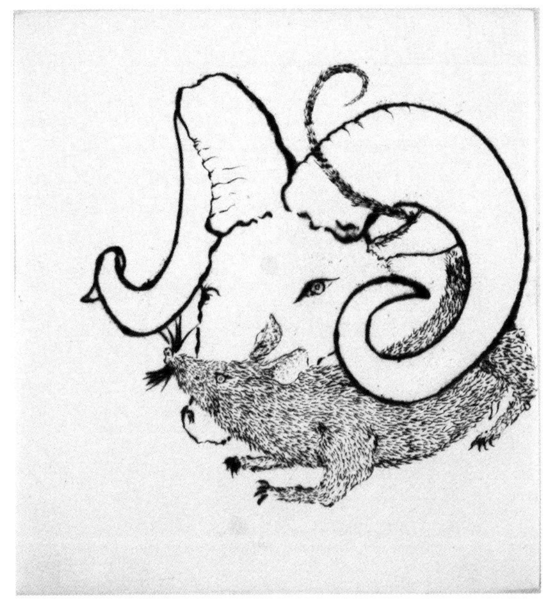
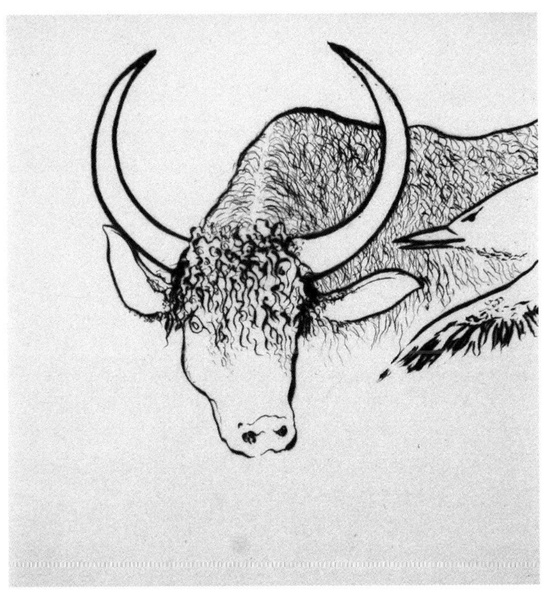
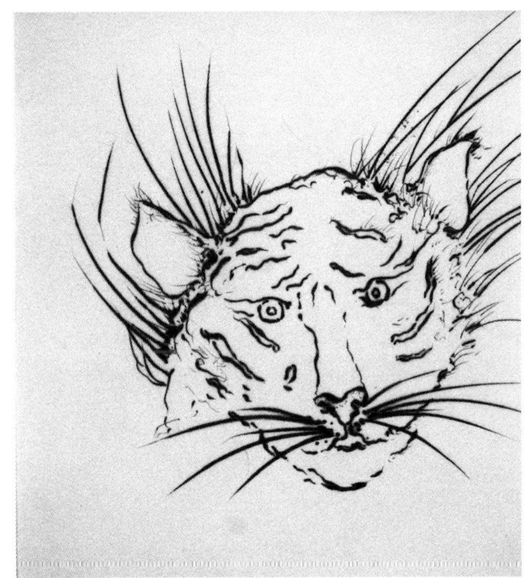

PLATES 60–63
(from left to right, top to bottom)
Boar and Fish, Ram and Rat, Bull and Magpie, and *Tiger,* from *A Carousel at Birth*
1997
Drypoint
6¼ x 5¾ in. each

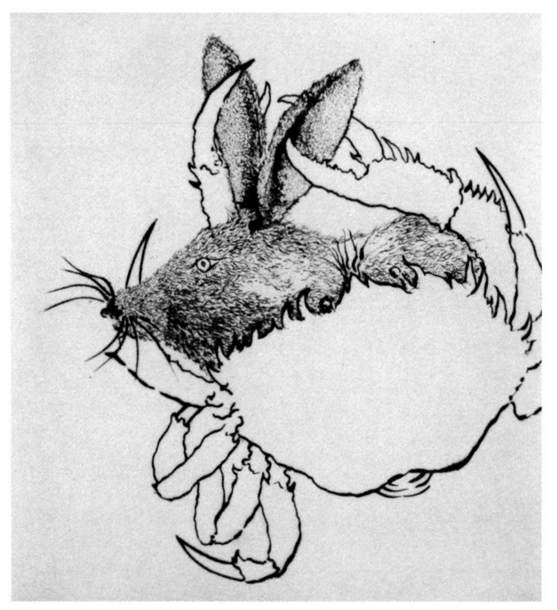

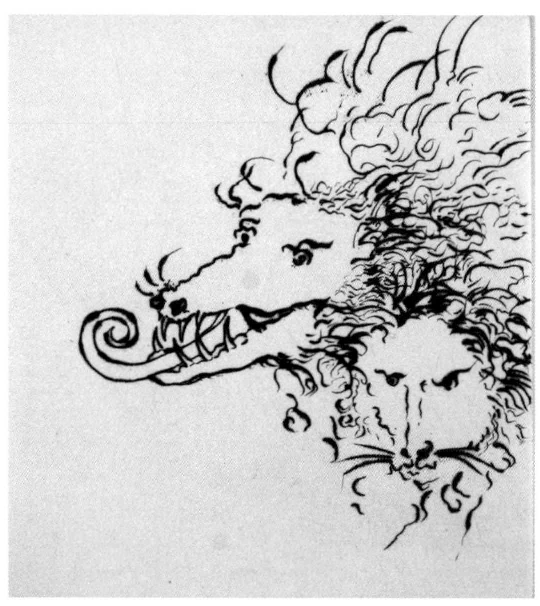

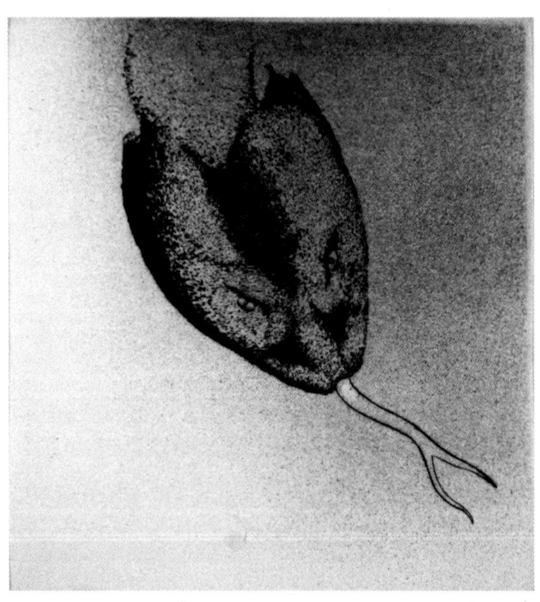

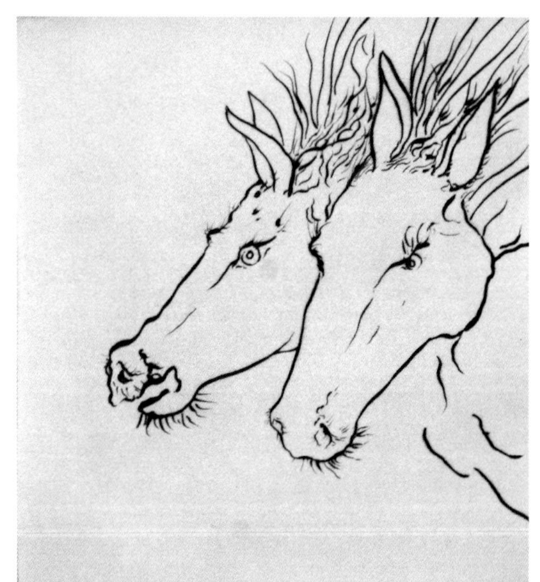

PLATES 64–67
(from left to right, top
to bottom)
Crab and Rabbit, Dragon and Lion, Snake, and *Horses,* from *A Carousel at Birth*
1997
Drypoint
6¼ x 5¾ in. each

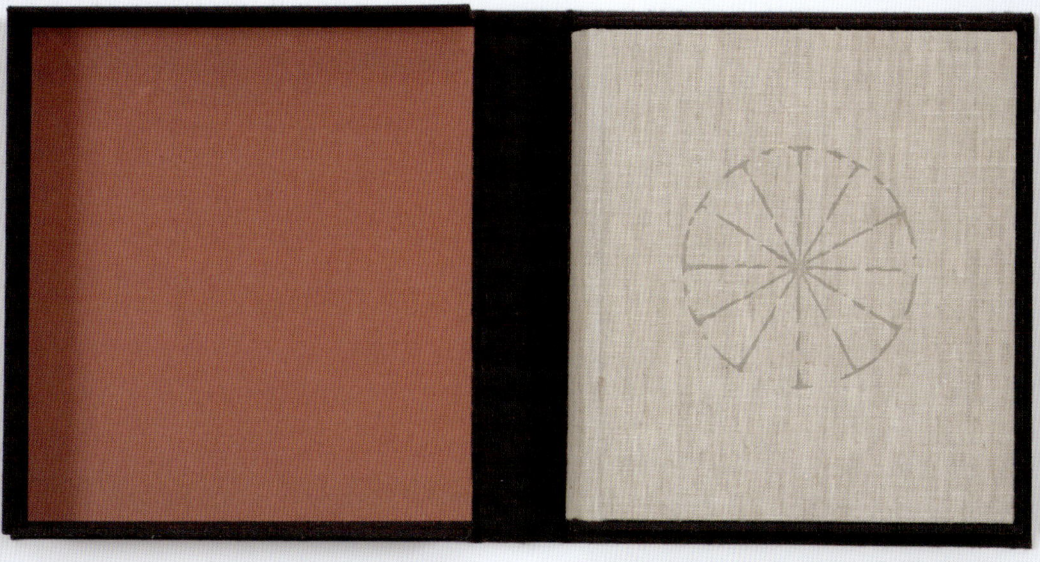

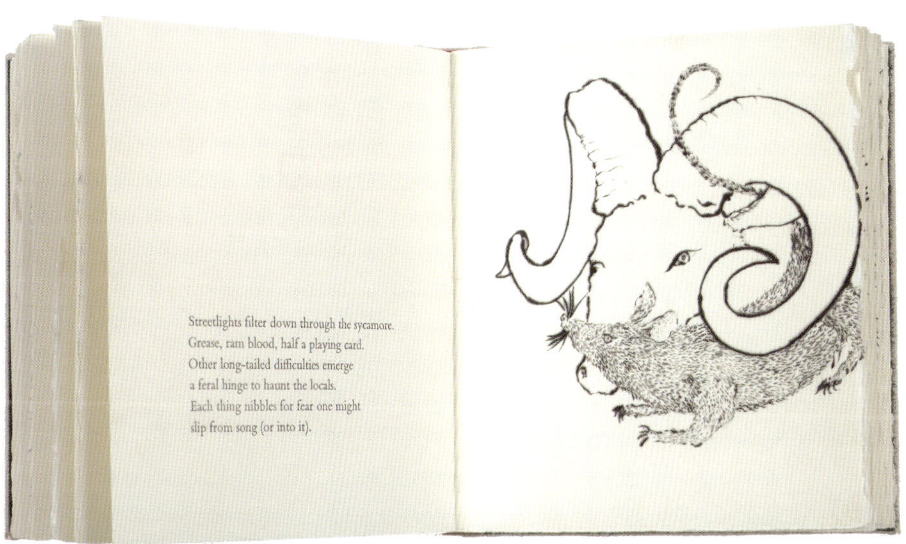
Streetlights filter down through the sycamore.
Grease, ram blood, half a playing card.
Other long-tailed difficulties emerge
a feral hinge to haunt the locals.
Each thing nibbles for fear one might
slip from song (or into it).

PLATES 68–69
A Carousel at Birth
Poem by Ian Boyden, prints by
Frank Boyden
1997
Published by Salient Seedling Press,
Portland, Oregon

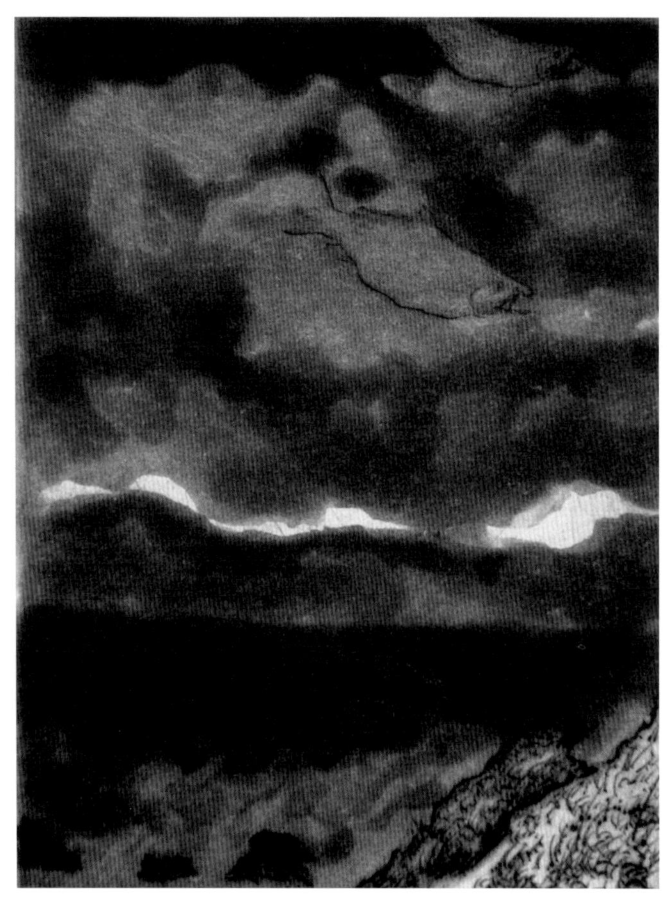

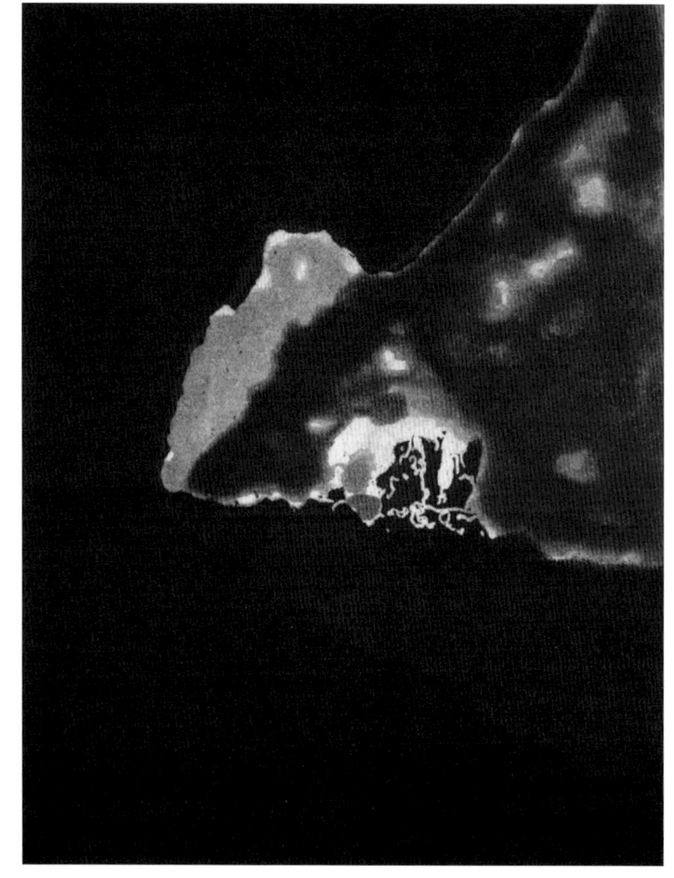

PLATE 70
Cascade Head 1
1997–1998
Ed. 10
Aquatint and drypoint
3¾ x 2¾ in.

PLATE 71
Cascade Head 3
1997–1998
Ed. 10
Aquatint
3¾ x 2¾ in.

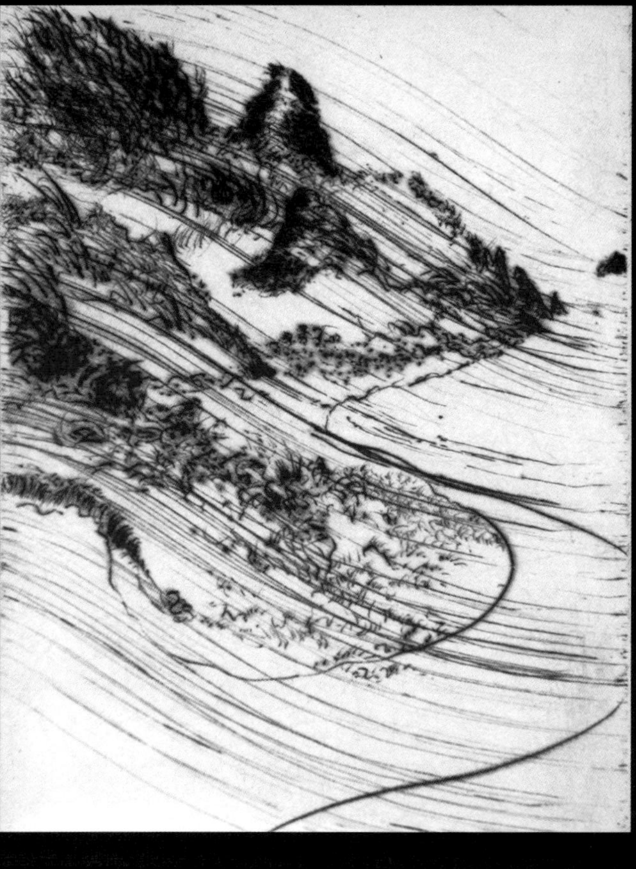

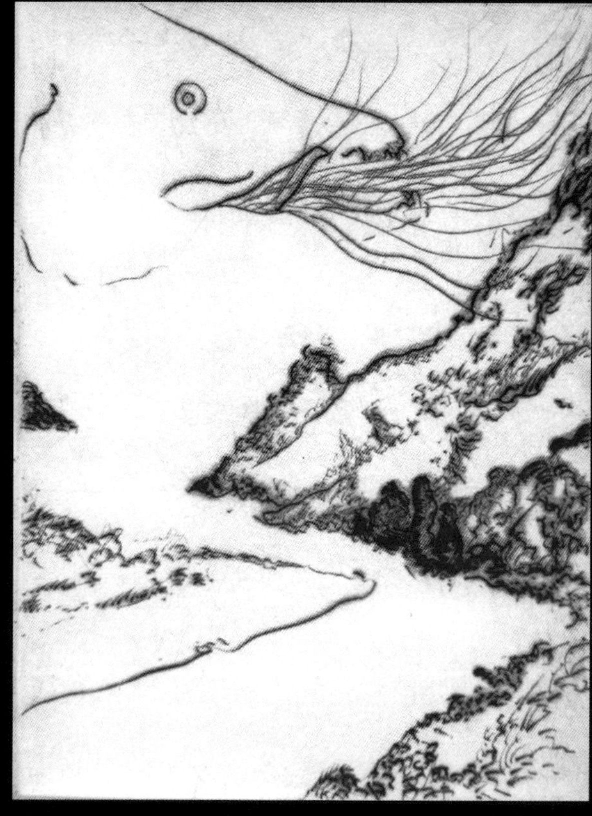

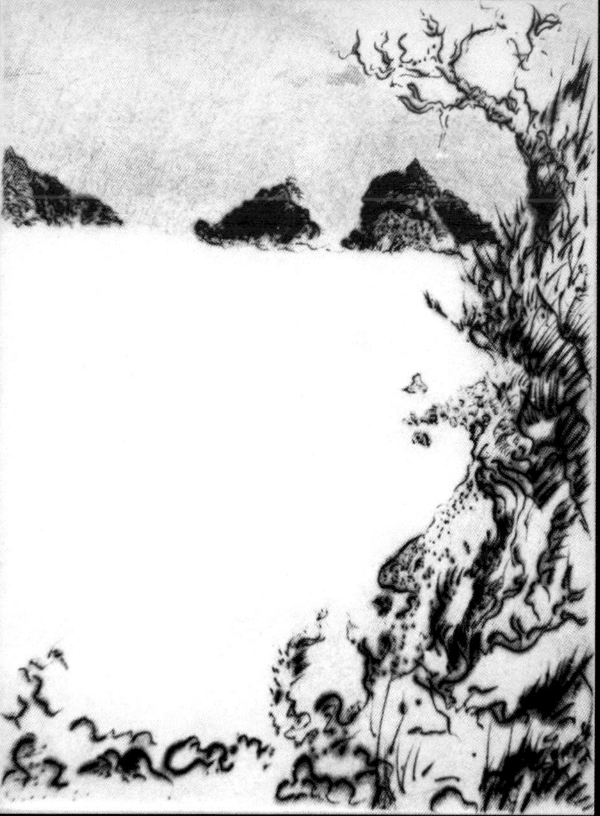

PLATES 72–74

(clockwise from top)

Cascade Head 2
1997–1998
Ed. 10
Drypoint
3¾ x 2¾ in.

Cascade Head 4
1997–1998
Ed. 10
Aquatint and drypoint
3¾ x 2¾ in.

Cascade Head 5
1997-1998
Ed. 10
Drypoint
3¾ x 2¾ in.

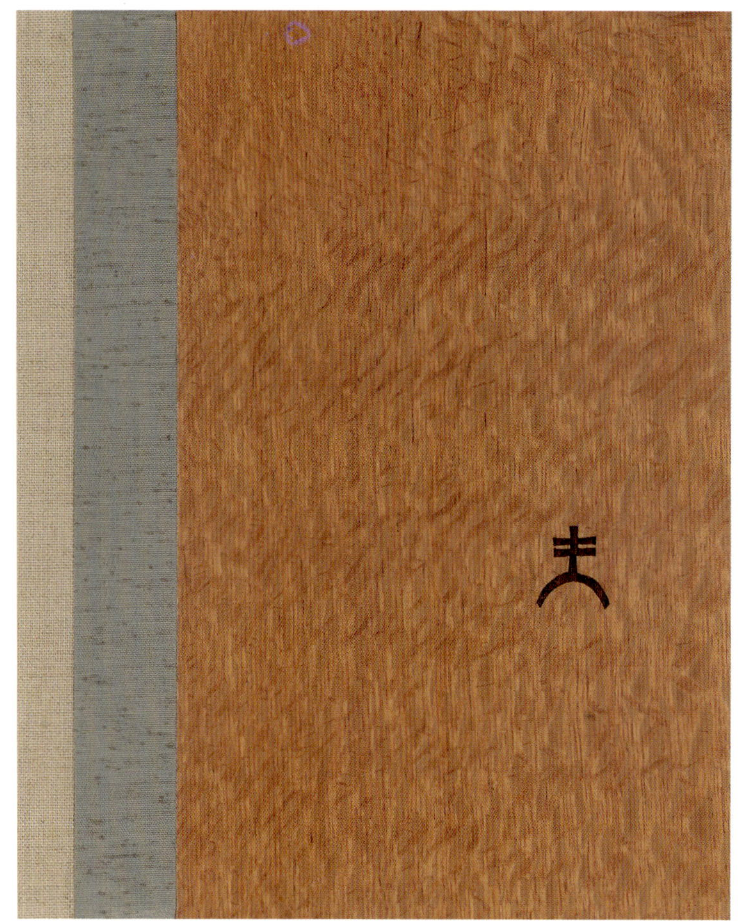

PLATES 75–76

Twenty Views of Cascade Head
Poems by J. Cailin Oakes and Ian Boyden, prints by Charles Chu and Frank Boyden
2001
Published by Crab Quill Press, Walla Walla, Washington
Ed. 10
Handmade book
8½ x 7 x 1¼ in.
Collection of Frank and Jane Boyden, Otis, Oregon

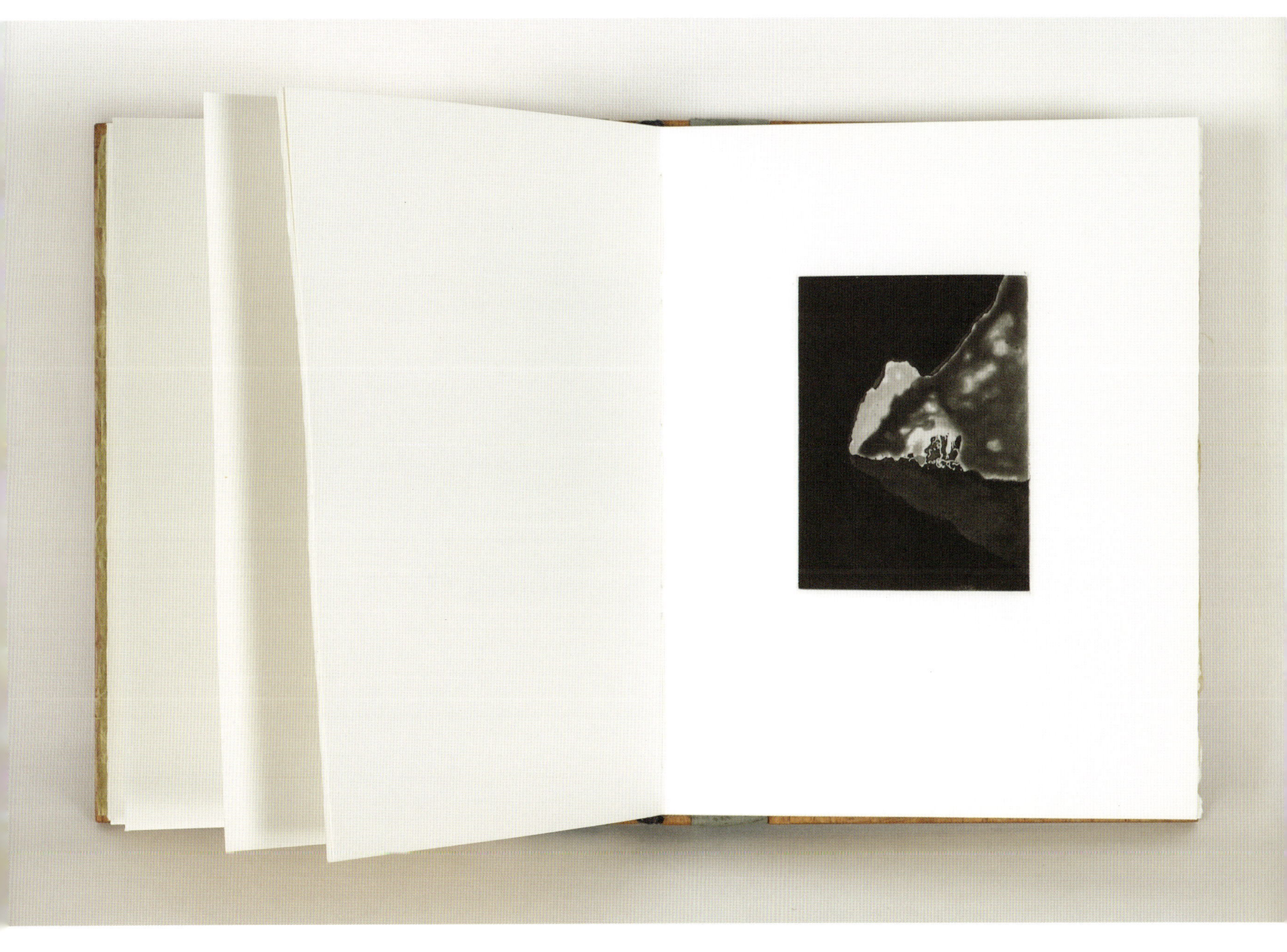

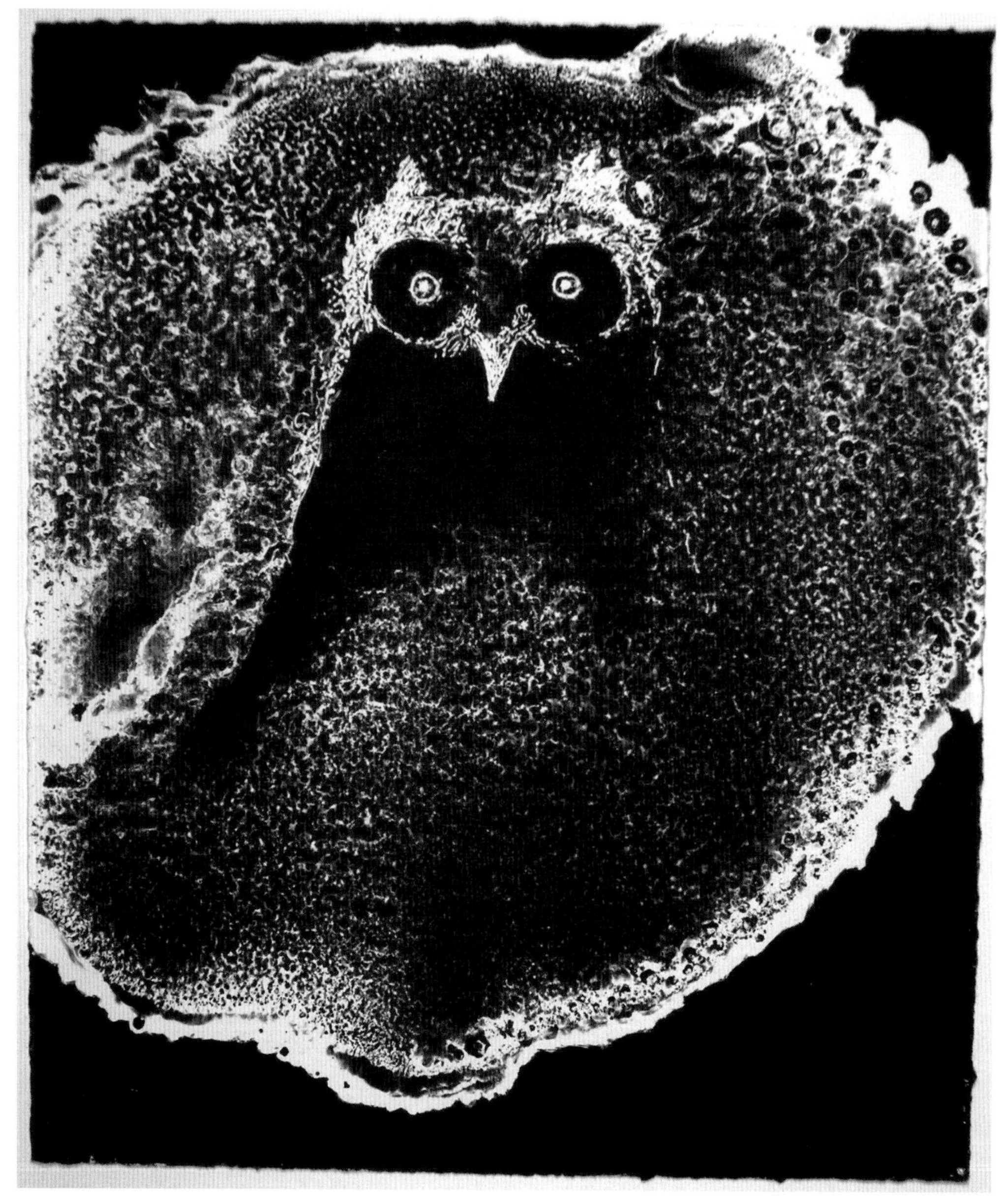

PLATE 77
Cave Owl
1998
Ed. 15
Cliché verre
10½ x 9 in.

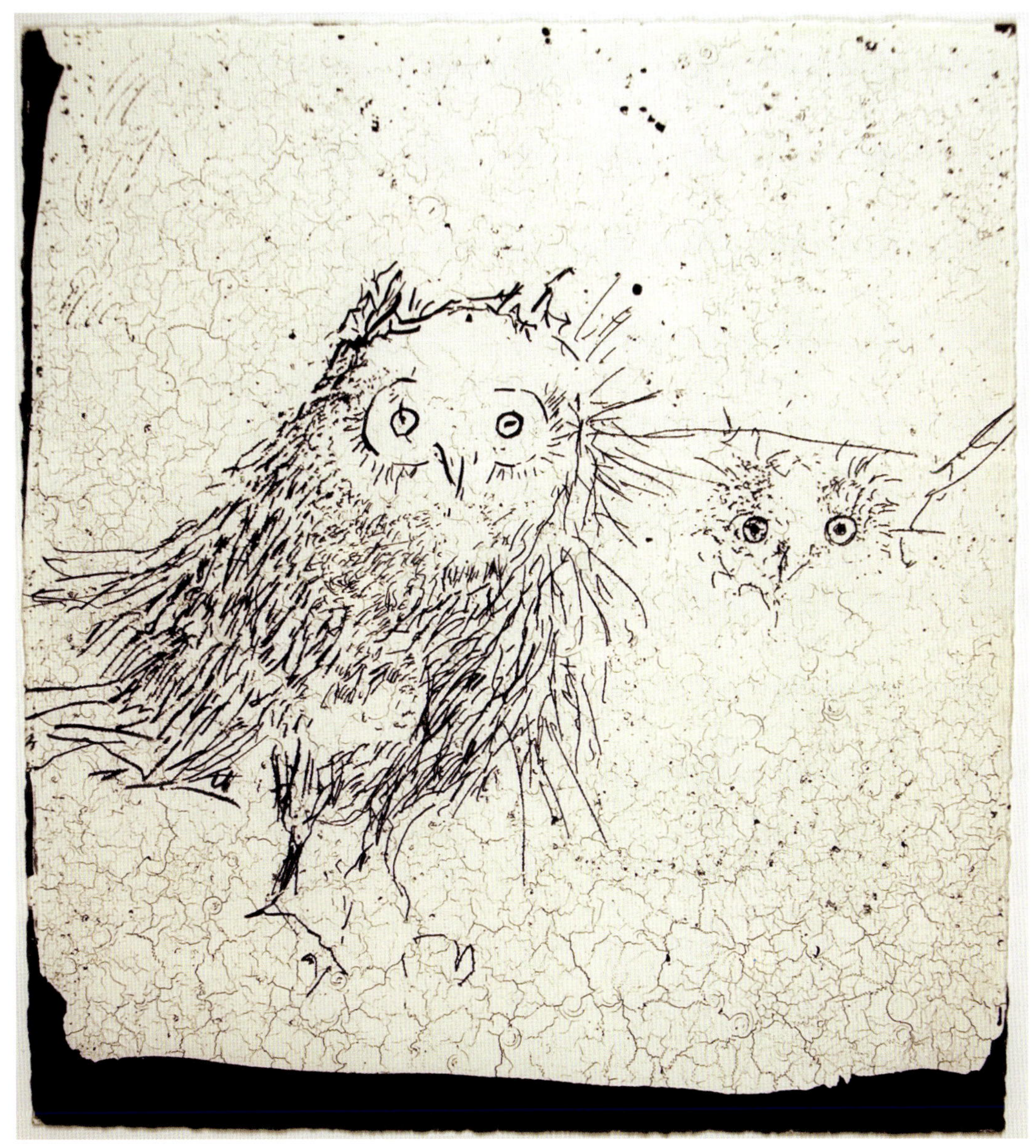

PLATE 78
Owl of the Crackling Plain
1998
Ed. 15
Cliché verre
9 x 8½ in.

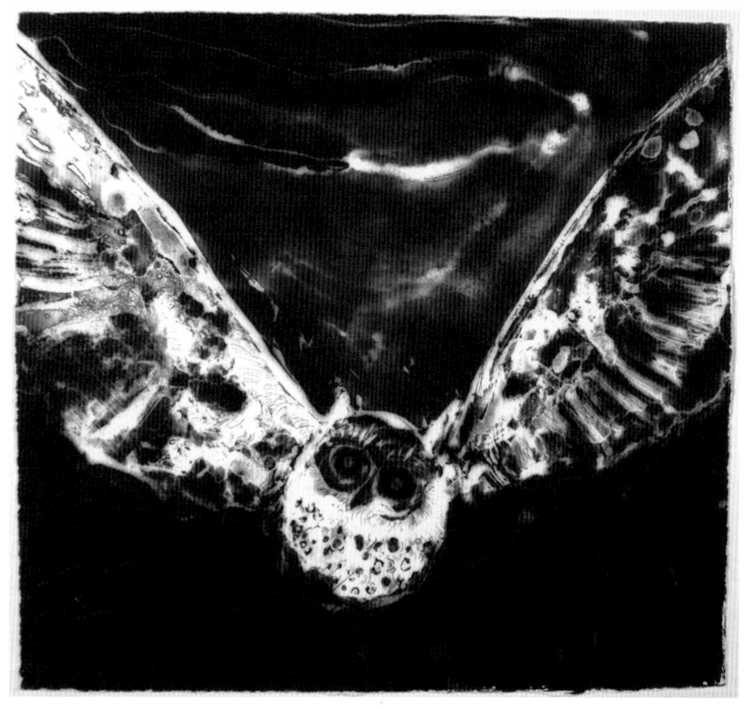

PLATE 79
Soft Owl Flying
1998
Ed. 10
Cliché verre
10 x 11 in.

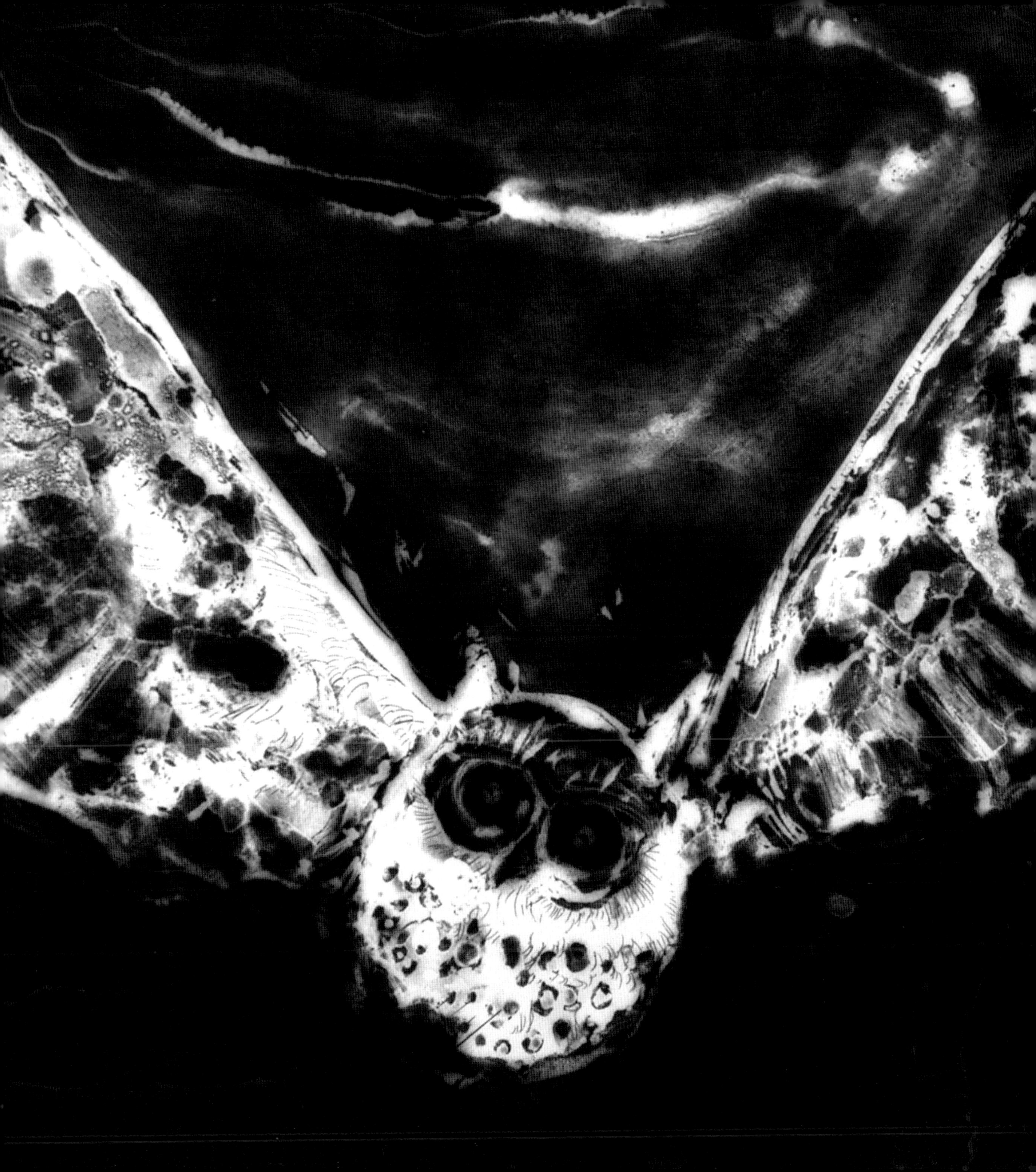

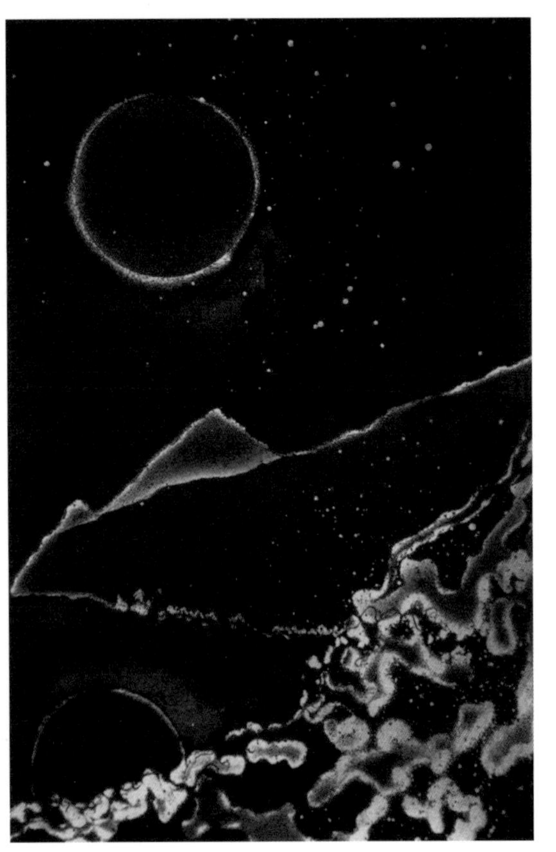

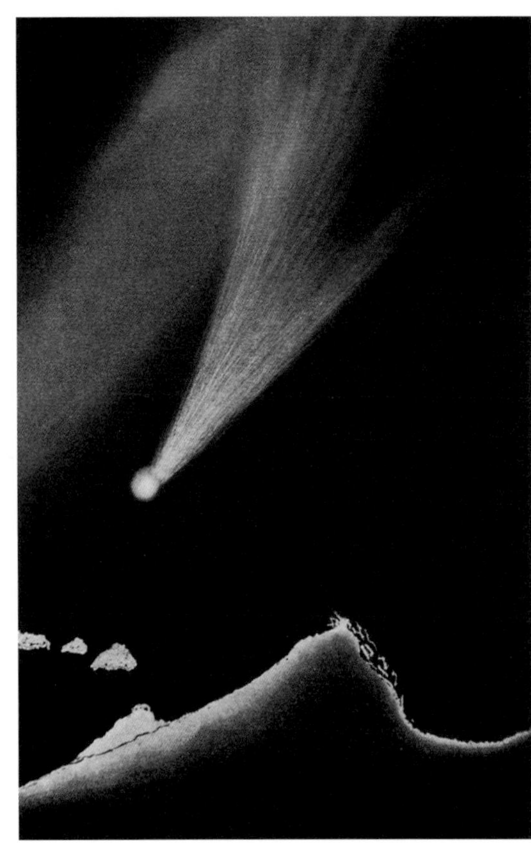

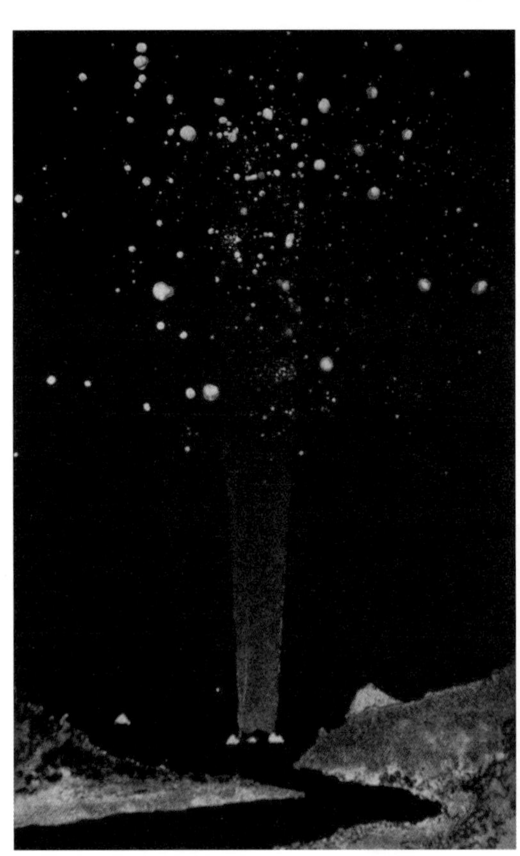

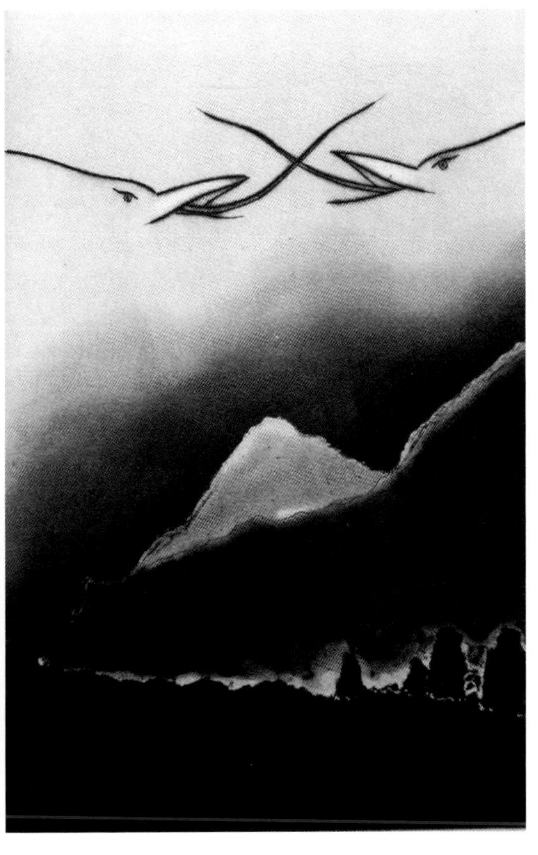

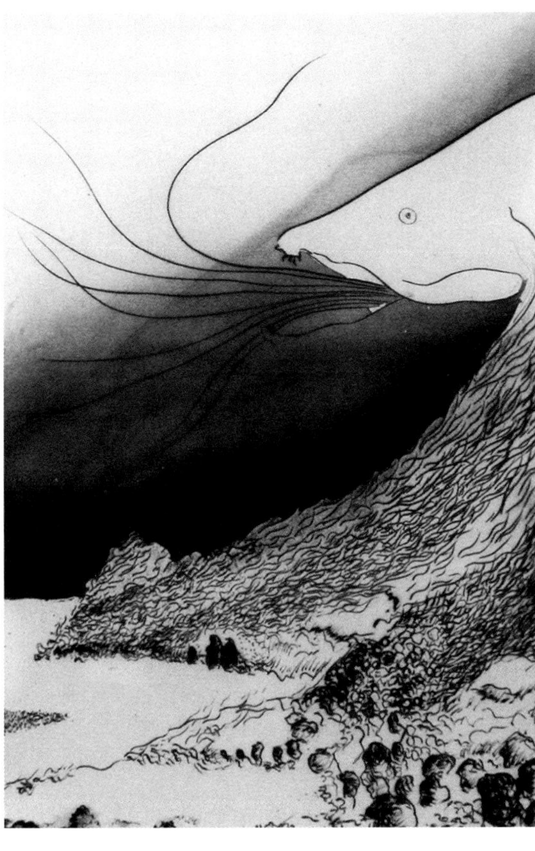

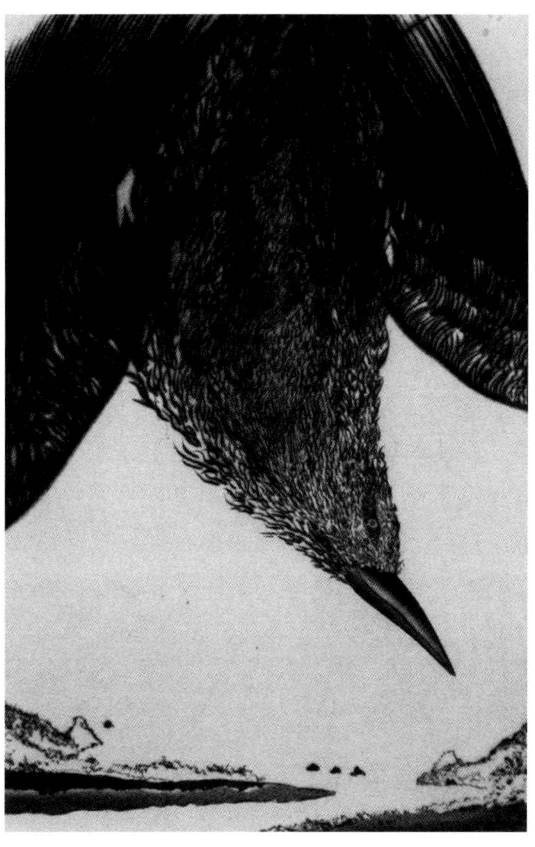

PLATES 80–85
Gifts of the Sky 1–6
1999
Ed. 15
Aquatint, drypoint,
spitbite, mezzotint
6¾ x 4½ in. each

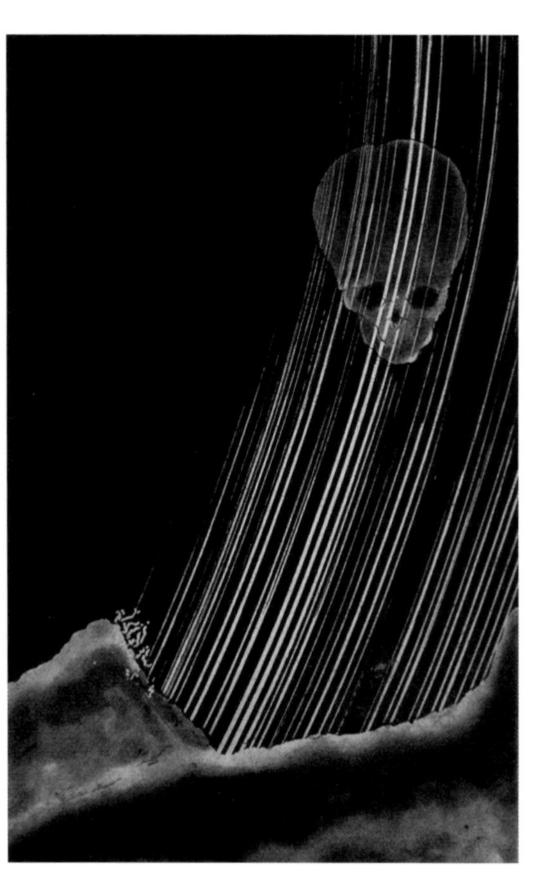

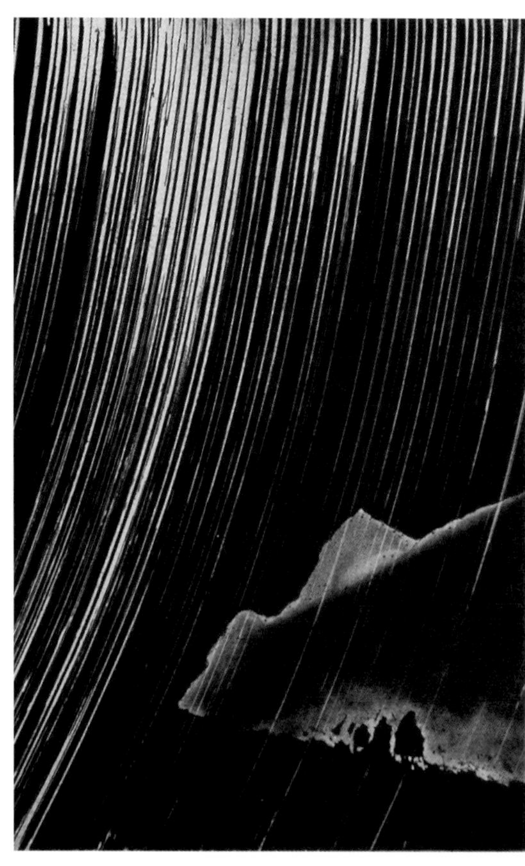

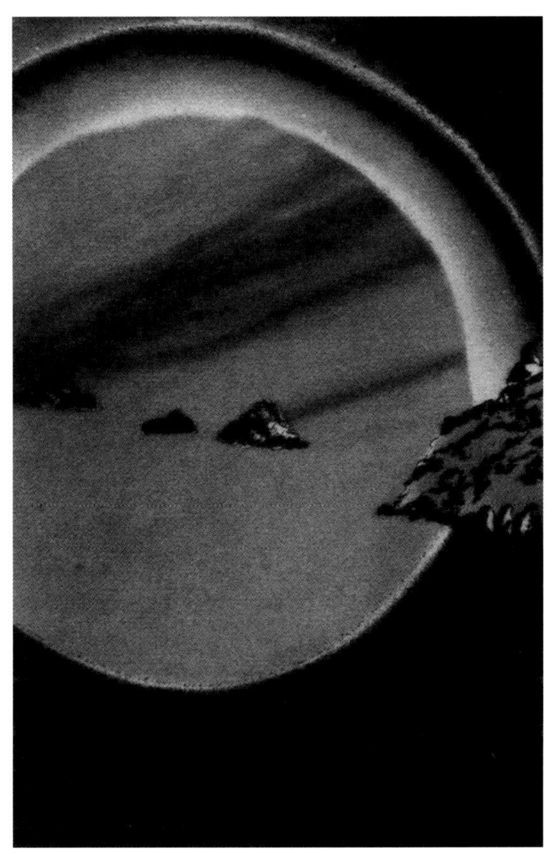

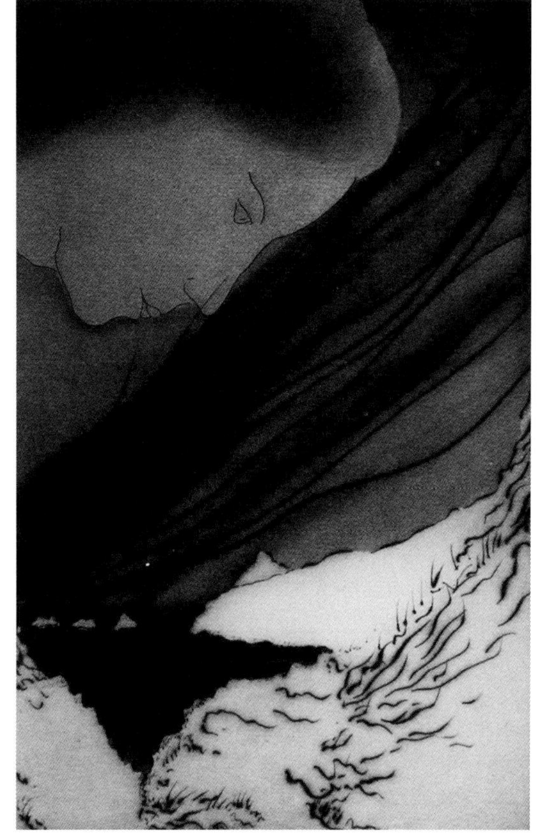

PLATE 86–89
Gifts of the Sky 7–10
1999
Ed. 15
Aquatint, drypoint,
spitbite, line etching
6¾ x 4½ in. each

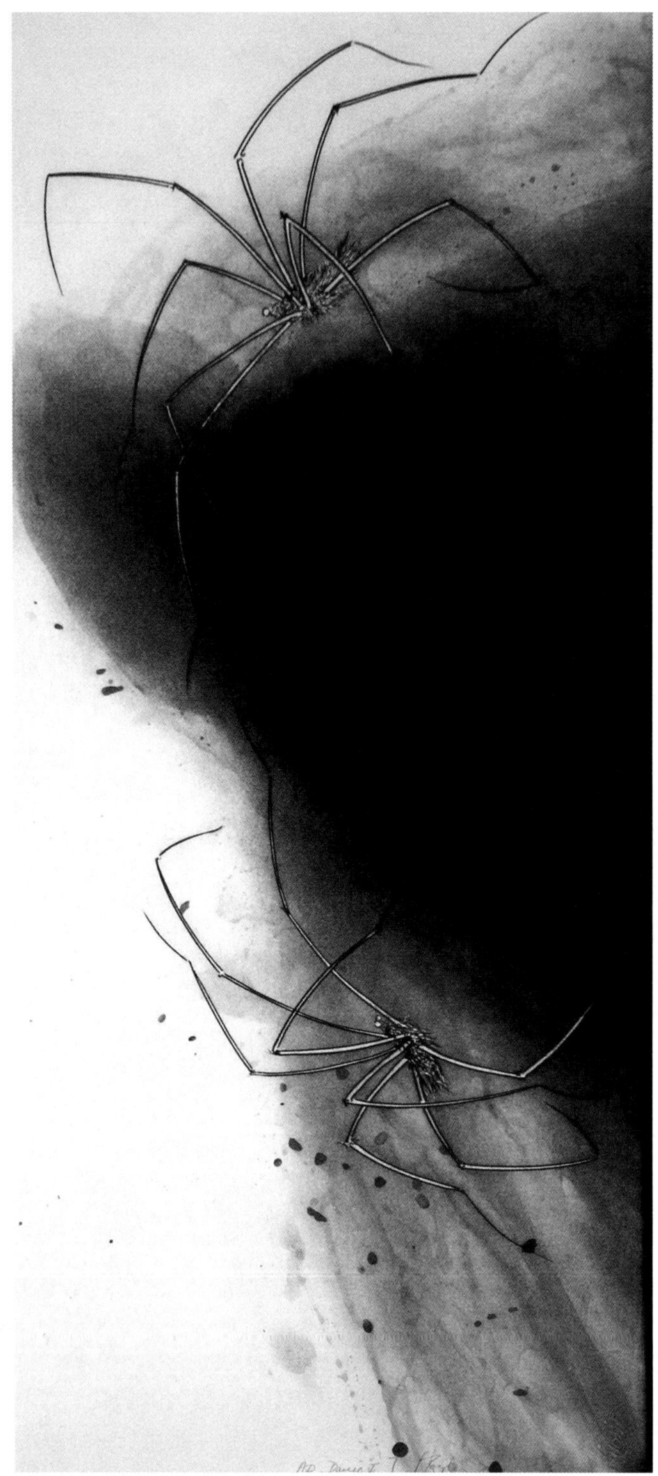

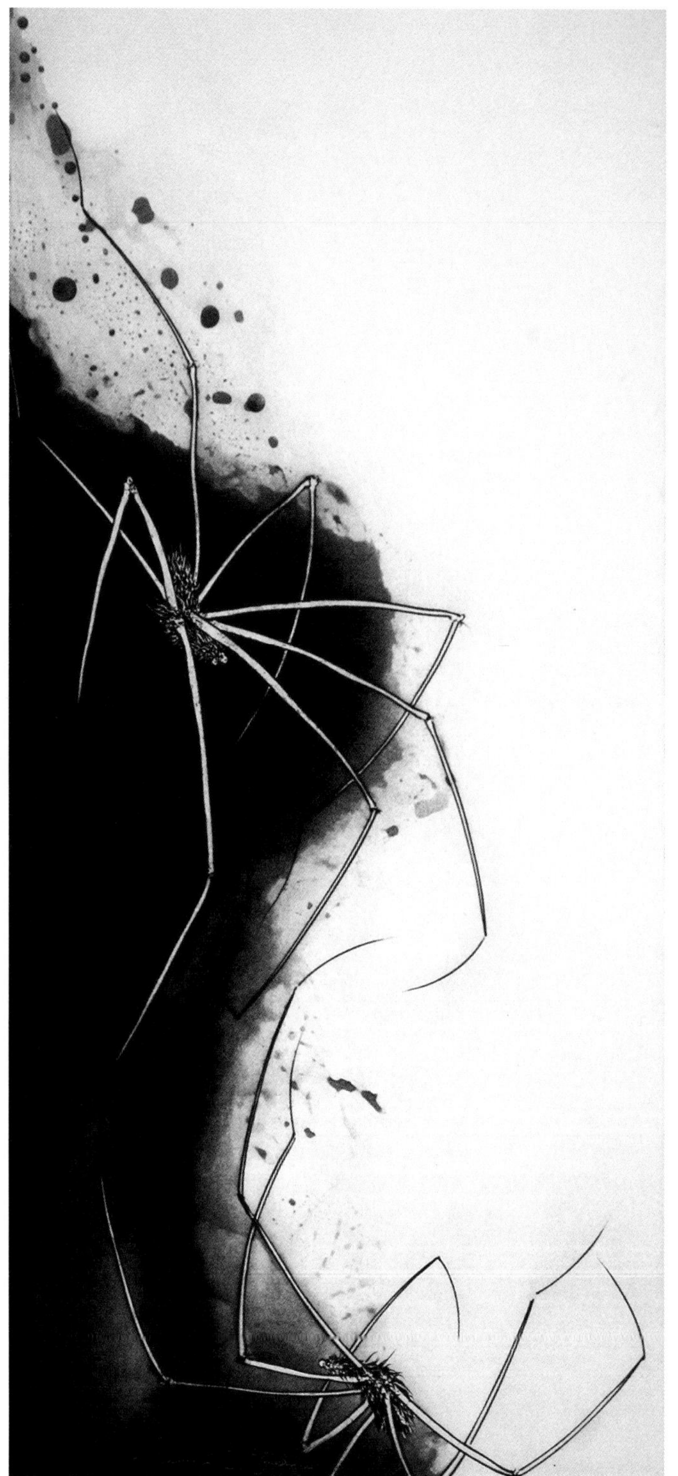

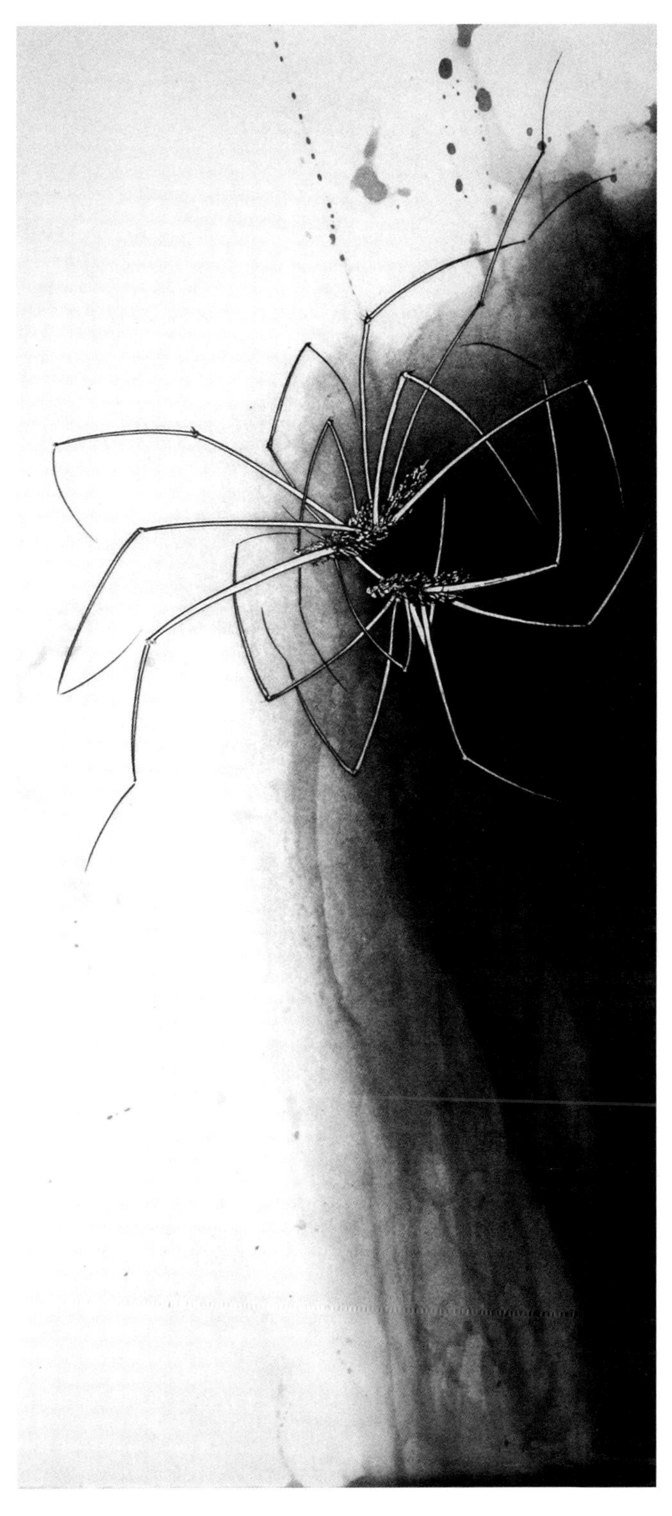

PLATES 90–92
Dance 1, 2, 3
1999–2000
Ed. 10
Drypoint, spitbite
23½ x 10¾ in. each

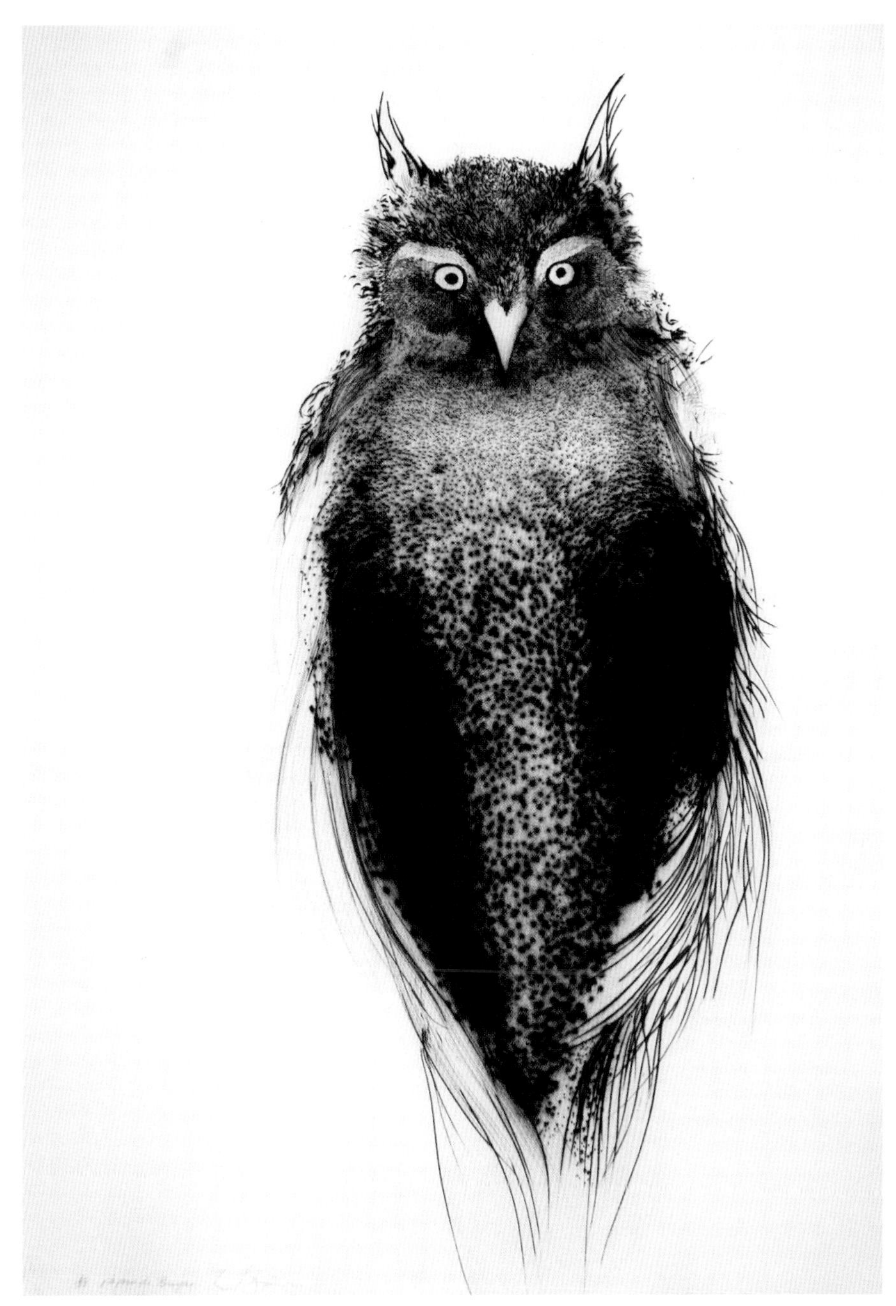

PLATE 93
Pajaro de Brujas
1999–2000
Ed. 23
Drypoint
31 x 22¼ in.

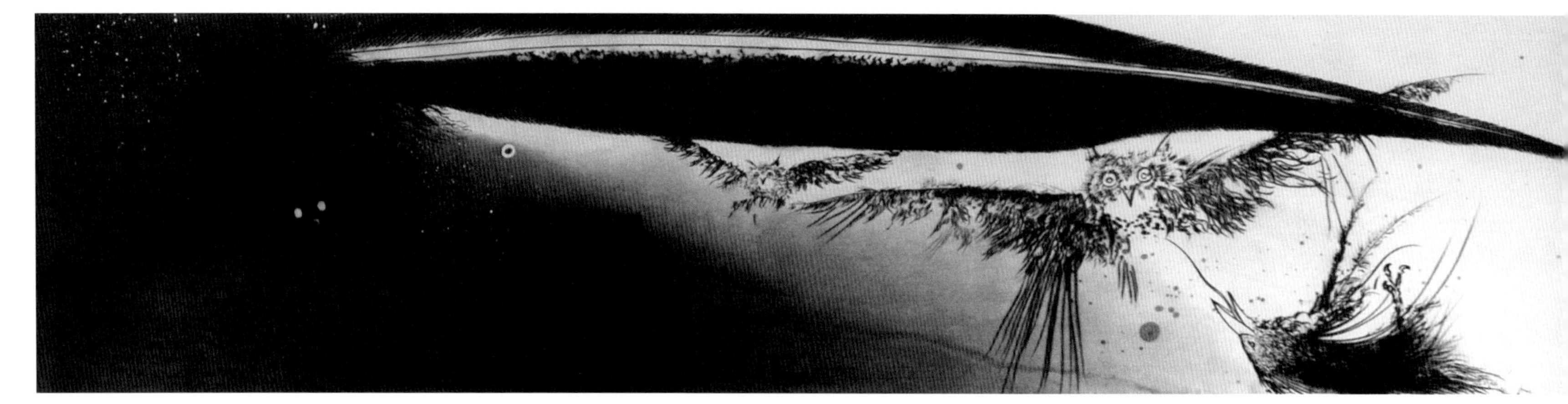

PLATE 94
Mockery of the Black Angel and Three Spanish Owls,
from the *Black Angel Suite*
2001
Ed. 12
Drypoint, spitbite
12 x 48 in.

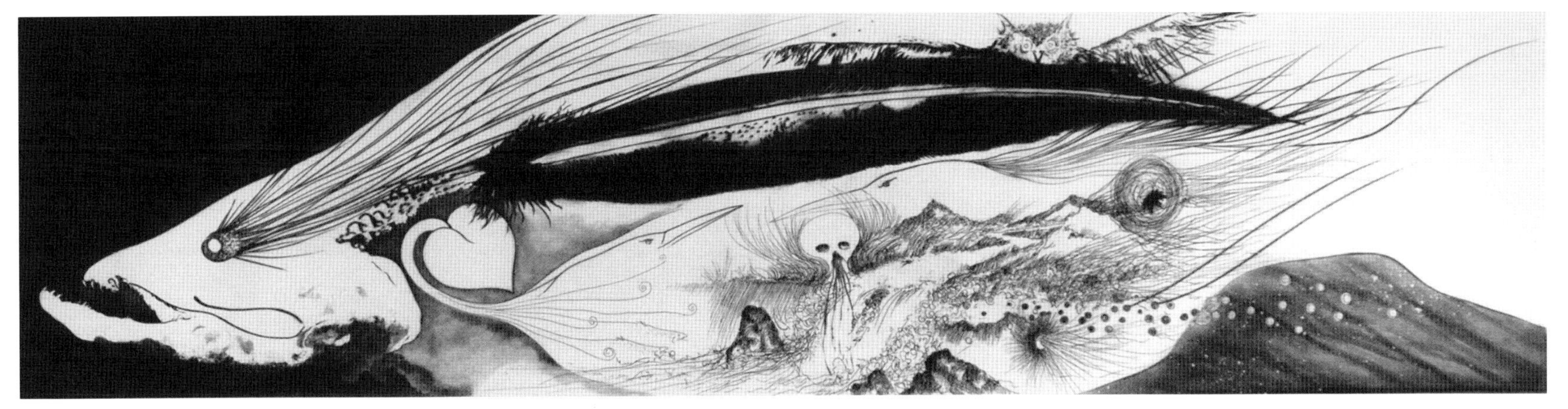

PLATE 95
Violation, from the *Black Angel Suite*
2001
Ed. 12
Drypoint, aquatint,
line etching
12 x 48 in.

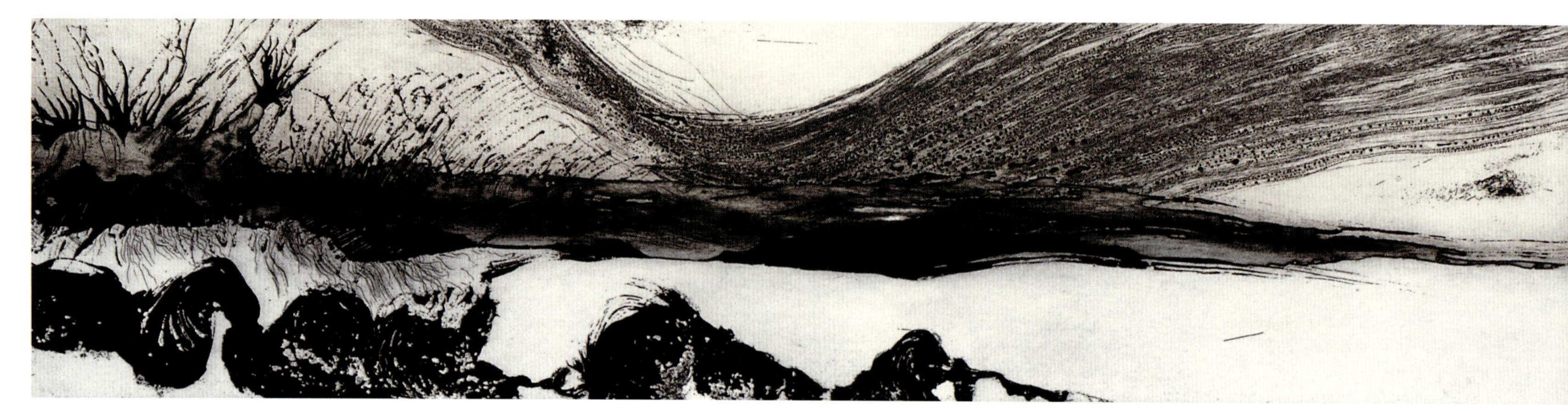

PLATE 96
Ascension
2001
Ed. 10
Spitbite, sugarlift
5⅞ x 24 in.

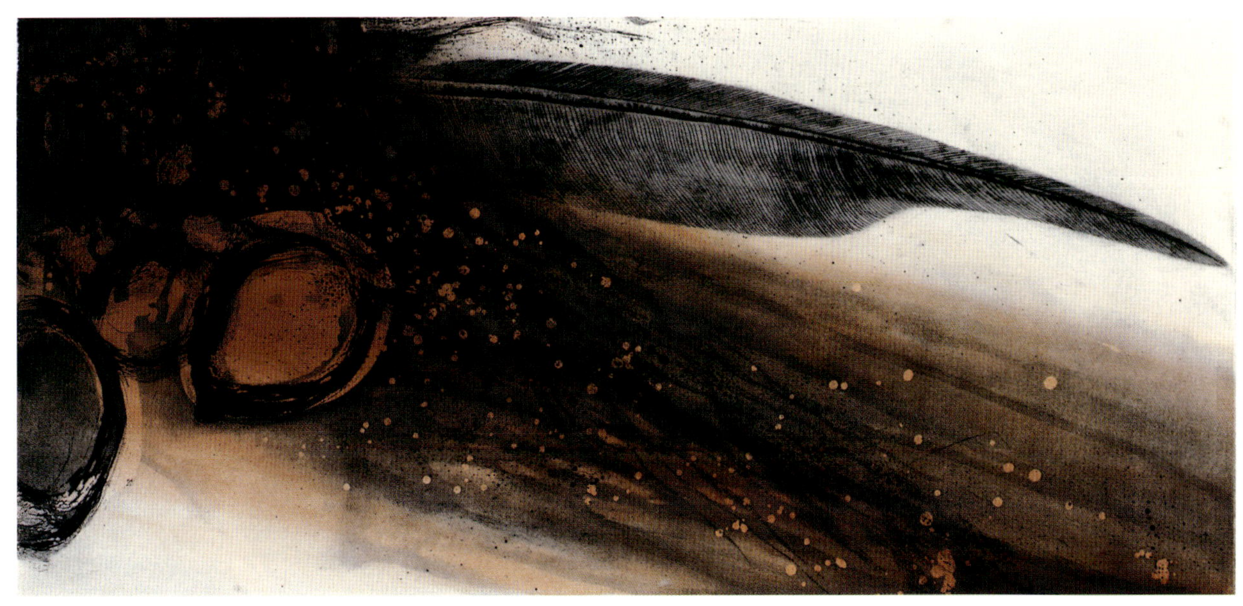

PLATE 97
Feather at Sandlake Wash
2001
Ed. 10
Drypoint, sugarlift,
spitbite
14½ x 31¼ in.

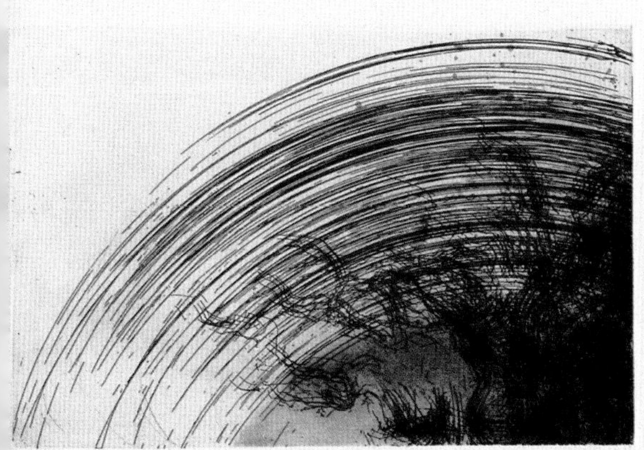
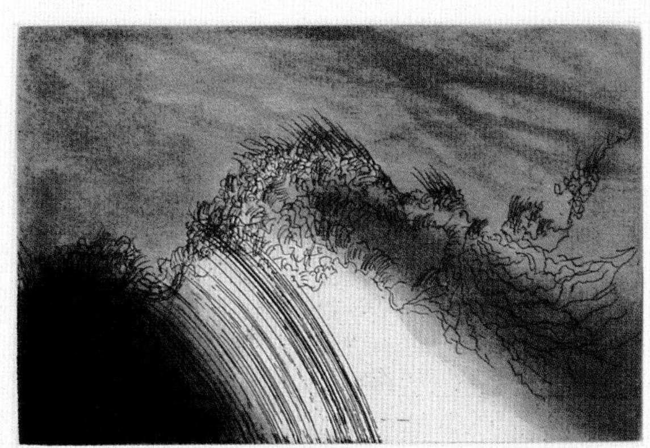
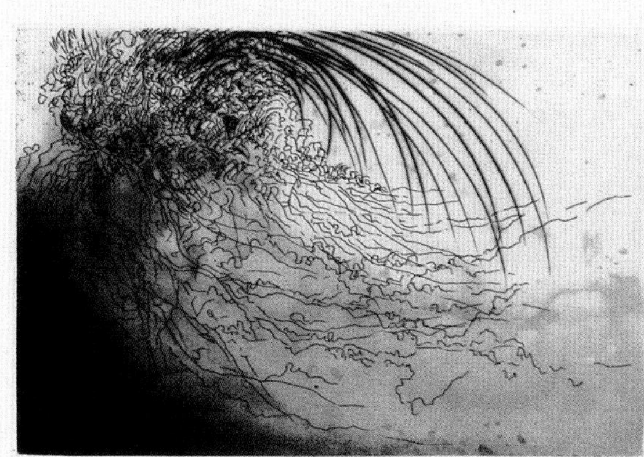

PLATE 98
Grass Dance
2001
Ed. 15
Drypoint, spitbite,
line etching
4½ x 21½ in.

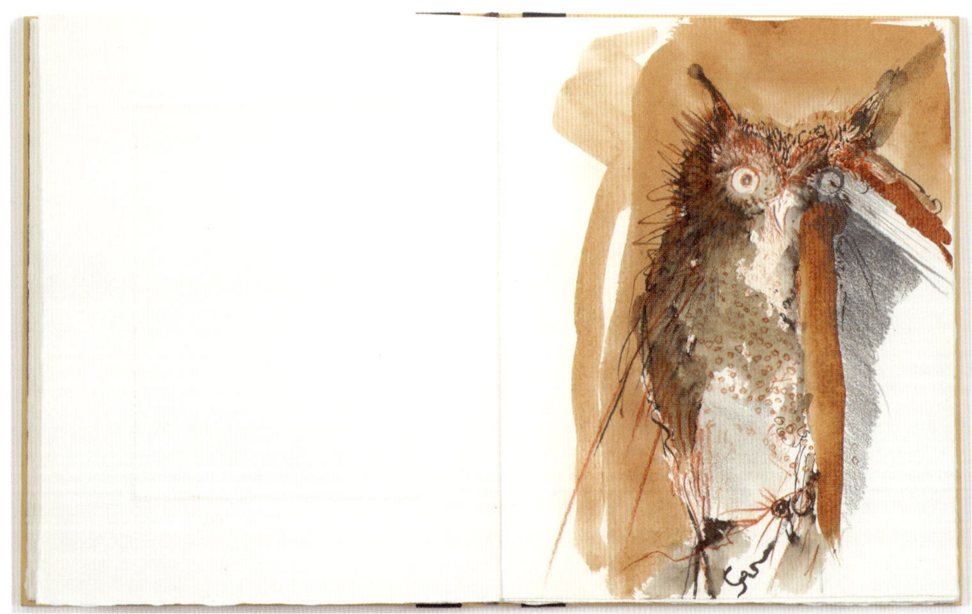

PLATES 99–104
Parts and Pieces: A Brief Bestiary
Prints and drawings by Rick Bartow and Frank Boyden
2001
Published by Crab Quill Press, Walla Walla, Washington
Ed. 6
Handmade book
11¼ x 9¼ x 1⅜ in.
Collection of Frank and Jane Boyden, Otis, Oregon

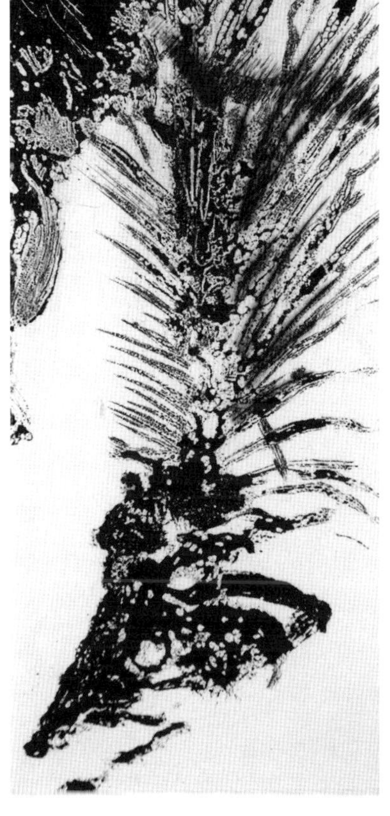

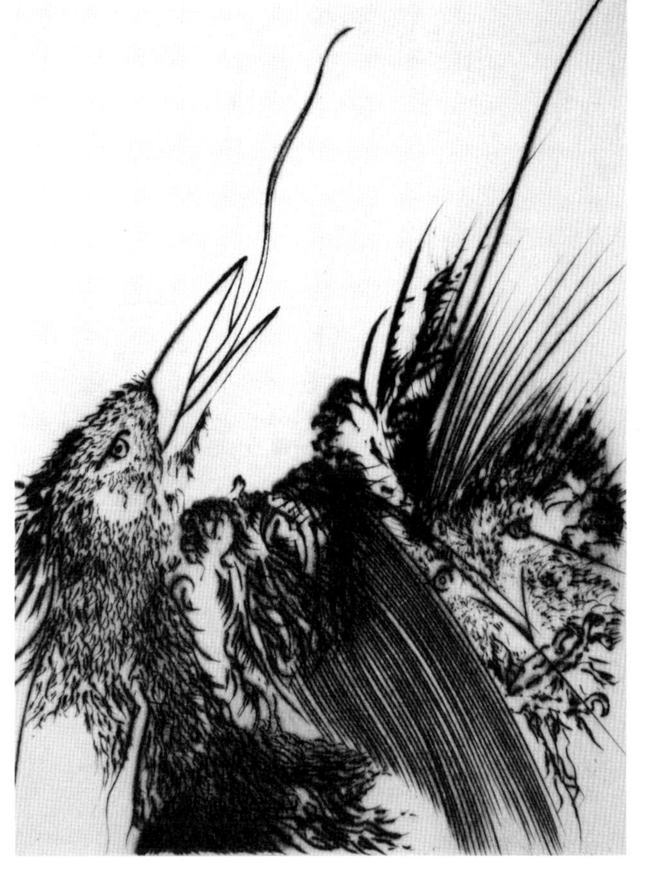

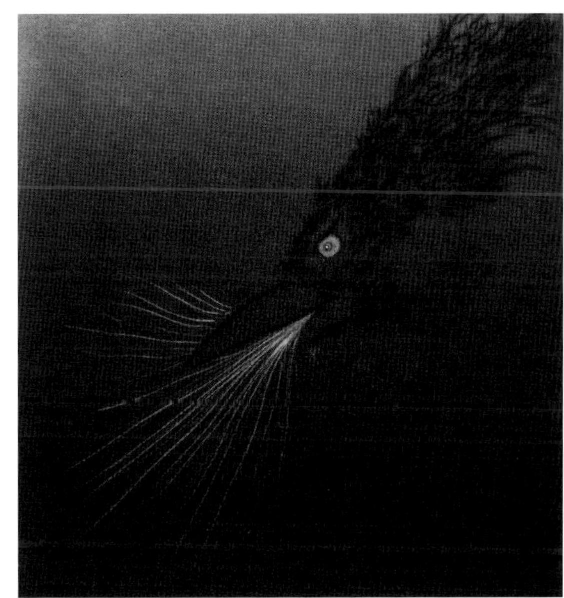

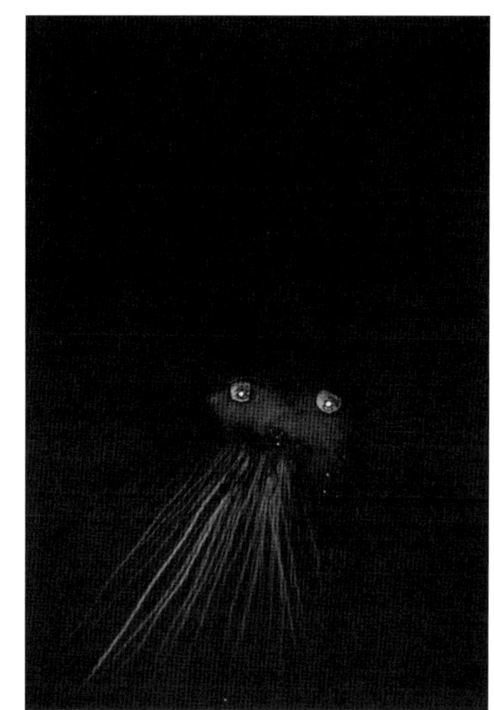

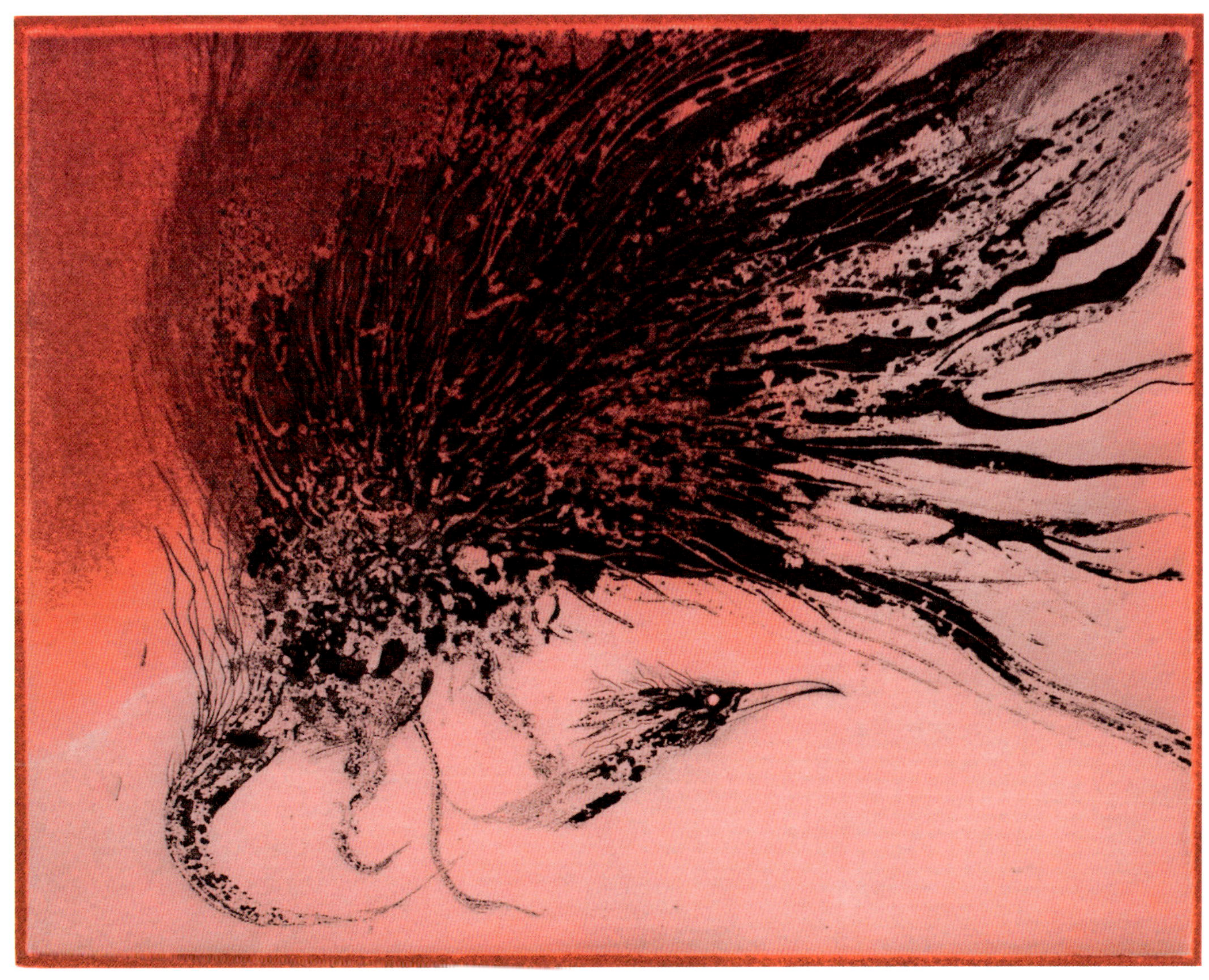

PLATE 105
Last Flight, from the *Phoenix Suite*
2001
Ed. 10
Sugarlift, drypoint, spitbite
5½ x 7⅛ in.

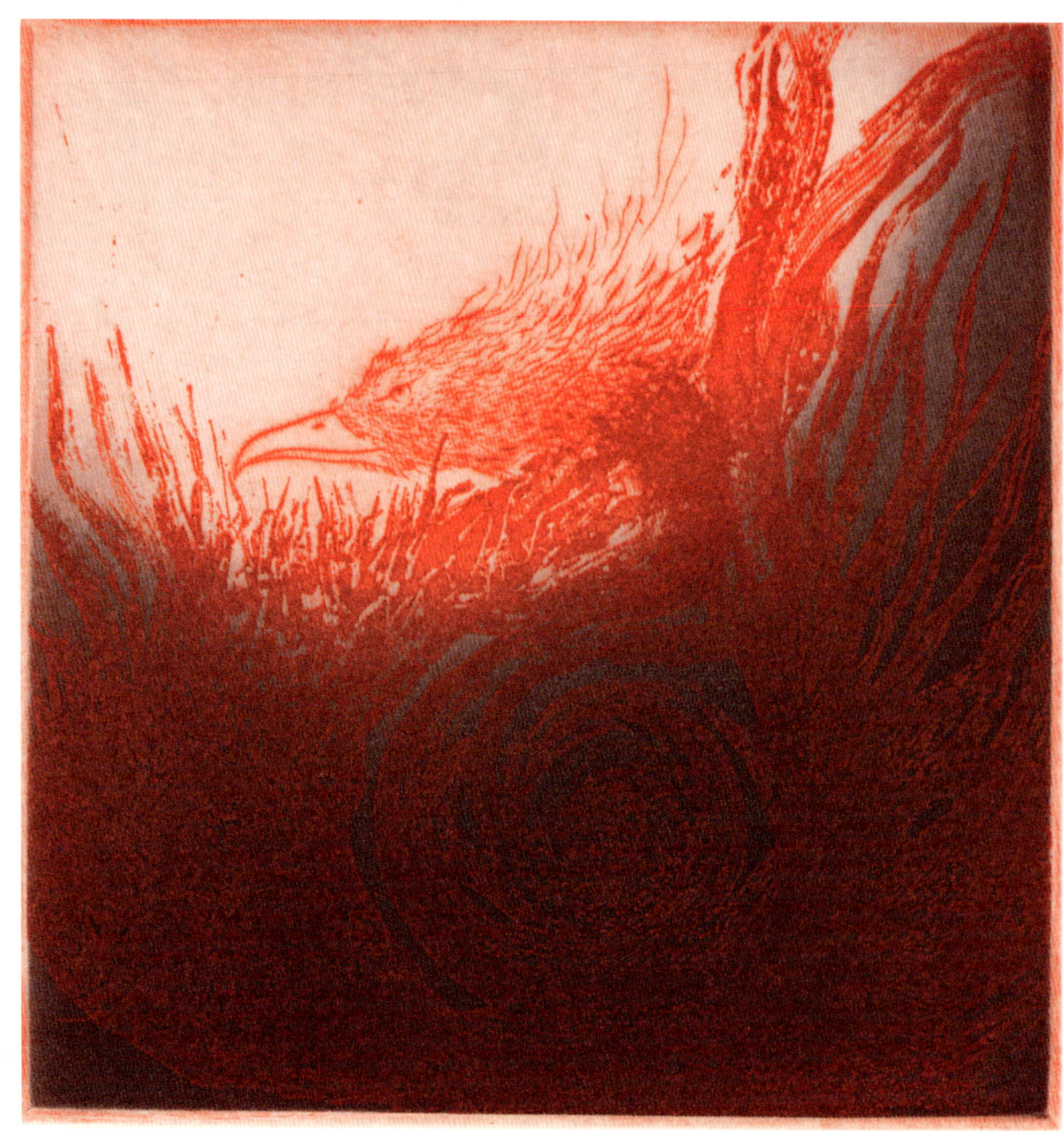

PLATE 106
Burning Nest, from the
Phoenix Suite
2001
Ed. 10
Sugarlift, drypoint,
spitbite
5⅞ x 5¾ in.

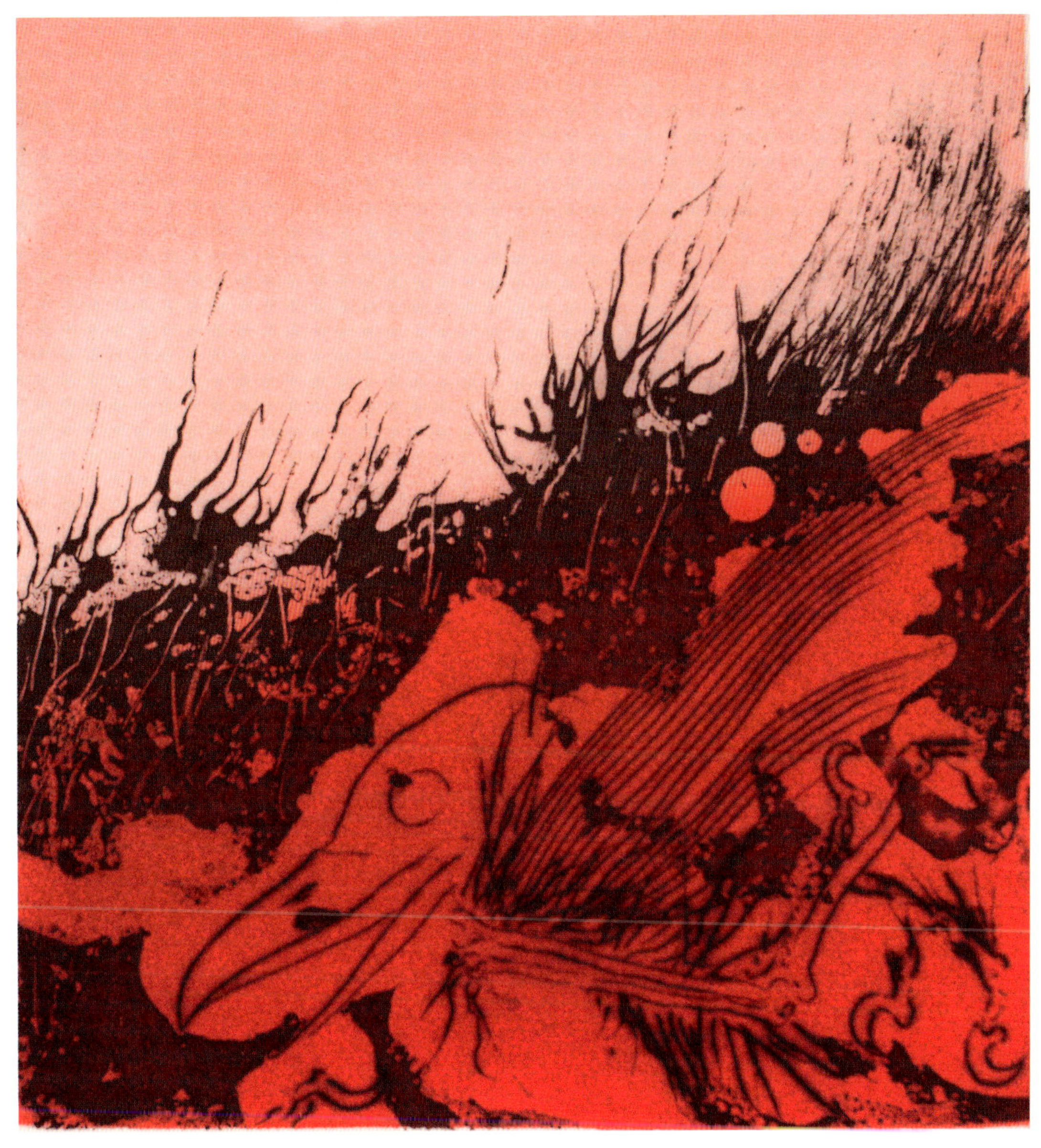

PLATE 107
Conflagration, from the
Phoenix Suite
2001
Ed. 10
Sugarlift, drypoint,
spitbite
6 x 5½ in.

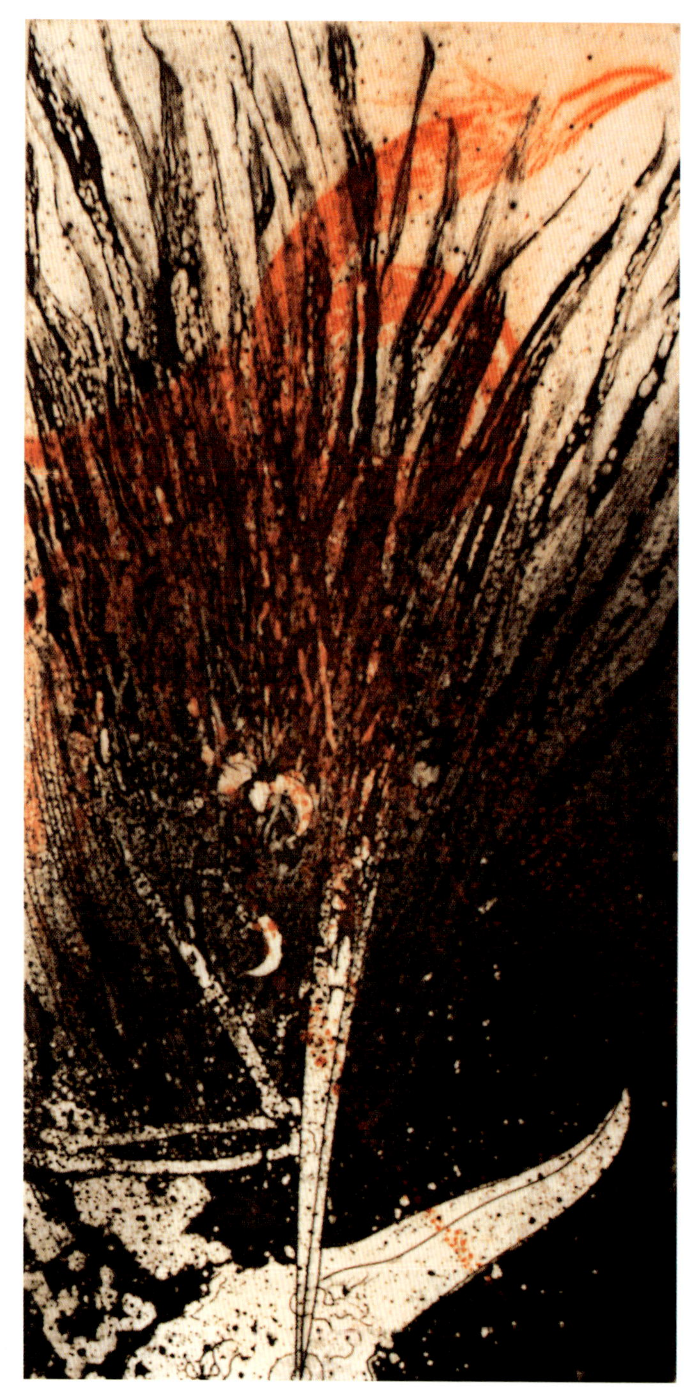

PLATE 108
Resurrection, from the
Phoenix Suite
2001
Ed. 10
Sugarlift, drypoint,
spitbite
7½ x 3¾ in.

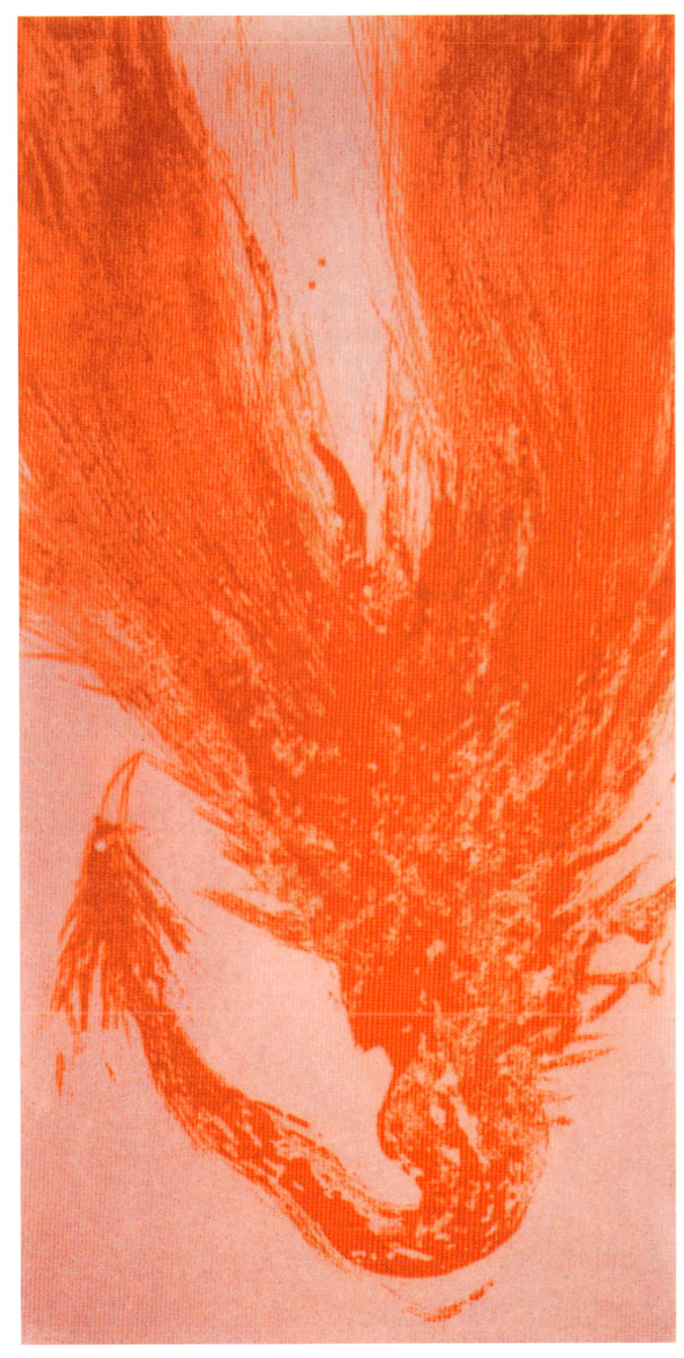

PLATE 109
First Flight of the Phoenix,
from the *Phoenix Suite*
2001
Ed. 10
Sugarlift, drypoint, spitbite
7½ x 3⅞ in.

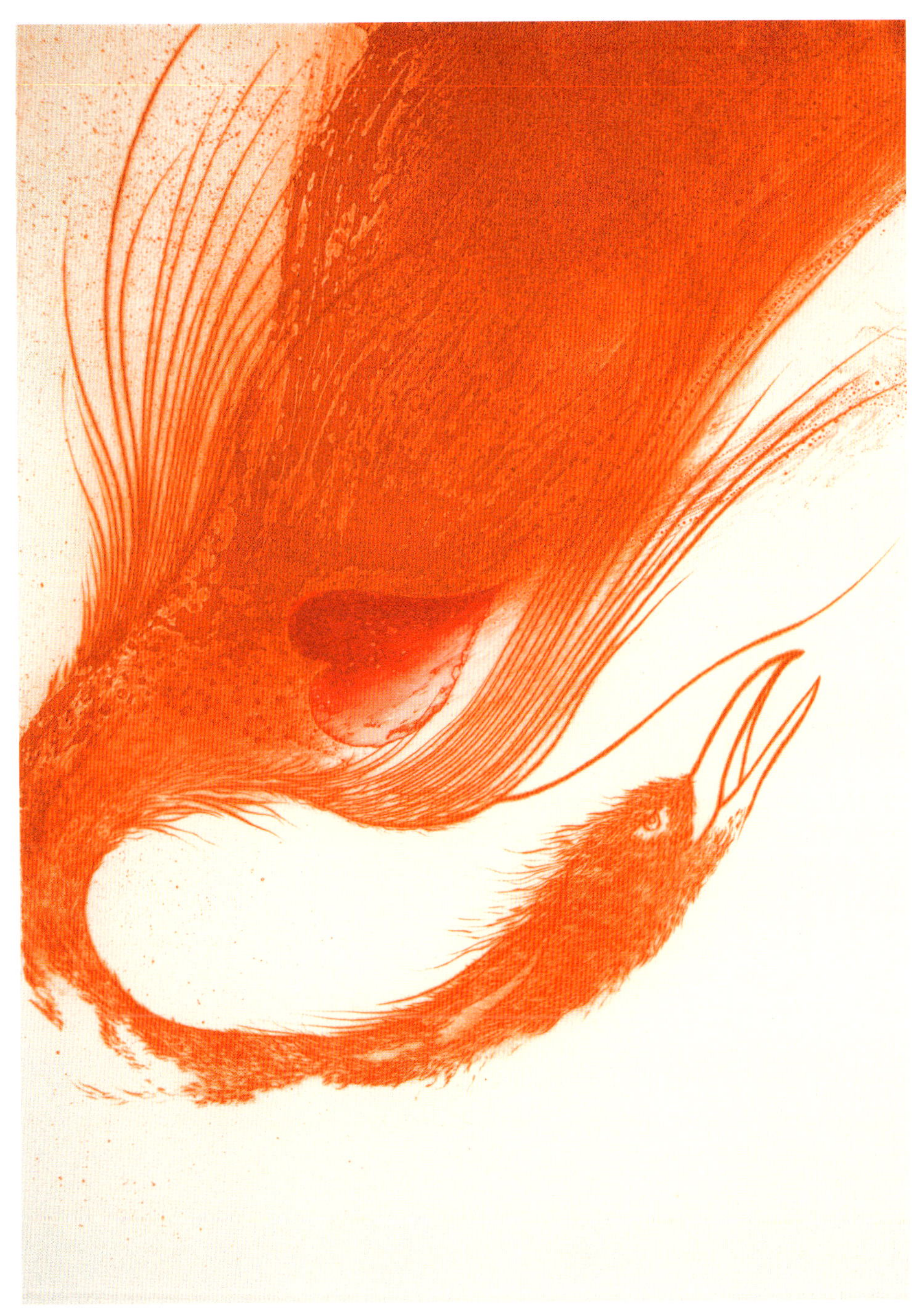

PLATE 110
Phoenix for Gordon
2001
Ed. 60
Drypoint, sugarlift
14¾ x 10¾ in.

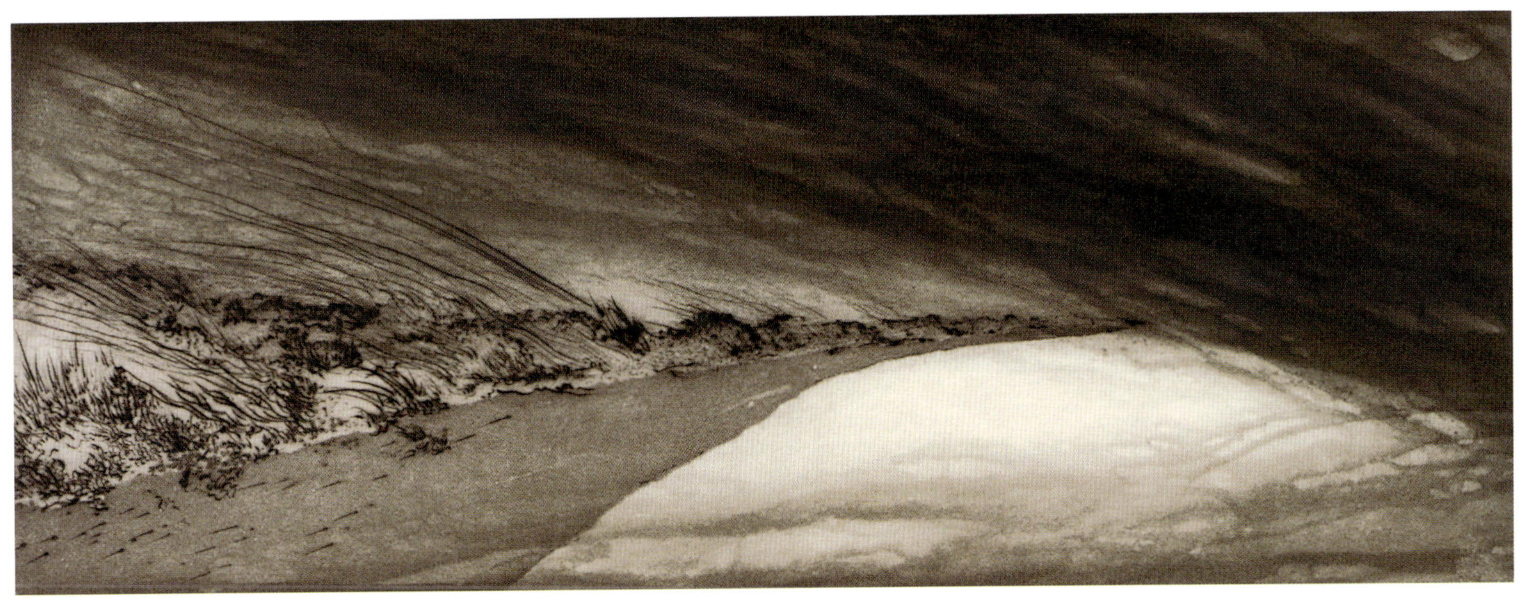

PLATE III
Wind, Fog, and Strange Light at Whiskey Run
2001
Ed. 16
Aquatint, drypoint, spitbite
8¾ x 22½ in.

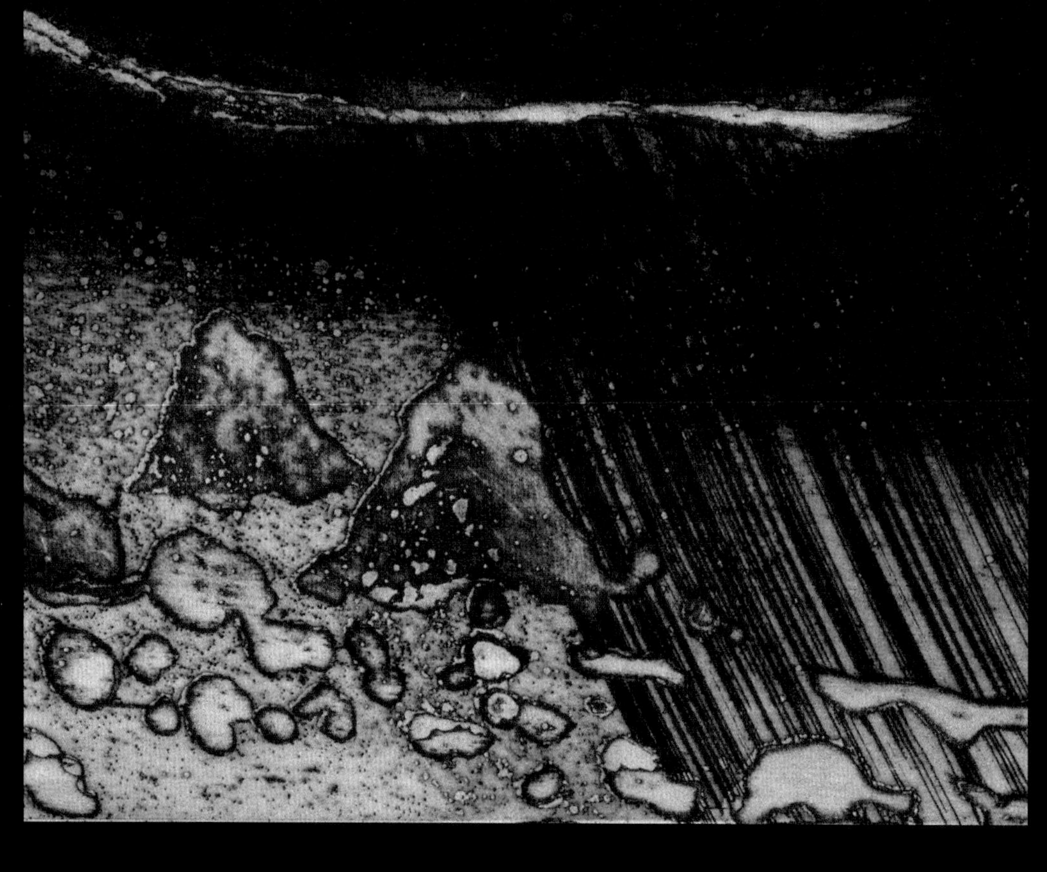

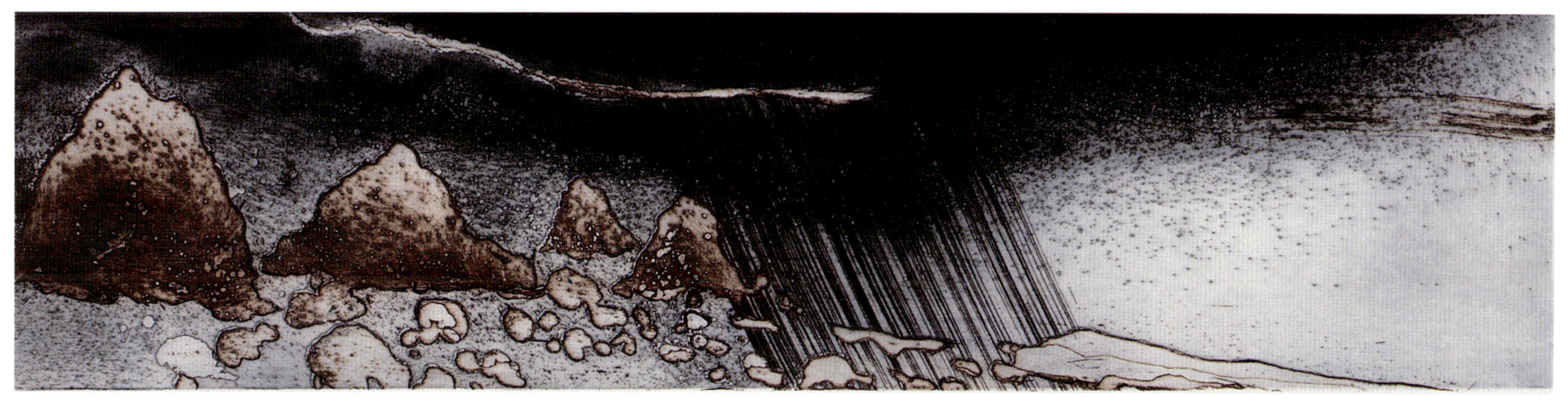

PLATE 112
Rain at Four Rocks
2001–2
Ed. 10
Sugarlift, line etching,
spitbite
6 x 24 in.

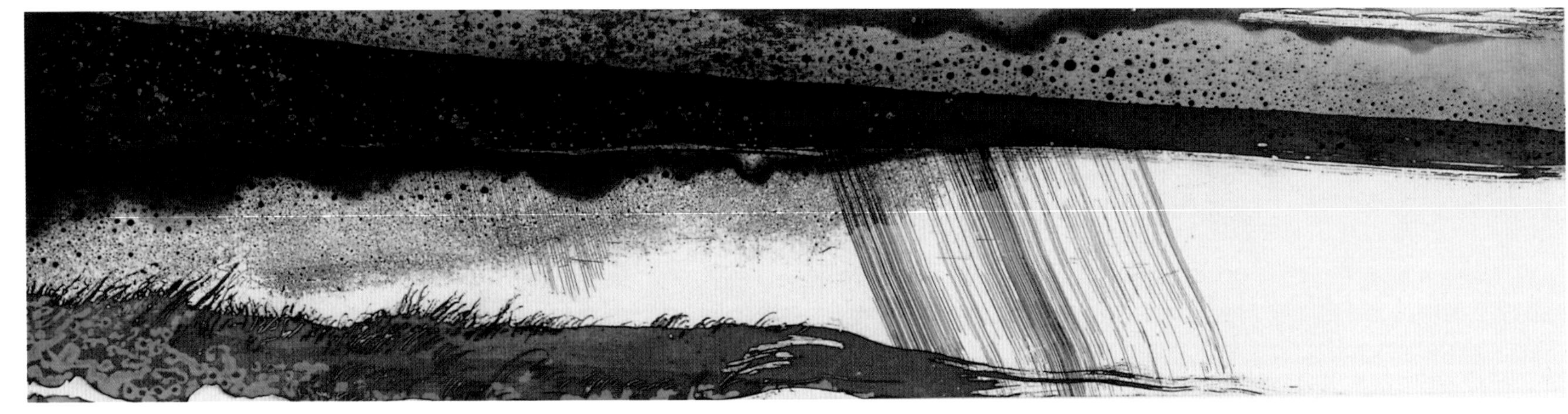

PLATE 113
Reflections at Nexo
2001–2
Ed. 10
Sugarlift, line etching, spitbite
6⅜ x 24 in.

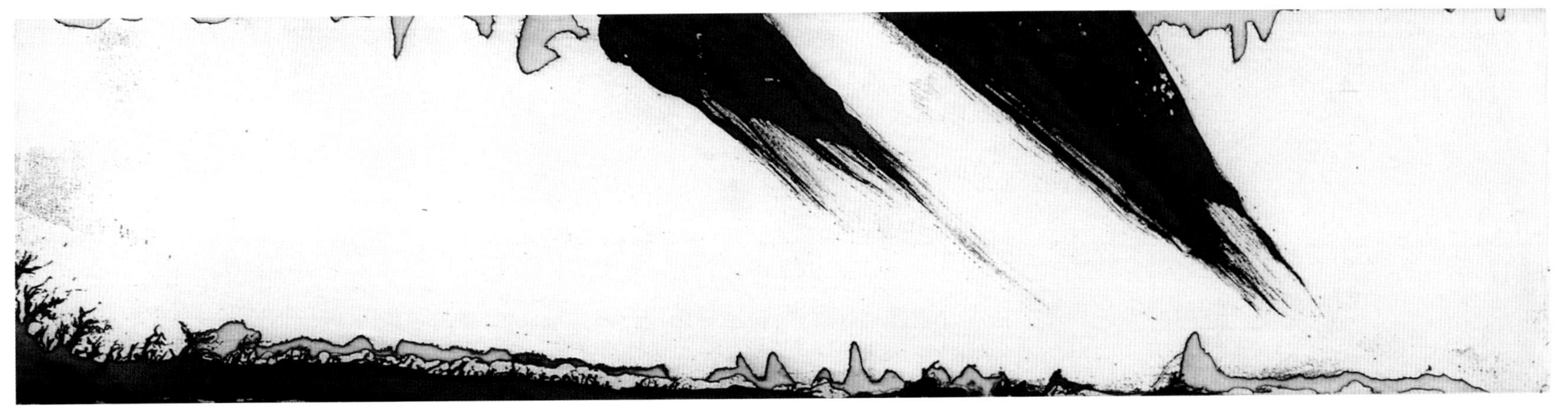

PLATE 114
River Sky across Karst
2001–2
Ed. 5/State 1
Sugarlift, spitbite
6 x 24 in.

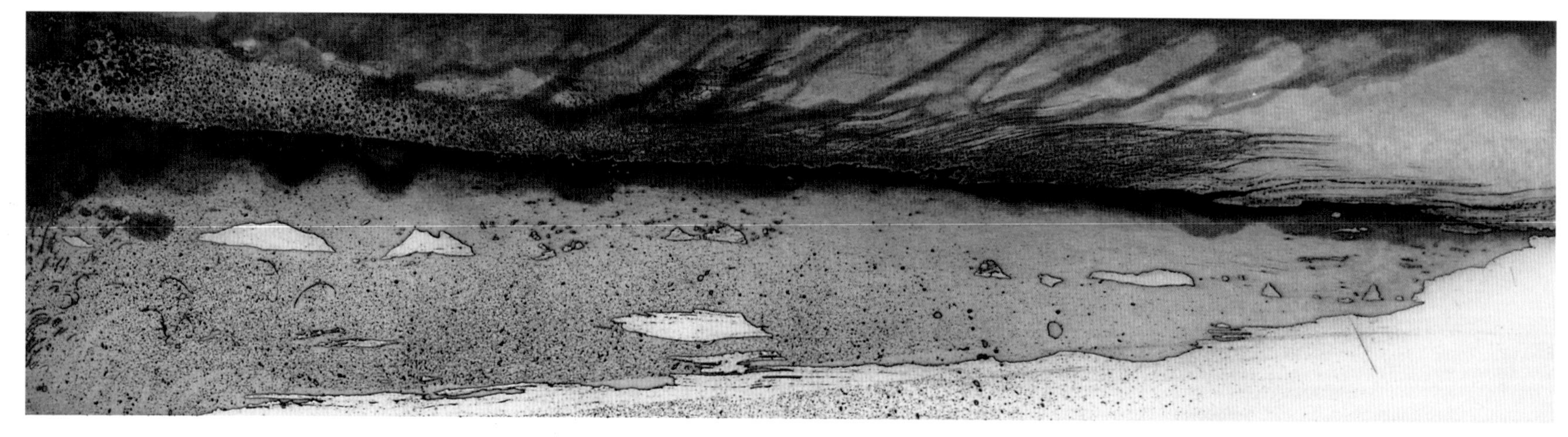

PLATE 115
Above and Below
2002
Ed. 10
Spitbite, sugarlift
6⅝ x 24 in.

PLATE 116
Arc at Hells Gap
2002
Ed. 10
Spitbite, sugarlift; 2 plates
6 x 21 in.

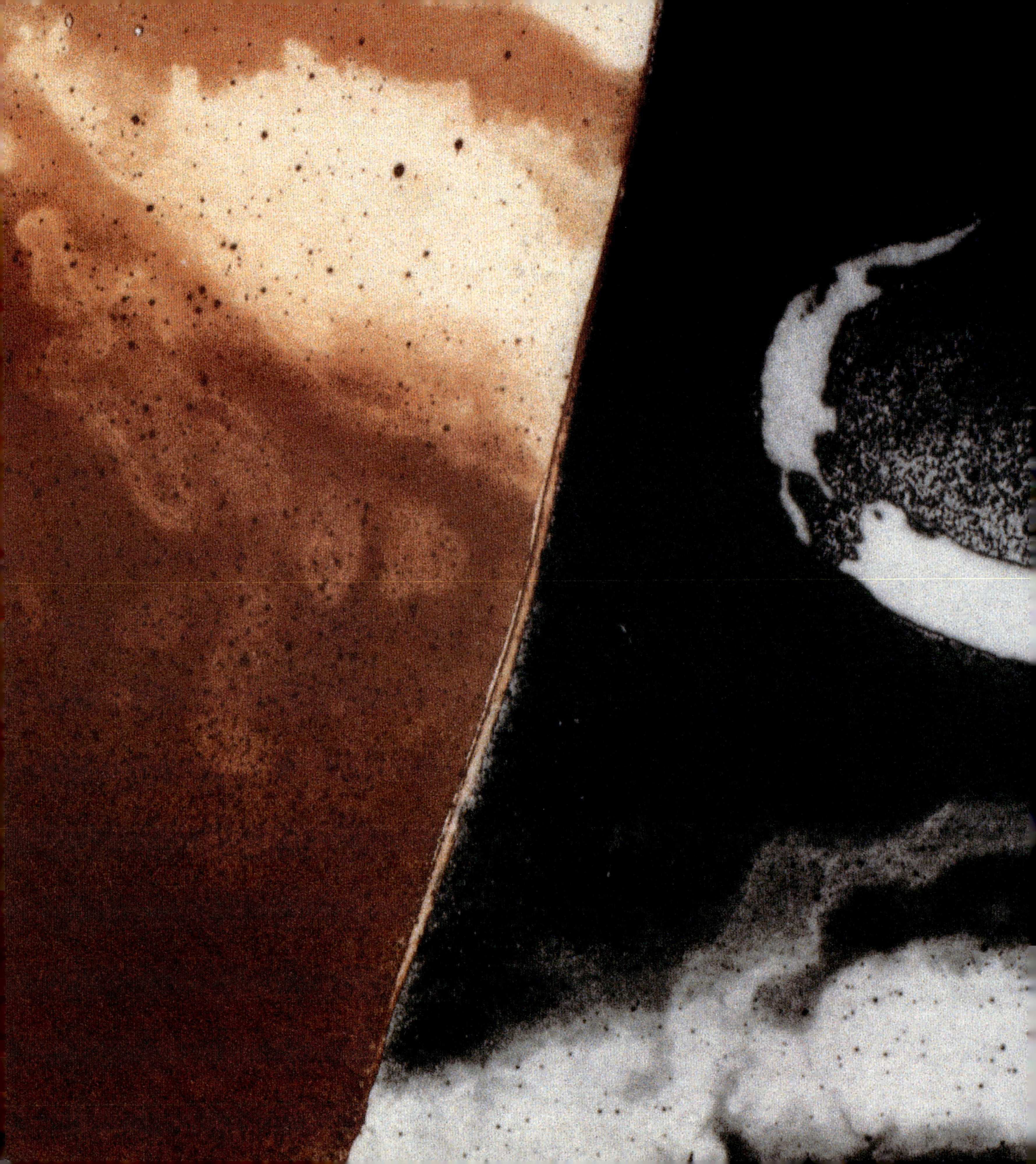

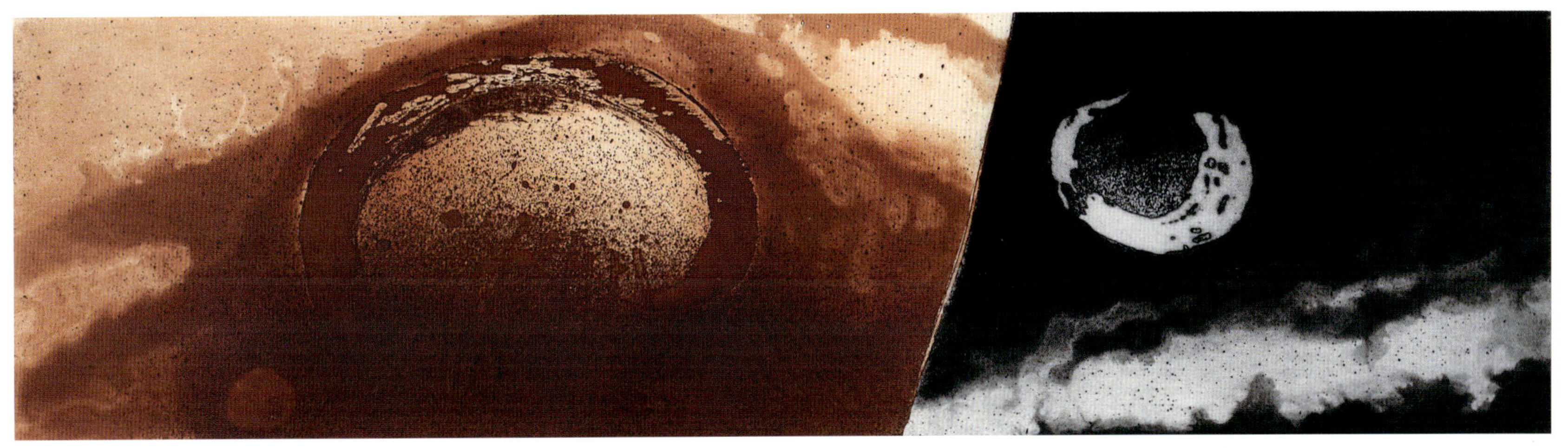

PLATE 117
Arc
2002
Ed. 10
Spitbite, sugarlift; 2 plates
6 x 21 in.

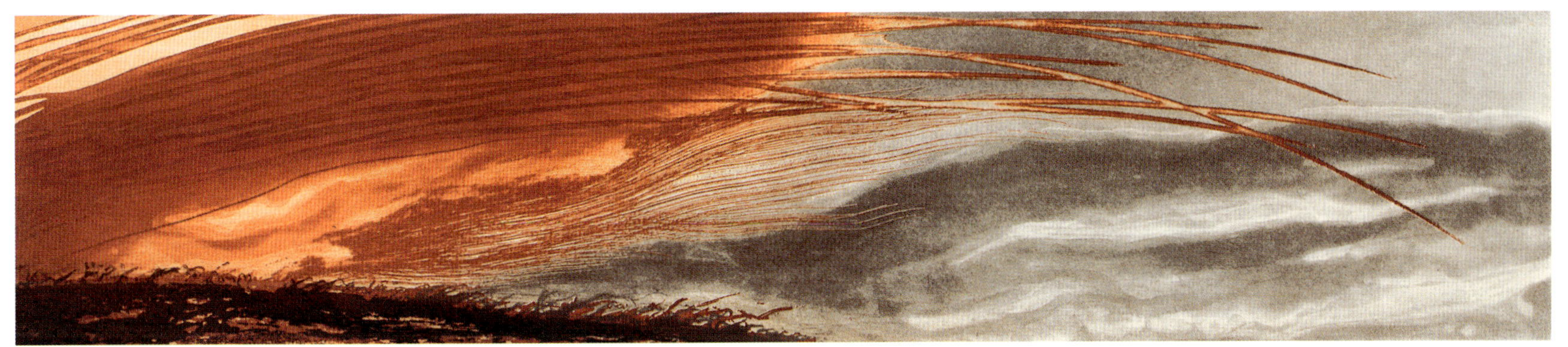

PLATE 118
Crowning
2002
Ed. 10
Line etching, spitbite,
sugarlift; 2 plates
4⅝ x 21 in.

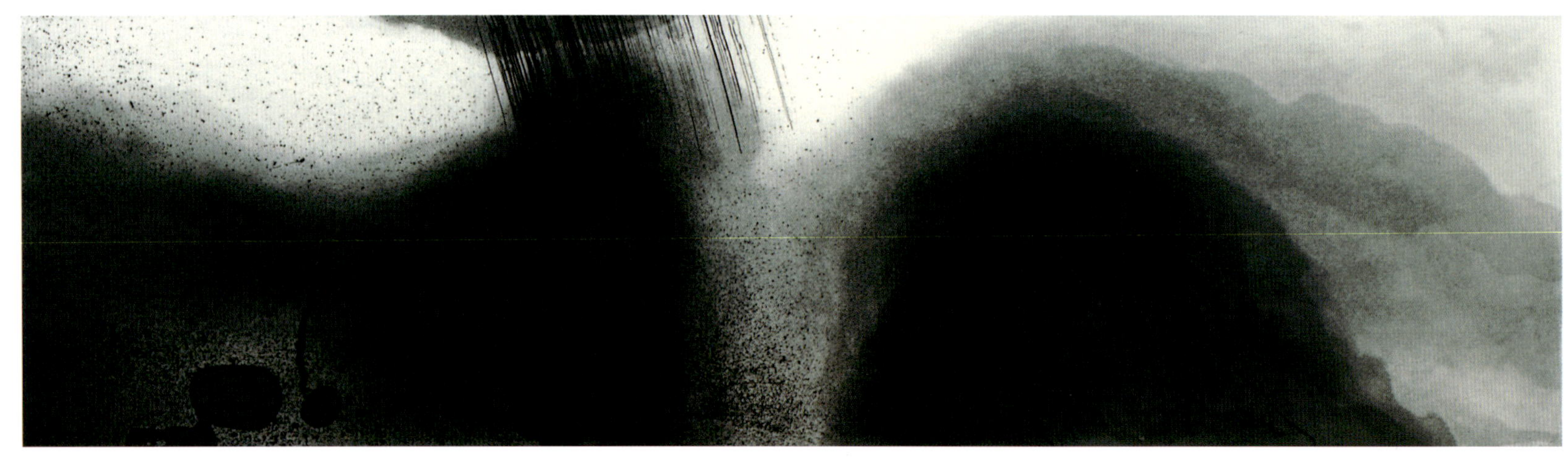

PLATE 119
Landscape with Densities
2002
Ed. 7
Spitbite, sugarlift,
line etching
6 x 20⅞ in.

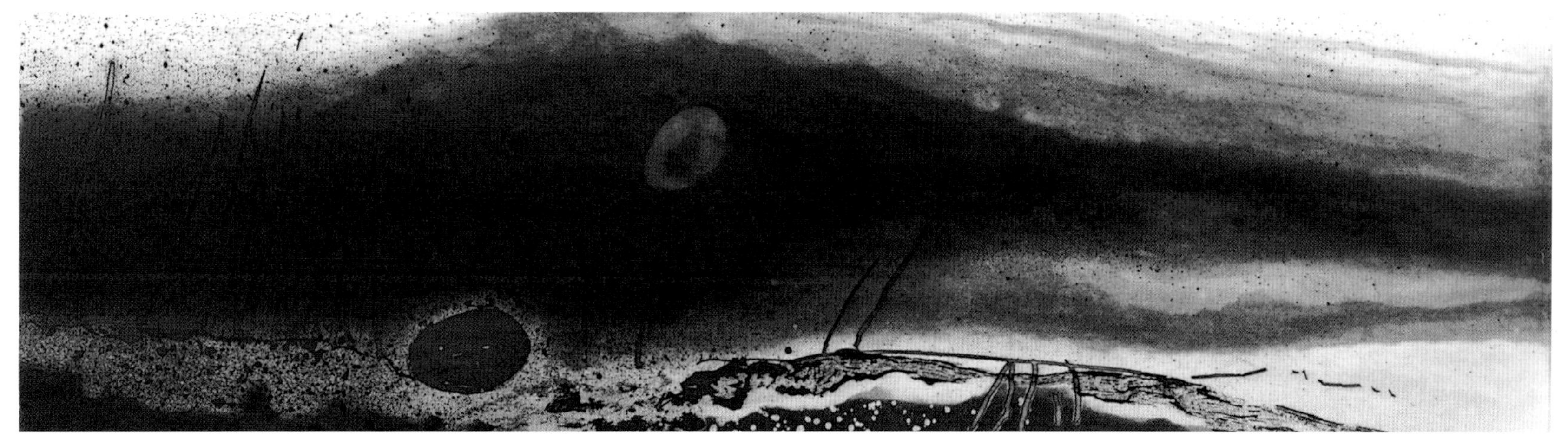

PLATE 120
Wasteland Caressed
2002
Ed. 10
Spitbite, sugarlift,
line etching
6⅞ x 21 in.

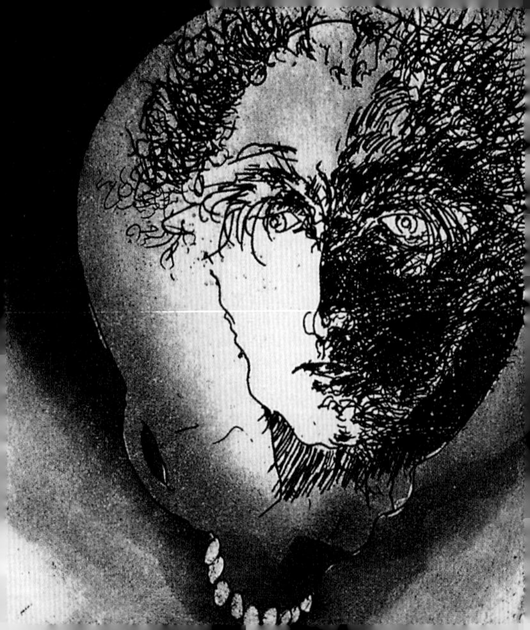

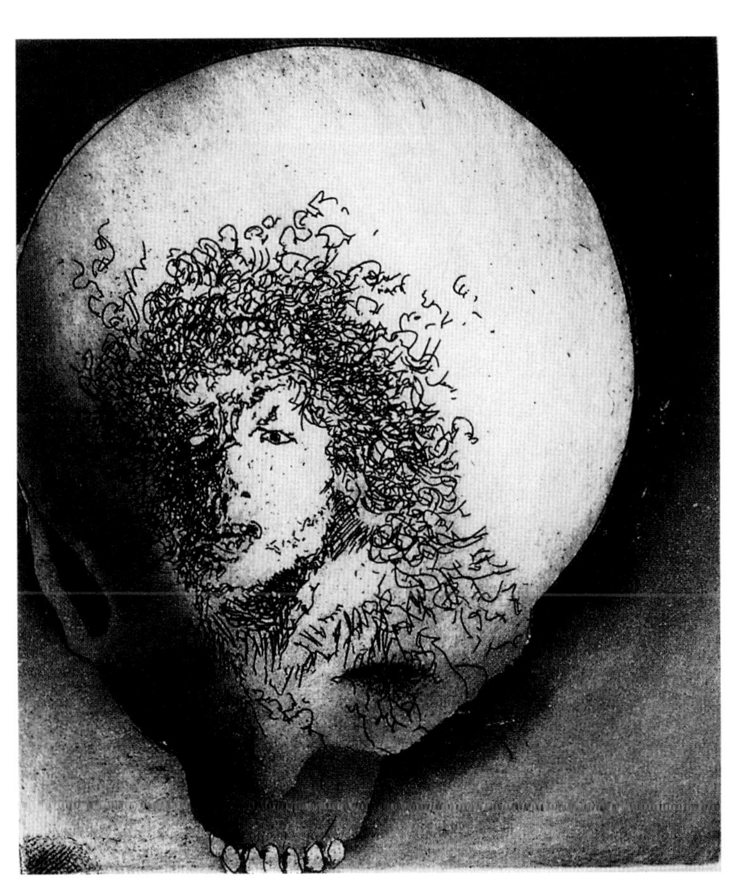

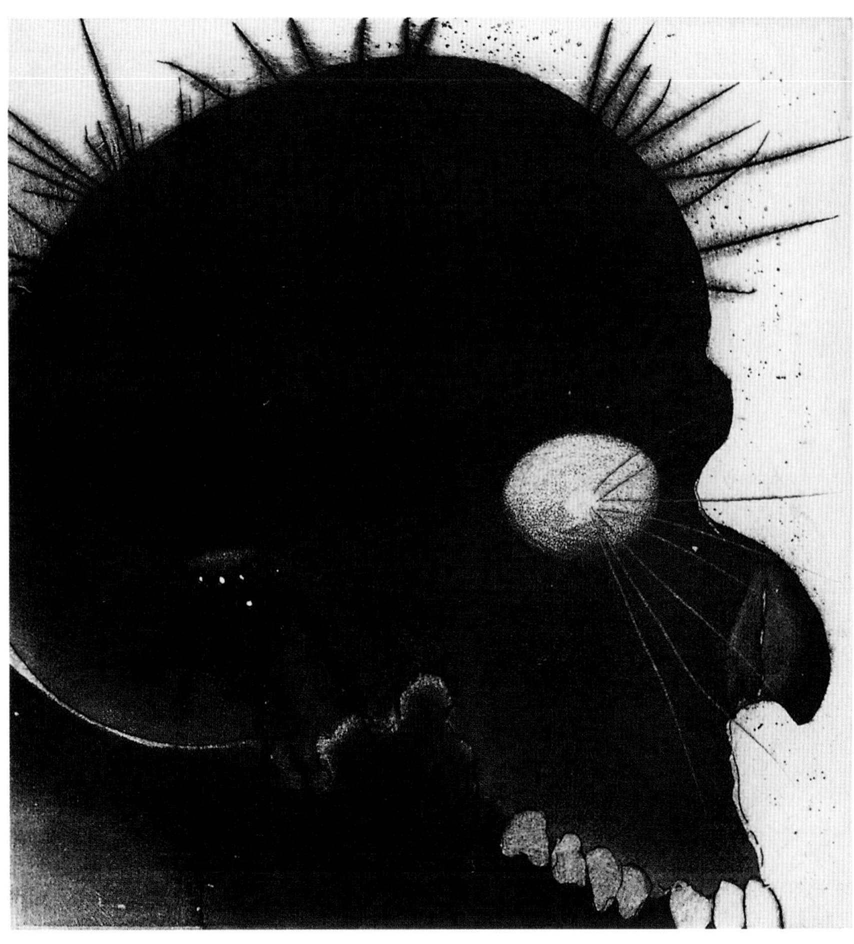

PLATE 122
Lens with Rembrandt, from the *Lenses Suite*
2002
Ed. 15
Spitbite, drypoint, line etching
3⅝ x 3⅛ in.

PLATE 123
Lens with Spines, from the *Lenses Suite*
2002
Ed. 15
Spitbite, drypoint, line etching
4⅜ x 4⅛ in.

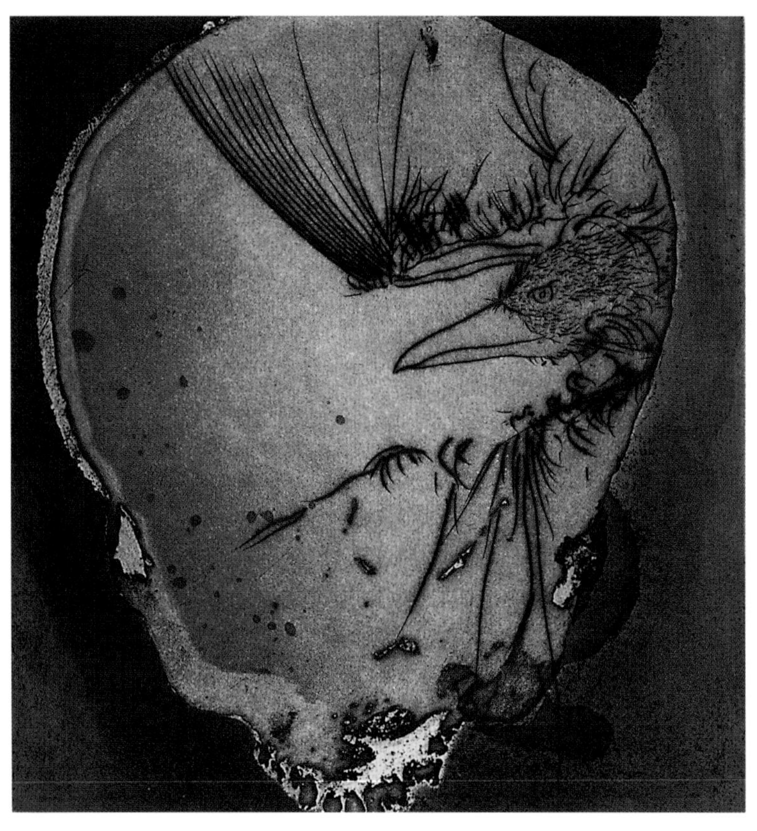

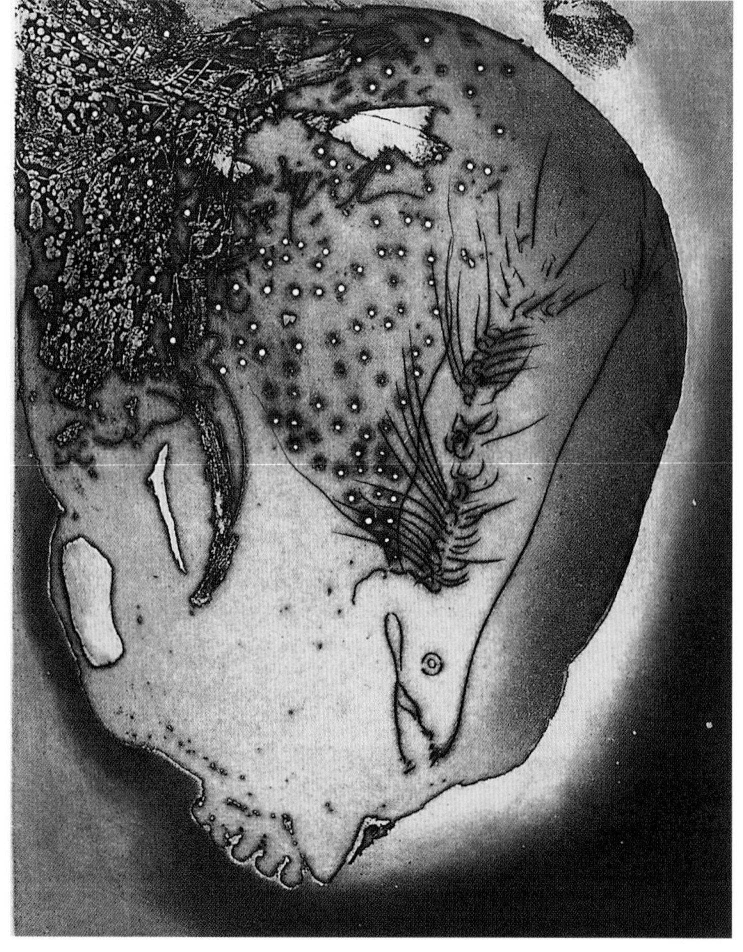

PLATE 124
Lens with Bird Spirit, from the *Lenses Suite*
2002
Ed. 15
Spitbite, drypoint, sugarlift
5¾ x 5⅜ in.

PLATE 125
Lens with Old Friend, from the *Lenses Suite*
2002
Ed. 15
Spitbite, drypoint, sugarlift
7⅜ x 5¾ in.

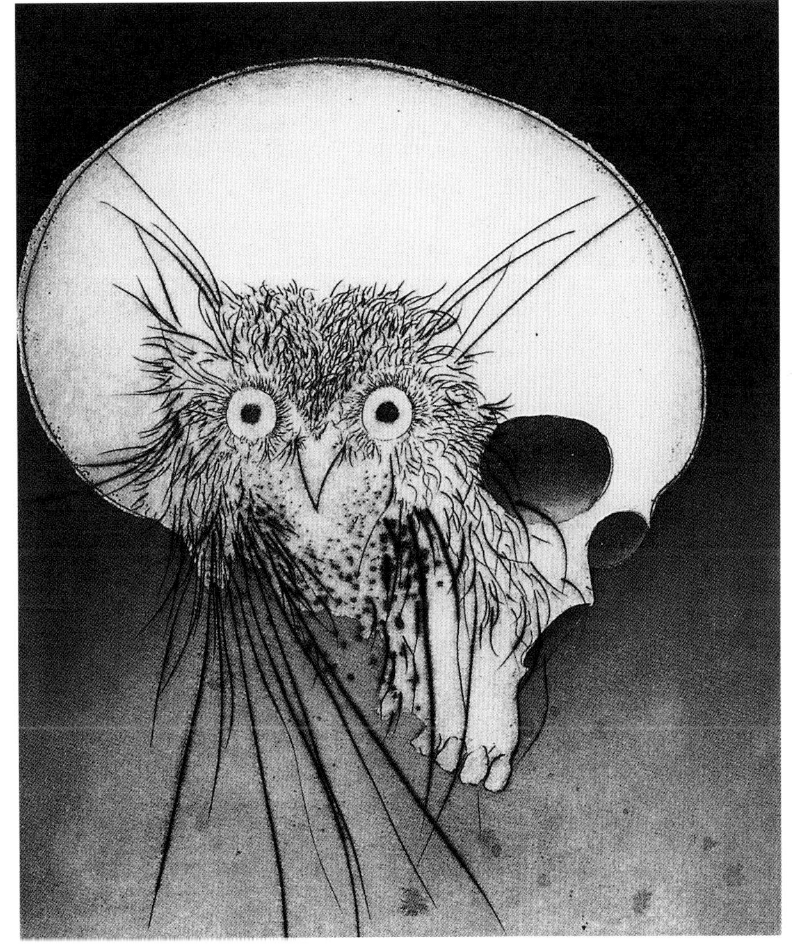

PLATE 126
Lens with Owl, from the *Lenses Suite*
2002
Ed. 15
Spitbite, drypoint, line etching
7¾ x 6⅝ in.

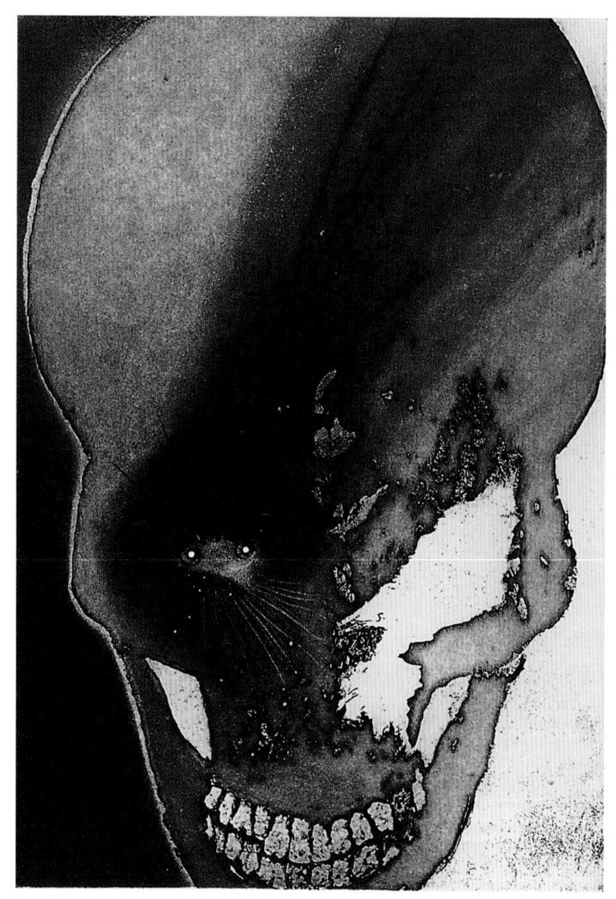

PLATE 127
Lens with Black Idea, from the *Lenses Suite*
2002
Ed. 15
Spitbite, drypoint, sugarlift
7½ x 5⅜ in.

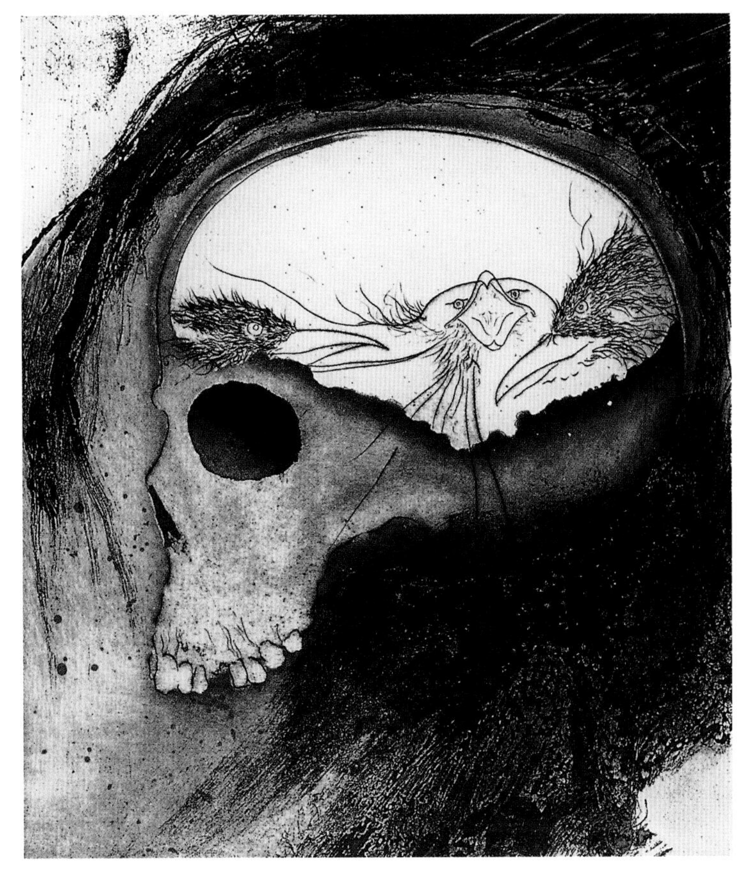

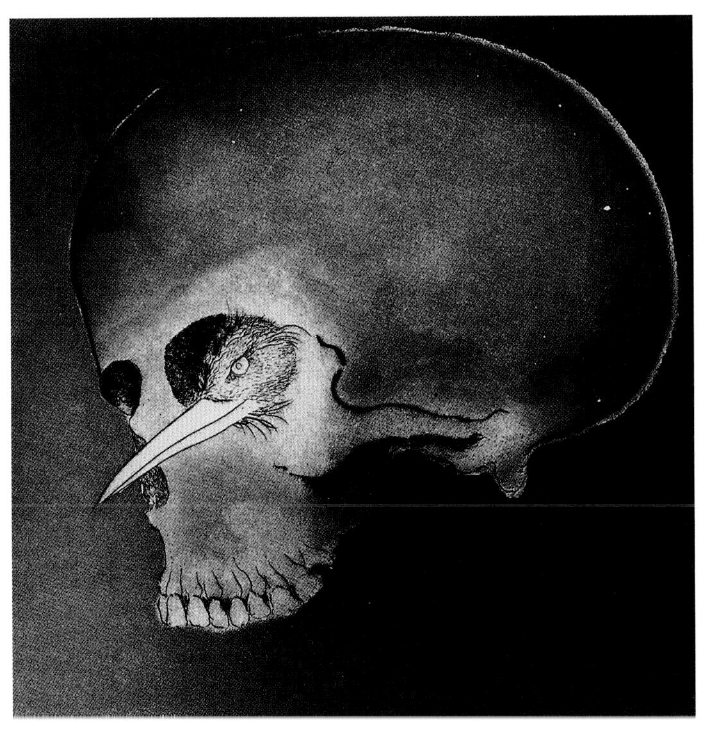

PLATE 128
Moon Lens with Heron, from the *Lenses Suite*
2002
Ed. 15
Spitbite, drypoint
8 x 8 in.

PLATE 129
Lens with Nest, from the *Lenses Suite*
2002
Ed. 15
Spitbite, drypoint, sugarlift
9¾ x 8½ in.

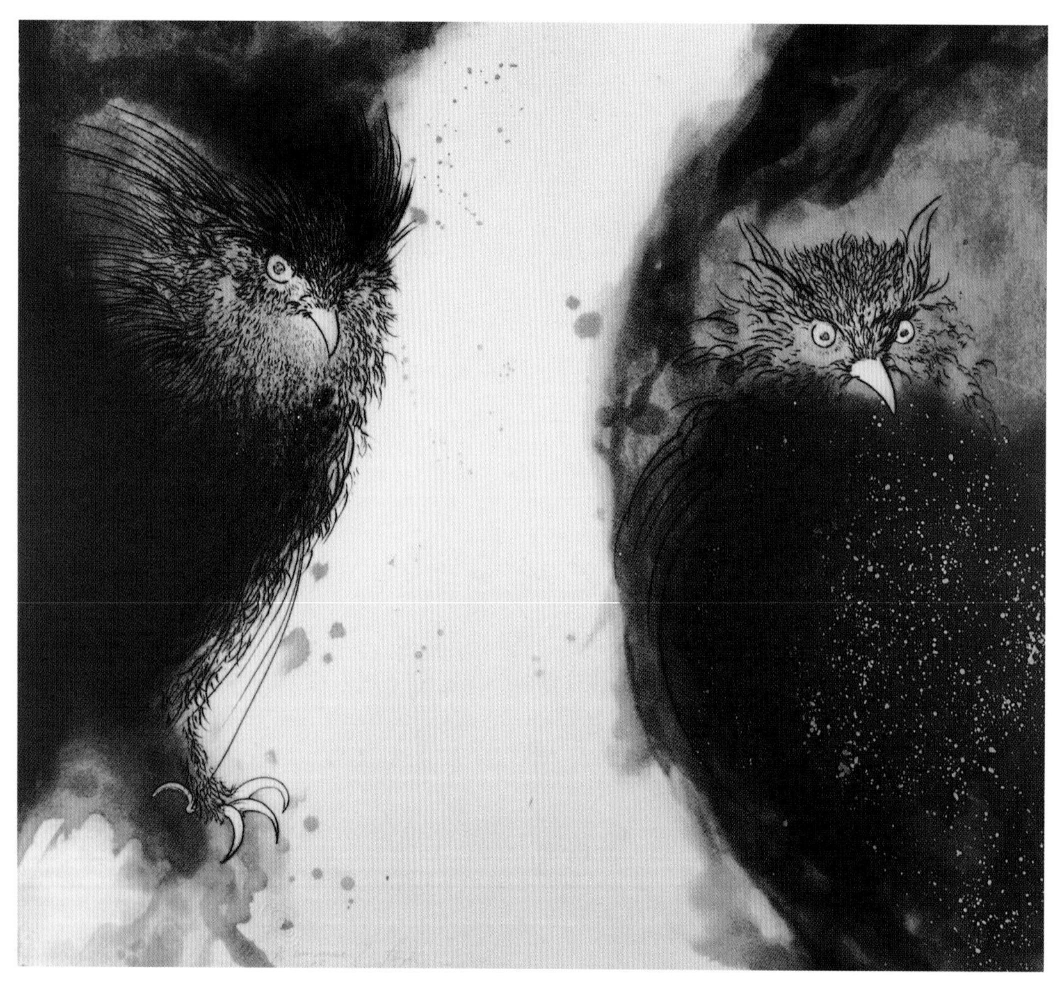

PLATE 130
Universe
2002
Ed. 10; 2 artist's proofs
Drypoint, spitbite
15½ x 17 in.

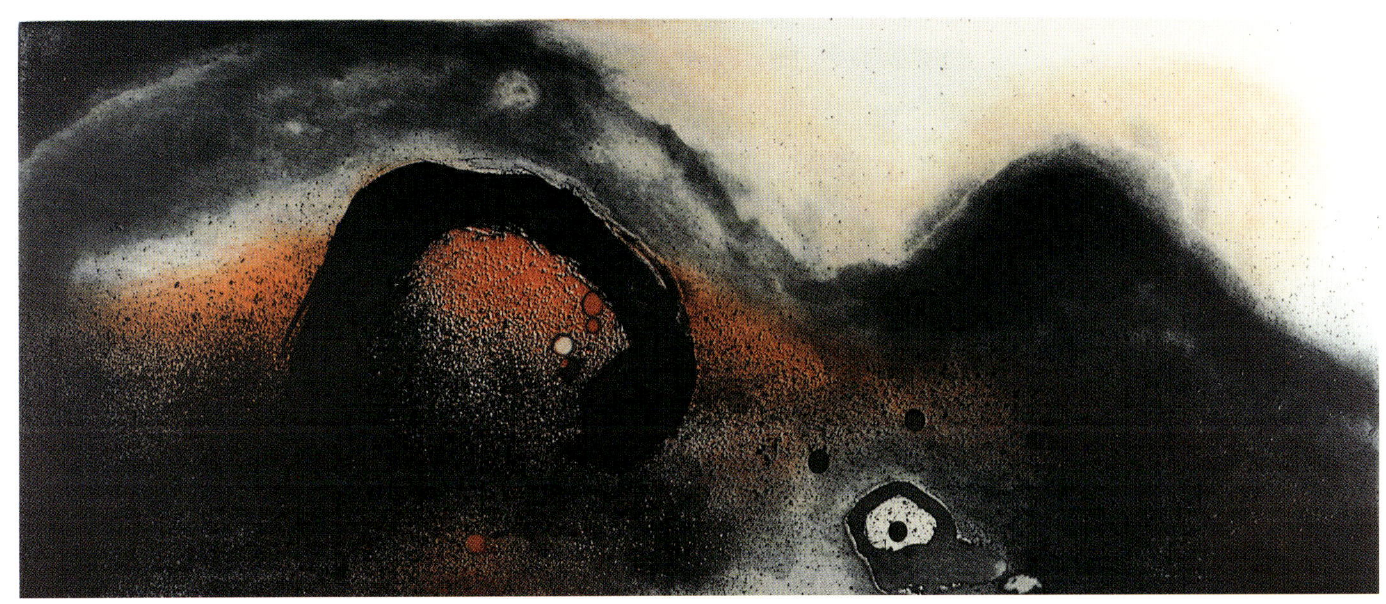

PLATE 131
Black Arc
2003
Ed. 12; 4 artist's proofs
Sugarlift, spitbite
7½ x 17⅞ in.

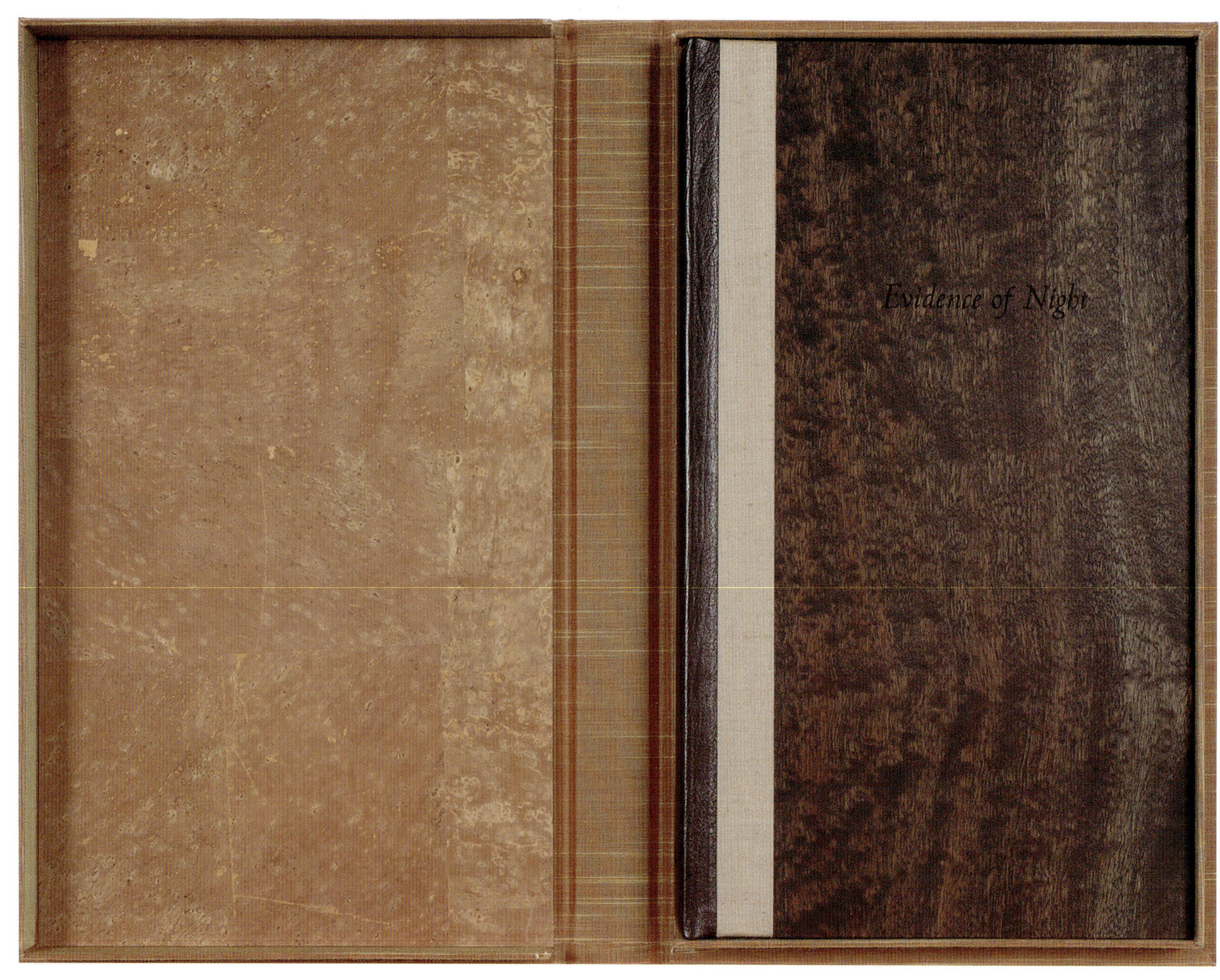

PLATES 132–133
Evidence of Night
Poems by Jennifer Boyden, prints and drawings by Frank Boyden
2003
Published by Crab Quill Press, Walla Walla, Washington
Ed. 15
Handmade book
15⅜ x 9 x 1 in.
Collection of Frank and Jane Boyden, Otis, Oregon

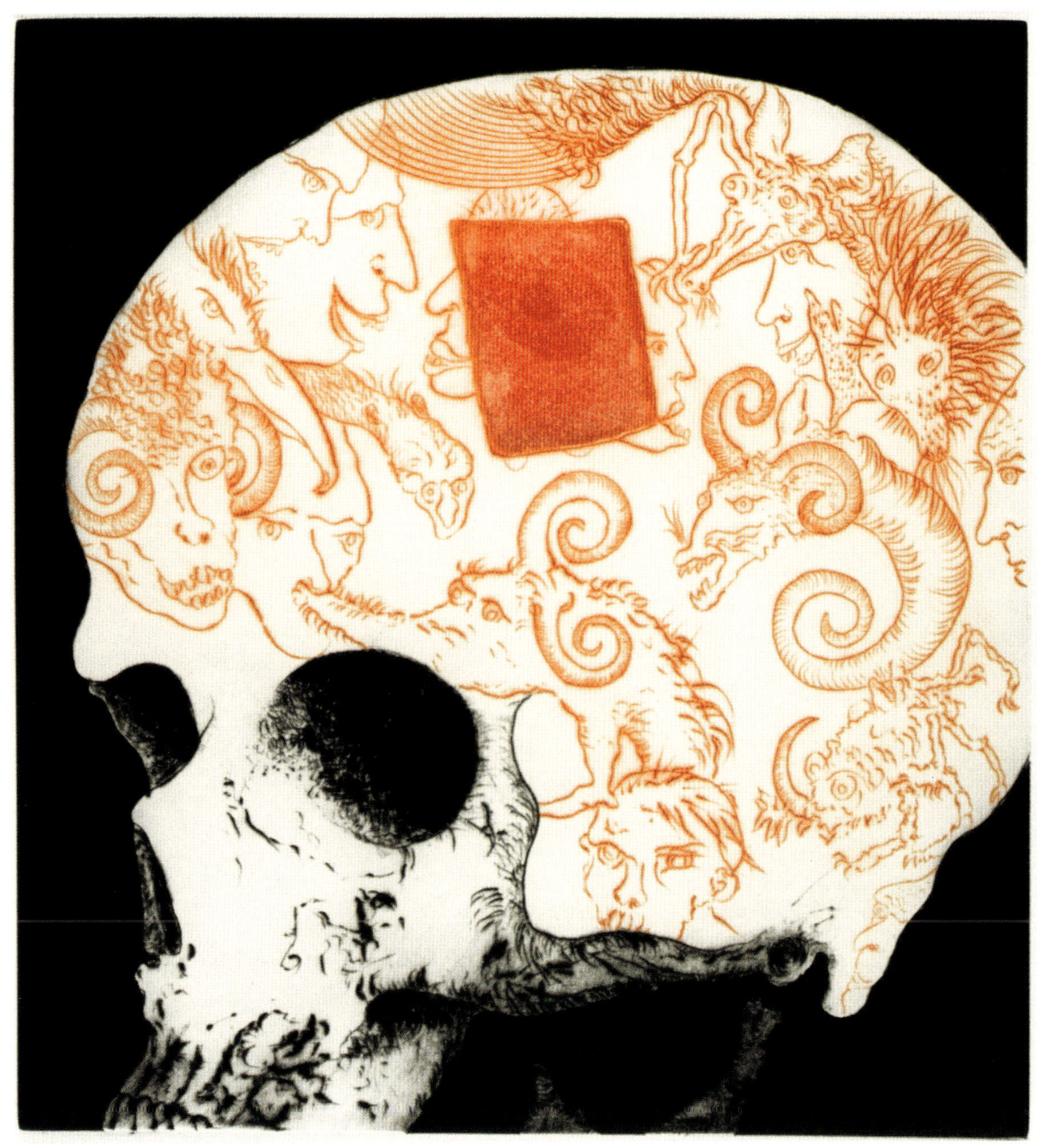

PLATE 135
The Possession of Uncle Skulky, from
The Irreverences, Provocations, &
Connivances of Uncle Skulky
2003
Ed. 16; 4 artist's proofs
Drypoint, aquatint; 2 copper
plates, one wiped "à la poupée"
8 x 7⅜ in.

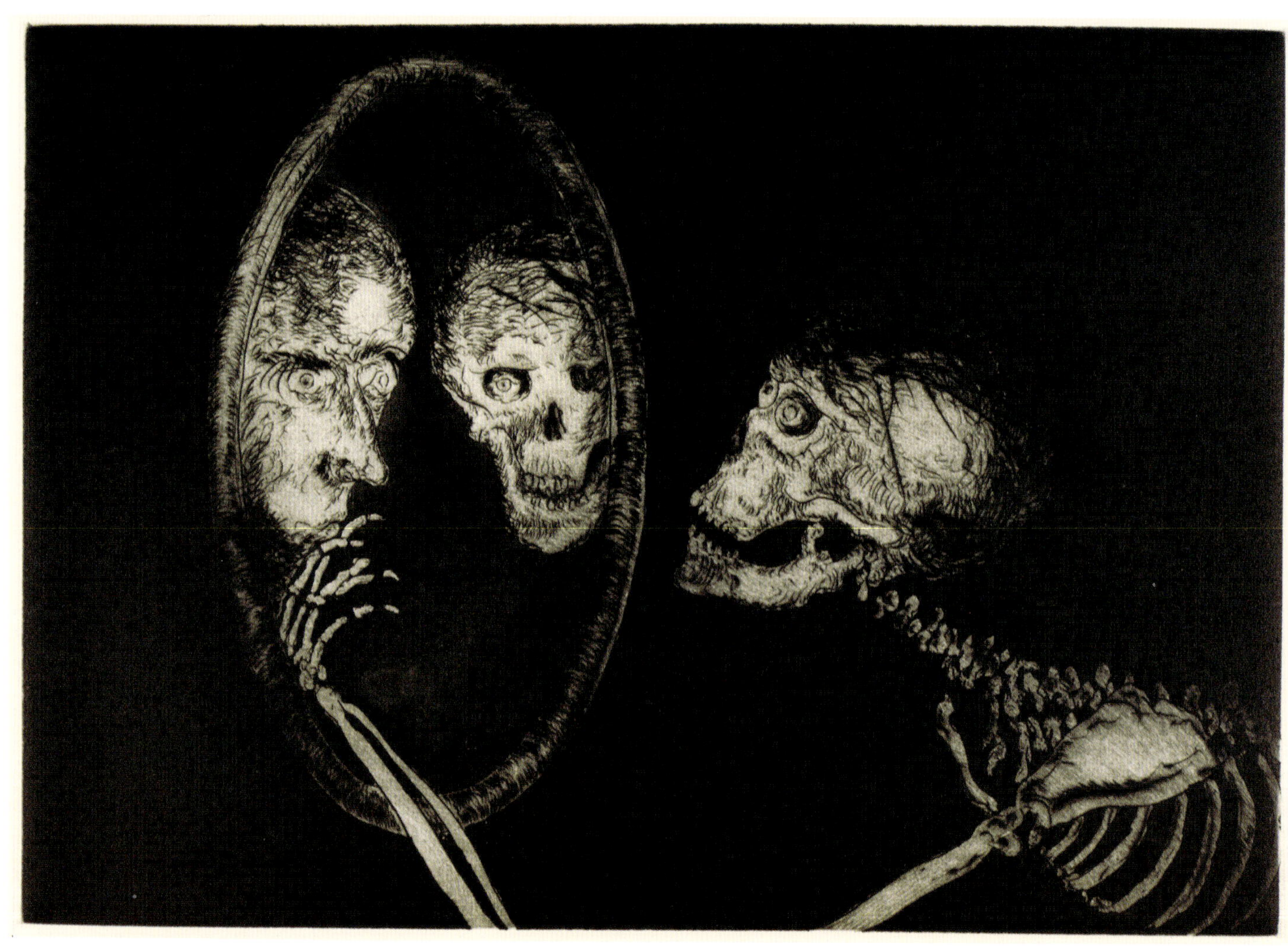

PLATE 136
Uncle Skulky bekons the artist from his mirror of illusions, from *The Irreverences, Provocations, & Connivances of Uncle Skulky*
2003
Ed. 16; 5 artist's proofs
Drypoint, aquatint, spitbite
5 x 7 in.

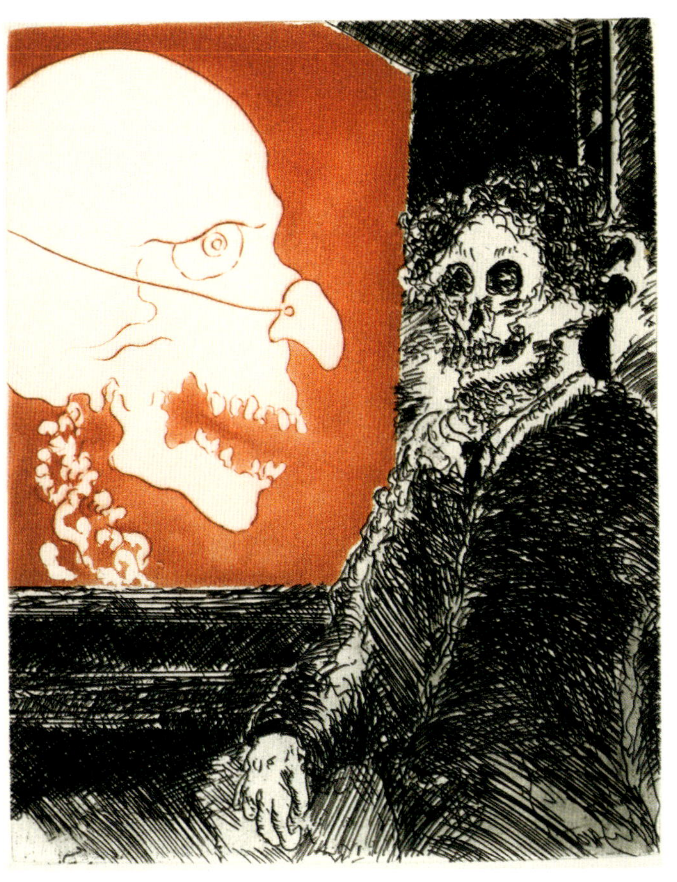

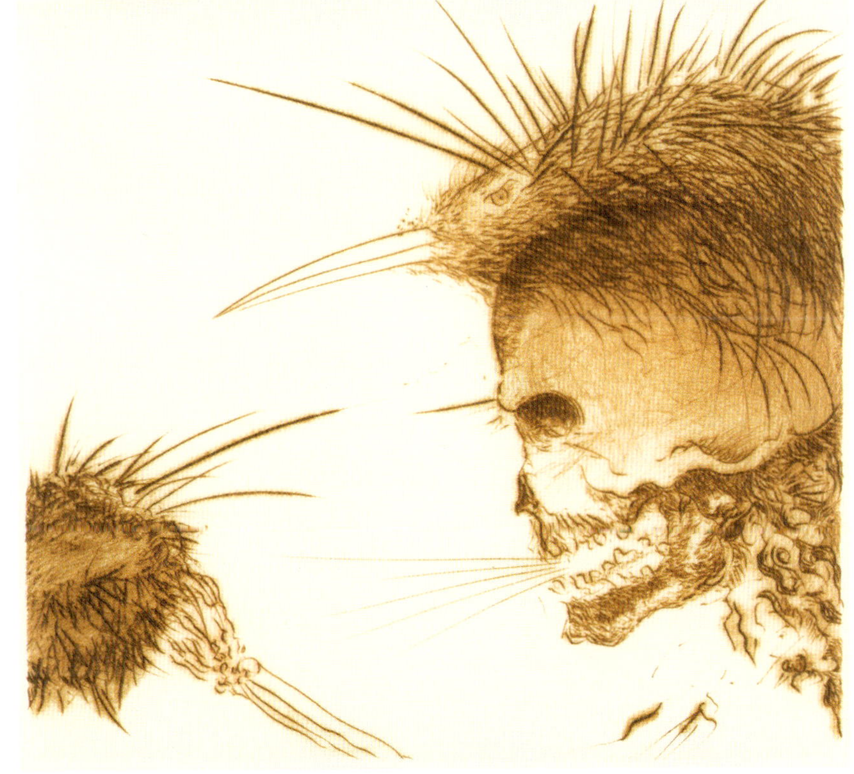

PLATE 137

(above) *Uncle Skulky appears to James Ensor and mocks him with a fake nose,* from *The Irreverences, Provocations, & Connivances of Uncle Skulky*
2003
Ed. 15; 4 artist's proofs
Line etching, drypoint, spitbite; 2 copper plates
5 x 4 in.

PLATE 138

(right) *Uncle Skulky examines some fluff,* from *The Irreverences, Provocations, and Connivances of Uncle Skulky*
2003
Ed. 12; 6 artist's proofs
Drypoint; 1 copper plate
4½ x 5 in.

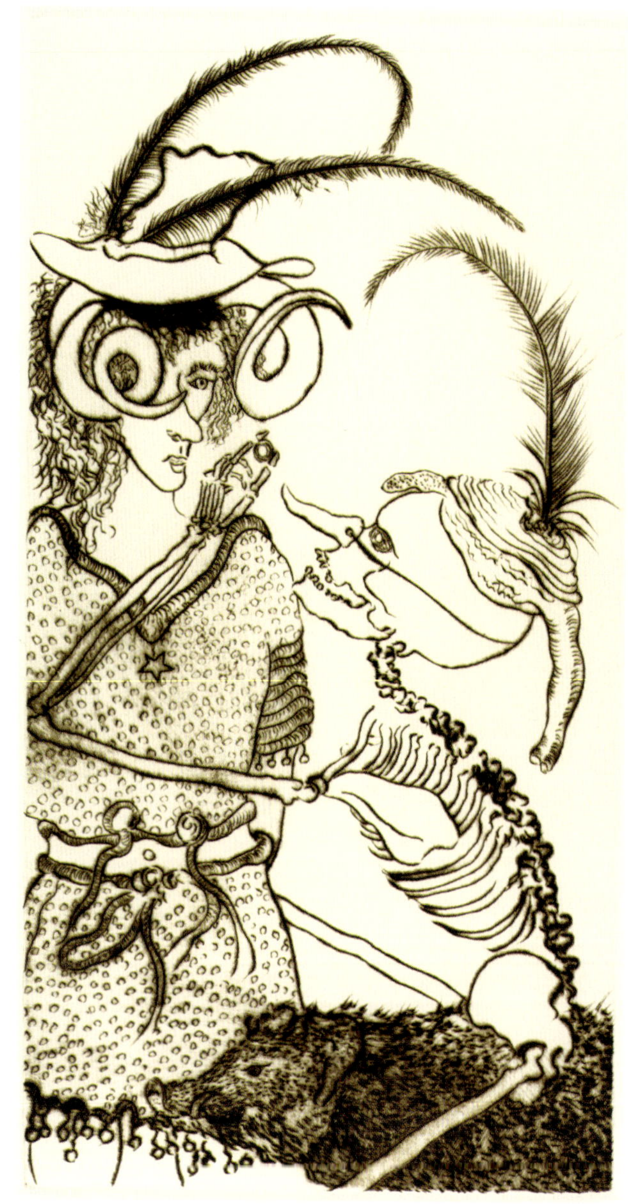

PLATE 139
The betrothal of Uncle Skulky, from
The Irreverences, Provocations, &
Connivances of Uncle Skulky
2003
Ed. 17; 3 artist's proofs
Drypoint
9 x 4¾ in.

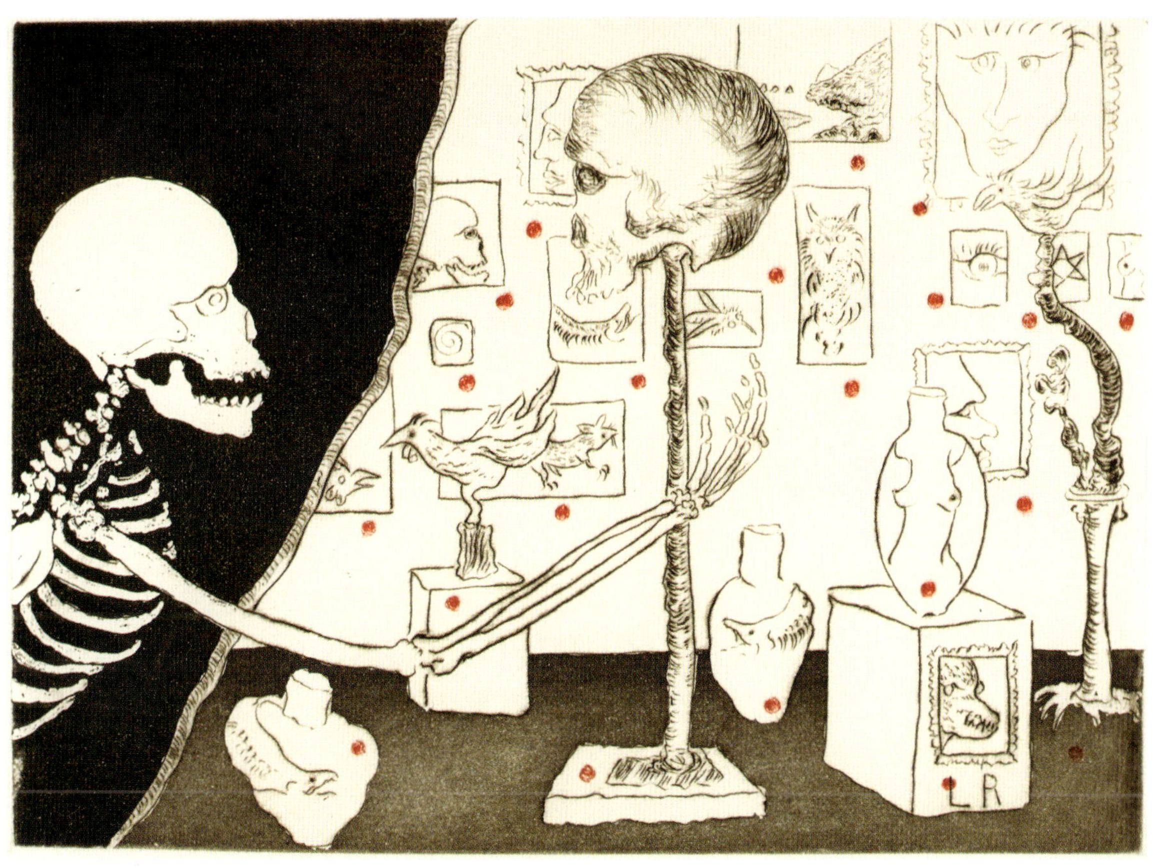

PLATE 140
The pompous, arrogant, copycat Uncle Skulky sells out another exhibition, from *The Irreverences, Provocations, & Connivances of Uncle Skulky*
2003
Ed. 15; 5 artist's proofs
Drypoint, spitbite; 2 copper plates
5 x 7 in.

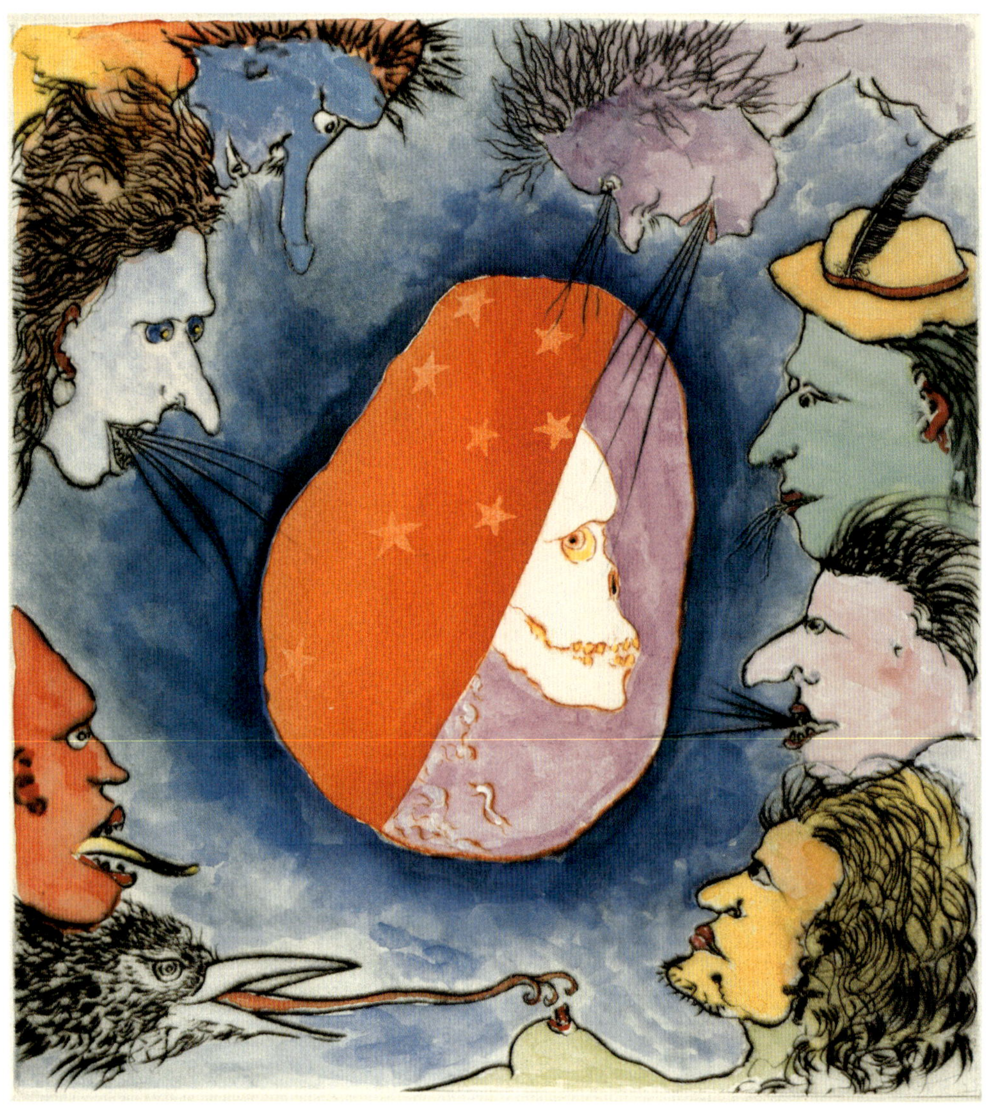

PLATE 141
The resplendent Uncle Skulky leers from behind his curtain of stars as his dolled-up and pompous detractors, like fetid bits of odium, gather to mock him, from *The Irreverences, Provocations, & Connivances of Uncle Skulky*
2003
Ed. 15; 3 artist's proofs
Drypoint, aquatint, spitbite, hand-colored with watercolor and colored pencils; 3 copper plates
7⅞ x 7¼ in.

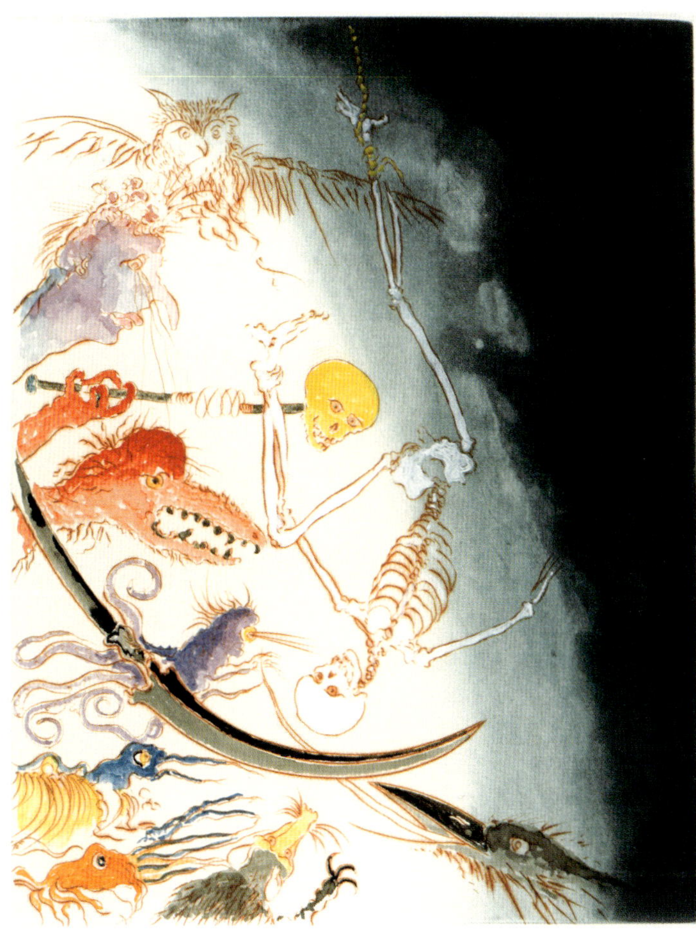

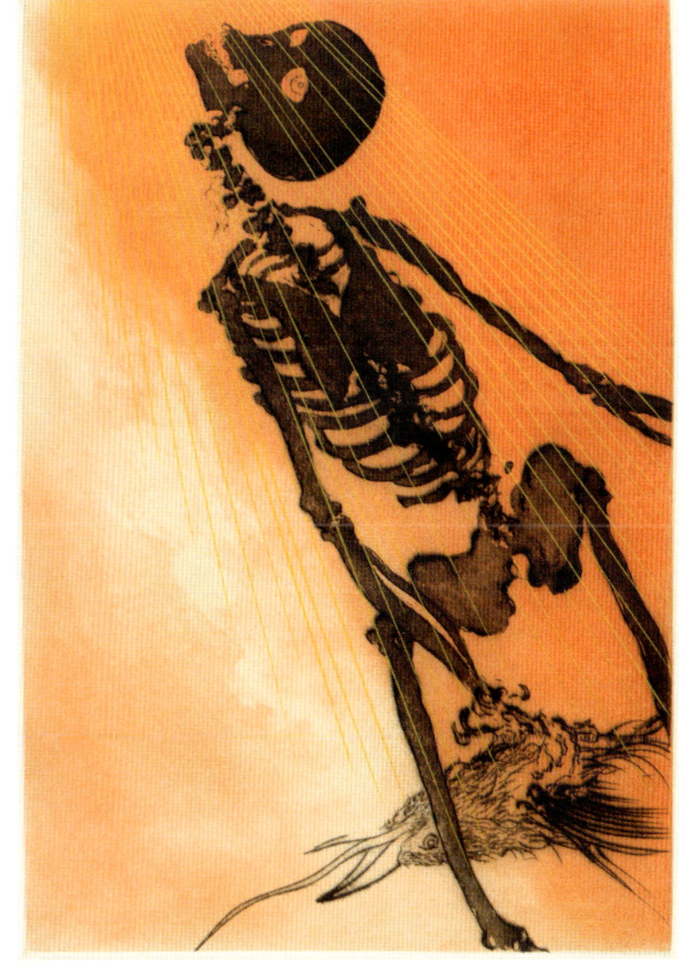

PLATE 142
Uncle Skulky is accosted by a few of his Demons, from *The Irreverences, Provocations, & Connivances of Uncle Skulky*
2003
Ed. 15; 3 artist's proofs
Drypoint, spitbite, hand-colored; 2 copper plates
9 x 7 in.

PLATE 143
The Transcendence of Uncle Skulky, from *The Irreverences, Provocations, & Connivances of Uncle Skulky*
2003
Ed. 15; 2 artist's proofs
Drypoint, spitbite; 3 copper plates
7⅛ x 5 in.

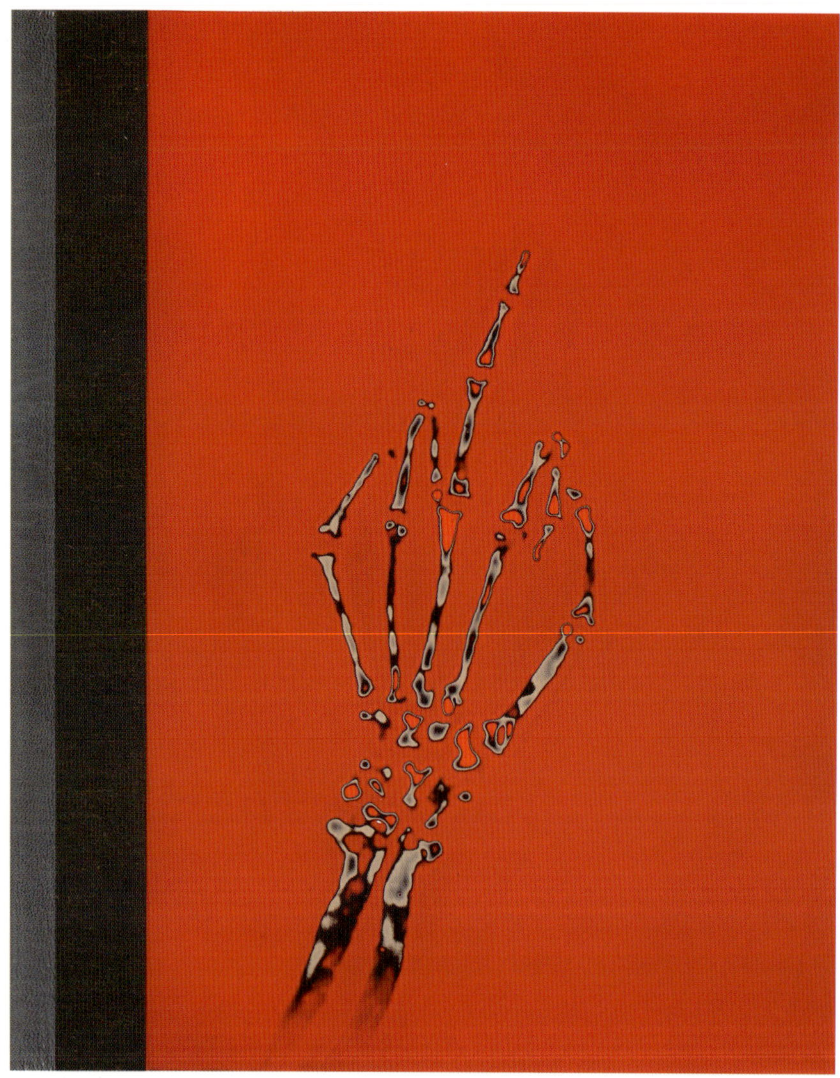

PLATES 144–145
Uncle Skulky
2004
Published by Crab Quill Press, Walla Walla, Washington
Ed. 6
Handmade book with lacquer cover
14⅜ x 11⅝ x 1⅞ in.
Collection of Frank and Jane Boyden, Otis, Oregon

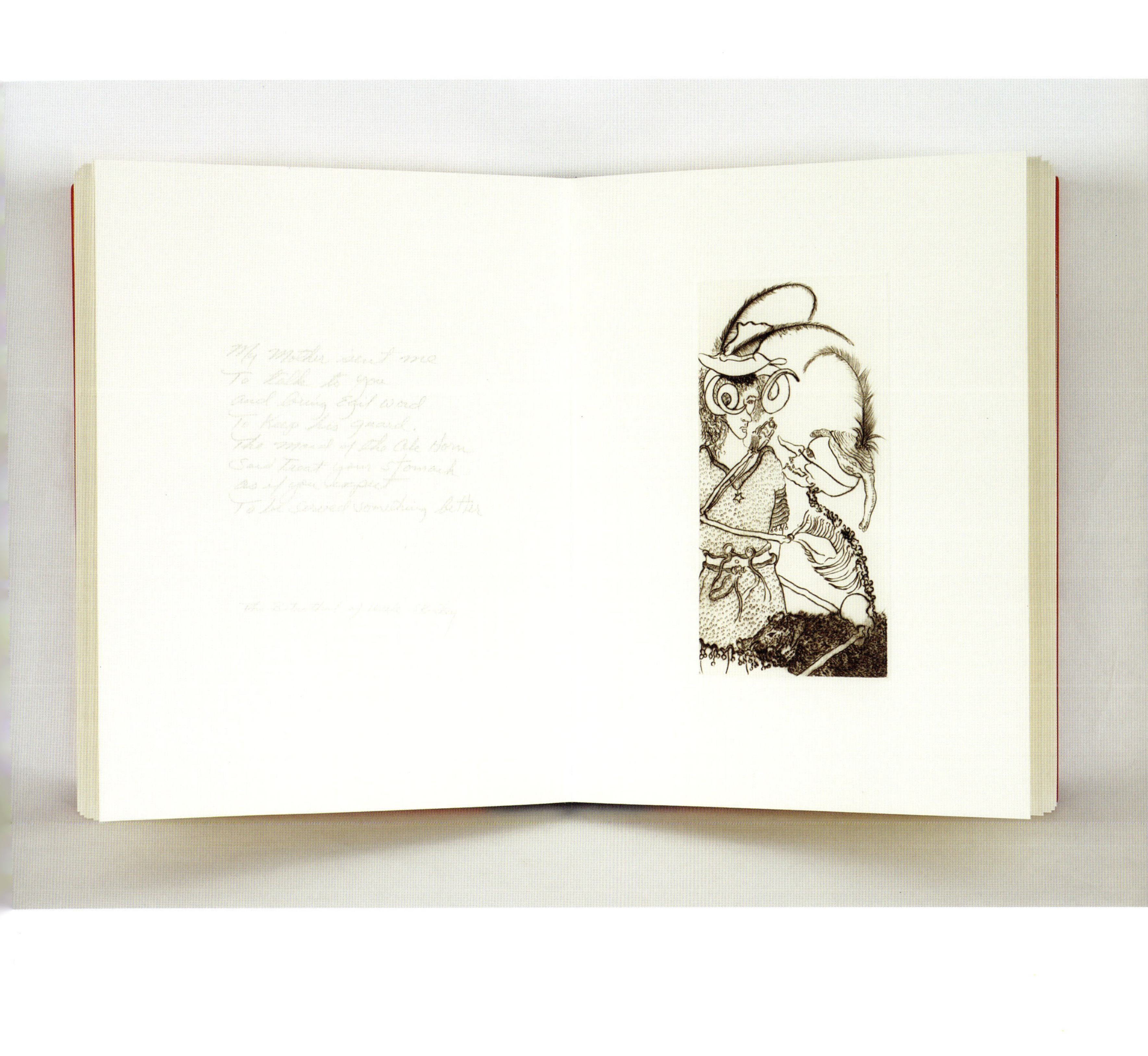
My Mother sent me
To talk to you
And bring Evil word
To keep his guard.
Said Treat your stomach
as if you expect
To be served something better

PLATE 146
The Field of Aki: A Translation of a Poem by Kakinomoto no Asomi Hitomaro
Translation by Edward Morris, prints by Frank Boyden
2004
Published by Crab Quill Press, Walla Walla, Washington
Ed. 6
Handmade book
$10\frac{3}{4}$ x 29 x $1\frac{1}{2}$ in.
Collection of Frank and Jane Boyden, Otis, Oregon

Frank Boyden: A Chronology

1942

Born to Allen and Margery Boyden of Portland, Oregon. Father was a surgeon raised in Pendleton; mother was originally from Philadelphia. Frank is the oldest of three sons; his brothers are Allen and Bradley. Frank attends the Gable School (now Catlin Gable) through the eighth grade.

1957–1960

Attended The Taft School, in Watertown, Connecticut. At Taft, met art instructor Mark Potter. With Potter, learned about painting and drawing. Began painting seriously.

1960

Returned to Portland and spent senior year at Lincoln High School. Met Oregon artist LaVerne Krause, who introduced him to Louis Bunce, William Givler, and Carl and Hilda Morris. Painted at Sauvie Island with Krause and other artists.

His painting was juried into Oregon Artists exhibition, Portland Art Museum (work also accepted for the 1963, 1966, 1970, and 1972 shows).

1961–1965

Attended Colorado College, Colorado Springs. Teachers include Bernard Arnest, Herman Snyder, and Mary Chenoweth. Focused on painting. Made first print in 1963.

Married Jane Humphrey in 1965.

1965–1968

Frank and Jane attended Yale University, where she received her MA in music; he graduated with his BFA and MFA degrees. Frank intended to study printmaking but shifted his major to painting. Studied with Jack Tworkov and Al Held; took seminars with Helen Frankenthaler, Robert Motherwell, and Clement Greenberg.

1968–1971

Had first one-person exhibition of paintings at the Portland Art Museum.

Taught painting and contemporary art history, University of New Mexico, Albuquerque.

Continues painting, began making ceramics with Jenny Lind.

Spent two months visting the caves of central and southern France.

1970

With Jane, conceived, organized, and built Sitka Center for Art and Ecology, Otis, Oregon.

1971

Settled on Oregon coast and continued building Sitka.

Son Ian born.

Moved away from painting to focus on ceramics.

1976

Solo exhibition of ceramics at Hoffman Gallery, Oregon School of Arts and Crafts, Portland.

1977

Received Individual Artist Grant from the Oregon Arts Commission; studied ceramics in jungles of Peru and Ecuador.

Exhibited in group shows in Oregon and Washington.

1978

Received award for excellence in ceramics, Oregon Crafts.

Exhibited in solo and group shows in California, Oregon, and Japan.

Studied ceramics in the jungles of Peru and Ecuador for three months.

1979

Exhibited in solo and group shows in Oregon, Washington, and Japan.

1980

Received commission for steel-and-clay wall relief sculptures at the Hult Performing Arts Center, Eugene, Oregon.

Exhibited in solo and group shows in California, Oregon, Washington, and Washington, D.C.

1981

Received National Endowment for the Arts Crafts Fellowship.

Completed corten steel piece for park at mouth of Siletz River, Lincoln City, Oregon.

Exhibited in solo and group shows in New York, North Carolina, Oregon, and Washington, D.C.

1982

Exhibited in solo and group shows in California, New Mexico, New York, North Carolina, Oregon, and Washington.

1983

Commissioned to make 1983 Governor's Arts Awards.

Exhibited in solo and group shows in California, Montana, New Mexico, and Oregon.

1984

Constructed the first anagama kiln in Oregon.

Began making prints at North Light Editions with Myrna Burkes and Vicki Vanderslice.

Exhibited in solo and group shows in California, New Mexico, New York, Oregon, Vermont, and Washington.

1985

Began making drypoints with Tom Prochaska and Martha Pfanschmidt (who would go on to found MARS Atelier in Portland).

Exhibited in solo and group shows in California, Ohio, Oregon, Canada, and Ireland.

Headed ceramics section at two-week conference "Craftsmen and their Environments," in Ballyvaughan, Ireland.

Artist-in-residence, National College of Art and Design, Oslo, Norway.

1986

Works at Arabia Porcelein factory in Finland.

Visits Soviet Union where he meets with clay artists in Leningrad and subsequently publishes their work in *Studio Potter* periodical.

1988

Lectures and conducts workshops throughout Australia.

1991

Received Oregon Arts Commission grant to travel to Russia.

Began showing at Laura Russo Gallery, Portland.

Edition of prints for Oregon State Department of Corrections.

Conceived and organized the Margery Davis Boyden Writer's Residency Program with his brother Bradley Boyden.

Exhibited in solo and group shows in Arizona, Iowa, Nevada, Oregon, the Netherlands, and Norway.

Works in Riga, Latvia.

1992

Commissions to make bronze sculptures for the Oregon State Hospital Forensic Center; the Oregon Coast Aquarium, Newport; and the Vietnam Memorial Park, Newport.

Commission for marble sculptures for new concert hall, Krasnoyarsk, Russia (Siberia). Not completed due to political environment.

Lectured in Helsinki and Posio, Finland, and in Krasnoyarsk, Russia.

Exhibited in solo and group shows in Missouri, Oregon, Washington, D.C., and Finland.

1993

Exhibited in solo and group shows in Arizona, Connecticut, Oregon, and Denmark.

1995

Received Oregon Governor's Art Award.

Commission for three bronze sculptures, Portland Community College, Rock Creek Campus.

Designed and built exterior of kiln and foundry facility at Western Oregon University, Monmouth.

Began working with Julia D'Amario.

Exhibited in solo and group shows in Oregon and Denmark.

1996

25 Years of Clay, a retrospective at Contemporary Crafts Gallery, Portland.

Exhibited *Triumph Suite* (prints and bronzes) at Laura Russo Gallery (this suite includes *Stances*) .

Commission for Doernbecher Children's Hospital entry and lobby, Portland.

Exhibited in solo and group shows in Idaho, Kentucky, Montana, and Oregon.

Traveled to China to visit son Ian, who was studying there.

1997

Collaborated with son Ian on the book *A Carousel at Birth*, with poetry by Ian and prints by Boyden. Printed at Salient Seedling Press, Portland. (As of 2006, there have been seven such projects.)

Ian Boyden founded Crab Quill Press, Walla Walla, Washington.

Commission for Justice Center Complex Sculpture Park, Hillsboro, Oregon.

Exhibited in solo and group shows in Oregon, Missouri, and Washington.

1998

Commission for Washington Park Zoo, Portland.

Exhibited in solo and group shows in Illinois, Maryland, Washington, and the Netherlands.

Gordon Gilkey asked Boyden to make an archive of his prints at the Portland Art Museum's Vivian and Gordon Gilkey Center for Graphic Arts.

Makes a major donation of prints to the Hallie Ford Museum of Art, Willamette University, in honor of Maribeth Collins.

1999

Built printmaking studio with press designed by Ray Trayle.

Exhibited in solo and group shows in Iowa and England.

2000

Commission for Tri Met, Portland.

Participated in Open Fire, a five-week symposium held at the International Ceramics Center, Skaelskor, Denmark.

Collaborated with composer William Balcom and son Ian on *Bird Spirits*, printed at Crab Quill Press.

Exhibited in solo and group shows in Oregon, Washington, and Denmark.

2001

Residency at The Glass and Ceramic School on Bornholm, Denmark.

Created patron print for the Vivian and Gordon Gilkey Center for the Graphic Arts, Portland Art Museum (pictured on the cover of this book).

Collaborated with painter and calligrapher Charles Chu and poets Ian Boyden and Jennifer Oakes on *20 Views of Cascade Head*. Printed at Crab Quill Press.

Exhibited in solo and group shows in New Mexico, Oregon, and Vermont.

2002

Commission for City of Bend, Oregon.

Participated in symposium "The Magnificent 5," Seabeck, Washington.

Exhibited in solo and group shows in Florida, Missouri, New York, and Oregon.

Collaborated with artist Rick Bartow on *Parts and Pieces*, a book that includes eight drawings and eight prints by each artist. Printed at Crab Quill Press.

Makes a second major donation of prints to the Hallie Ford Museum of Art, Willamette University, in honor of Maribeth Collins.

2003

Residency with Tom Coleman and Janet Mansfield, Finch Pottery, Bailey, North Carolina.

Commission to make commemorative sculpture for poet William Stafford.

Commission for Tri Met, Portland.

Prints selected for Oregon Governor's Arts Award.

Collaborated with poet (and daughter-in-law) Jennifer Boyden on *Evidence of Night*. Printed at Crab Quill Press.

Joined Davidson Galleries, Seattle, Washington.

Made fourteen prints for *The Field of Aki*, based on a poem written in 693 by Hitomaro, translated by Ed Morris. Printed at Crab Quill Press.

Exhibits in solo and group shows in Ohio, Oregon, and London.

2004

Commissions for Washington State Police Forensic Crime lab building, Cheney, and for Kincade Curlicue Corridor Stones, Lake Oswego, Oregon.

Exhibited in solo and group shows in Oregon and Washington.

Exhibited the Uncle Skulky suite at Laura Russo Gallery and Davidson Galleries; exhibition accompanied by catalogue, *The Irreverences, Provocations, & Connivances of Uncle Skulky*, designed by Ian Boyden and published by the Portland Art Museum. The prints and two drawings were also published at Crab Quill Press in a limited-edition book with lacquer cover.

2005

Conceived and printed *The Empathies* suite.

Exhibited in solo and group shows in Maryland and Oregon.

Caught a lot of salmon.

2006

Retrospective exhibition of prints and books at the Hallie Ford Museum of Art, Willamette University, Salem, Oregon, accompanied by a major book.

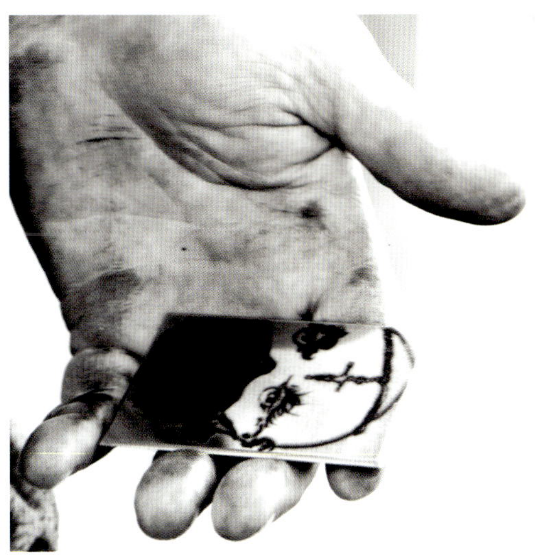

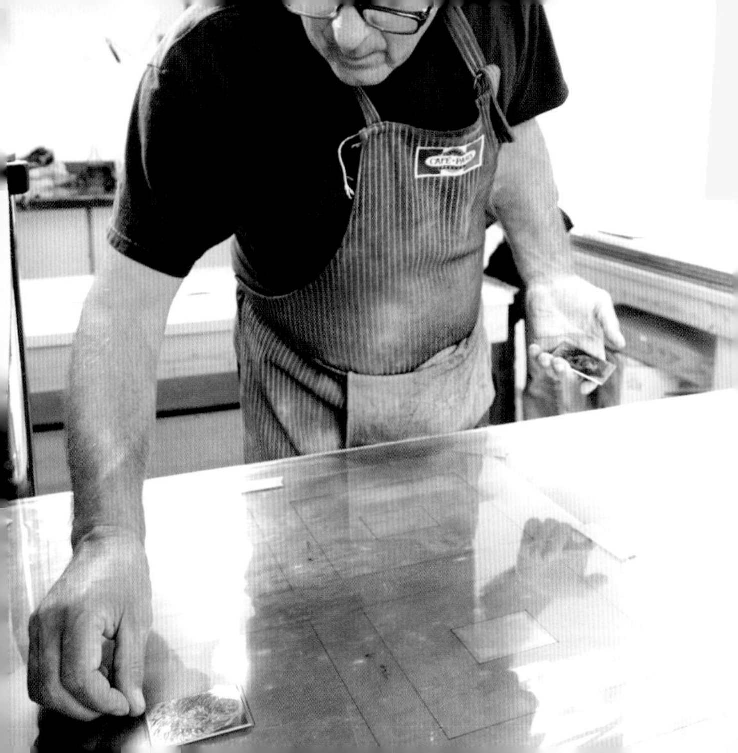

Checklist of the Exhibition

Height precedes width precedes depth.

All works are from the collection of the Hallie Ford Museum of Art, Willamette University, Salem, Oregon, gift of Frank and Jane Boyden in honor of Maribeth Collins unless otherwise noted.

Birth of Fossils
1984–85
Ed. 40
3-color lithograph
22½ x 30 in.
PLATE 1

Changes 1
1984–85
Ed. 40
2-color lithograph
8⅛ x 9⅞ in.
PLATE 2

Changes 2
1984–85
Ed. 40
2-color lithograph
9¼ x 8⅛ in.
PLATE 3

Changes 3
1984–85
Ed. 30
2-color lithograph
9 x 7¾ in.
PLATE 4

Changes 4
1984–85
Ed. 30
2-color lithograph
9 x 7¾ in.
PLATE 5

Changes 9
1984–85
Ed. 40
2-color lithograph
7½ x 9⅝ in.
PLATE 10

Changes 10
1984–85
Ed. 40
2-color lithograph
7 x 9¼ in.
PLATE 11

Heron Reflections 1
1984–85
Ed. 19
2-color lithograph
11¼ x 11⅝ in.
PLATE 12

Heron Reflections 2
1984–85
Ed. 24
2-color lithograph
11½ x 11 in.
PLATE 13

Tule
1984–85
Ed. 20
Lithograph
22 x 24 in.
PLATE 15

Dream Lightning
1985
Ed. 40
Drypoint
4¼ x 5½ in.
PLATE 16

Death Forming a Hummingbird Dream
1986–87
Ed. 40
Drypoint
9¾ x 11¾ in.
PLATE 17

Crow Foot
1991
Ed. 30
Drypoint, aquatint
17½ x 23½ in.
PLATE 18

Clock of Fall
1993–94
Ed. 45
Silkscreen
29½ x 42 in.
PLATE 19

Maelstrom for Shimmering Spines
1993–94
Ed. 14/State 1, 14/State 2
Silkscreen
32 x 38 in. each
PLATES 20–21

Much of What Is Seen Is Not
1993–94
Ed. 45
Silkscreen
29½ x 42 in.
PLATE 22

Traces 1
1994–95
Ed. 22
Drypoint
3¾ x 3¼ in.
PLATE 24

Traces 2
1994–95
Ed. 22
Drypoint
3¼ x 3¾ in.
PLATE 25

Traces 3
1994–95
Ed. 22
Drypoint
3¾ x 3¼ in.
PLATE 26

Traces 5
1994–95
Ed. 22
Drypoint
3¾ x 3¼ in.
PLATE 28

Traces 8
1994–95
Ed. 22
Drypoint
3¾ x 3¼ in.
PLATE 31

Traces 10
1994–95
Ed. 22
Drypoint
3¾ x 3¼ in.
PLATE 33

Interstices, A Conversation with Alders 1
1996
Ed. 10
Line etching
5¼ x 3½ in.
PLATE 34

Interstices, A Conversation with Alders 3
1996
Ed. 10
Line etching
5¼ x 3½ in.
PLATE 36

Interstices, A Conversation with Alders 5
1996
Ed. 10
Line etching
5¼ x 3½ in.
PLATE 38

Interstices, A Conversation with Alders 6
1996
Ed. 10
Sugarlift
5¼ x 3½ in.
PLATE 39

Interstices, A Conversation with Alders 8
1996
Ed. 10
Line etching
5¼ x 3½ in.
PLATE 41

Interstices, A Conversation with Alders 12
1996
Ed. 10
Aquatint
5¼ x 3½ in.
PLATE 45

Stances 1
1996
Ed. 30
Drypoint printed on tan flat
6⅜ x 8 in.
PLATE 46

Stances 2
1996
Ed. 30
Drypoint printed on tan flat
6⅜ x 8 in.
PLATE 47

Stances 4
1996
Ed. 30
Drypoint printed on tan flat
6⅜ x 8 in.
PLATE 48

Stances 5
1996
Ed. 30
Drypoint printed on tan flat
8 x 6⅜ in.
PLATE 49

Stances 8
1996
Ed. 30
Drypoint printed on tan flat
6⅜ x 8 in.
PLATE 50

Stances 9
1996
Ed. 30
Drypoint printed on tan flat
6⅜ x 8 in.
PLATE 51

Dead Raven
1996–97
Ed. 20
Drypoint
10 x 22¼ in.
PLATE 54

A Carousel at Birth
Poem by Ian Boyden, prints by Frank Boyden
1997
Published by Salient Seedling Press, Portland, Oregon
Ed. 25
Handmade book
6¼ x 5¾ x ¾ in.
Collection of Frank and Jane Boyden, Otis, Oregon
PLATES 68–69

Cave Owl
1998
Ed. 15
Cliché verre
10½ x 9 in.
PLATE 77

Owl of the Crackling Plain
1998
Ed. 15
Cliché verre
9 x 8½ in.
PLATE 78

Soft Owl Flying
1998
Ed. 10
Cliché verre
10 x 11 in.
PLATE 79

Gifts of the Sky 1
1999
Ed. 15
Aquatint, spitbite
6¾ x 4½ in.
PLATE 80

Gifts of the Sky 2
1999
Ed. 15
Aquatint, drypoint, spitbite, mezzotint
6¾ x 4½ in.
PLATE 81

Gifts of the Sky 3
1999
Ed. 15
Aquatint, drypoint, spitbite
6¾ x 4½ in.
PLATE 82

Gifts of the Sky 4
1999
Ed. 15
Aquatint, drypoint, spitbite
6¾ x 4½ in.
PLATE 83

Gifts of the Sky 5
1999
Ed. 15
Drypoint, spitbite
6¾ x 4½ in.
PLATE 84

Gifts of the Sky 6
1999
Ed. 15
Drypoint, spitbite
6¾ x 4½ in.
PLATE 85

Gifts of the Sky 7
1999
Ed. 15
Aquatint, drypoint, spitbite
6¾ x 4½ in.
PLATE 86

Gifts of the Sky 8
1999
Ed. 15
Aquatint, drypoint, spitbite
6¾ x 4½ in.
PLATE 87

Gifts of the Sky 9
1999
Ed. 15
Aquatint, drypoint, spitbite
6¾ x 4½ in.
PLATE 88

Gifts of the Sky 10
1999
Ed. 15
Drypoint, line etching, spitbite
6¾ x 4½ in.
PLATE 89

Dance 1
1999–2000
Ed. 10
Drypoint, spitbite
23½ x 10¾ in.
PLATE 90

Dance 2
1999–2000
Ed. 10
Drypoint, spitbite
23½ x 10¾ in.
PLATE 91

Dance 3
1999–2000
Ed. 10
Drypoint, spitbite
23½ x 10¾ in.
PLATE 92

Pajaro de Brujas
1999–2000
Ed. 23
Drypoint
31 x 22¼ in.
PLATE 93

Bird Spirits: Nine Piano Pieces for Jane Boyden
Piano pieces by William Bolcom, prints by Frank Boyden
2000
Published by Crab Quill Press, Walla Walla, Washington
Ed. 15
Handmade book with lacquer cover
11¼ x 14⅜ x 1 in.
Collection of Frank and Jane Boyden, Otis, Oregon
PLATES 52–53

Mockery of the Black Angel and Three Spanish Owls, from the *Black Angel Suite*
2001
Ed. 12
Drypoint, , spitbite
12 x 48 in.
PLATE 94

Violation, from the *Black Angel Suite*
2001
Ed. 12
Drypoint, aquatint, line etching
12 x 48 in.
PLATE 95

Feather at Sandlake Wash
2001
Ed. 10
Drypoint, sugarlift, spitbite
14½ x 31¼ in.
PLATE 97

Parts and Pieces: A Brief Bestiary
Prints and drawings by Rick Bartow and Frank Boyden
2001
Published by Crab Quill Press, Walla Walla, Washington
Ed. 6
Handmade book
11¼ x 9¼ x 1⅜ in.
Collection of Frank and Jane Boyden, Otis, Oregon
PLATES 99–104

Last Flight, from the *Phoenix Suite*
2001
Ed. 10
Sugarlift, drypoint, spitbite
5½ x 7⅛ in.
PLATE 105

Burning Nest, from the *Phoenix Suite*
2001
Ed. 10
Sugarlift, drypoint, spitbite
5⅞ x 5¾ in.
PLATE 106

Conflagration, from the *Phoenix Suite*
2001
Ed. 10
Sugarlift, drypoint, spitbite
6 x 5½ in.
PLATE 107

Resurrection, from the *Phoenix Suite*
2001
Ed. 10
Sugarlift, drypoint, spitbite
7½ x 3¾ in.
PLATE 108

First Flight of the Phoenix, from the *Phoenix Suite*
2001
Ed. 10
Sugarlift, drypoint, spitbite
7½ x 3⅞ in.
PLATE 109

Twenty Views of Cascade Head
Poems by J. Cailin Oakes and Ian Boyden, prints by Charles Chu and Frank Boyden
2001
Published by Crab Quill Press, Walla Walla, Washington
Ed. 10
Handmade book
8½ x 7 x 1¼ in.
Collection of Frank and Jane Boyden, Otis, Oregon
PLATES 75–76

Wind, Fog, and Strange Light at Whiskey Run
2001
Ed. 16
Aquatint, drypoint, spitbite
8¾ x 22½ in.
PLATE 111

Reflections at Nexo
2001–2
Ed. 10
Sugarlift, line etching, spitbite
6⅜ x 24 in.
PLATE 113

River Sky across Karst
2001–2
Ed. 5/State 1
Sugarlift, spitbite
6 x 24 in.
PLATE 114

Above and Below
2002
Ed. 10
Spitbite, sugarlift
6⅝ x 24 in.
PLATE 115

Arc
2002
Ed. 10
Spitbite, sugarlift; 2 plates
6 x 21 in.
PLATE 117

Arc at Hells Gap
2002
Ed. 10
Spitbite, sugarlift; 2 plates
6 x 21 in.
PLATE 116

Crowning
2002
Ed. 10
Line etching, spitbite, sugarlift; 2 plates
4⅝ x 21 in.
PLATE 118

Landscape with Densities
2002
Ed. 7
Spitbite, sugarlift, line etching
6 x 20⅞ in.
PLATE 119

Lens with Rembrandt, from the *Lenses Suite*
2002
Ed. 15
Spitbite, drypoint, line etching
3⅝ x 3⅛ in.
PLATE 122

Lens with Spines, from the *Lenses Suite*
2002
Ed. 15
Spitbite, drypoint, line etching
4⅜ x 4⅛ in.
PLATE 123

Lens with Bird Spirit, from the *Lenses Suite*
2002
Ed. 15
Spitbite, drypoint, sugarlift
5¾ x 5⅜ in.
PLATE 124

Lens with Owl, from the *Lenses Suite*
2002
Ed. 15
Spitbite, drypoint, line etching
7¾ x 6⅝ in.
PLATE 126

Lens with Black Idea, from the *Lenses Suite*
2002
Ed. 15
Spitbite, drypoint, sugarlift
7½ x 5⅜ in.
PLATE 127

Moon Lens with Heron, from the *Lenses Suite*
2002
Ed. 15
Spitbite, drypoint
8 x 8 in.
PLATE 128

Wasteland Caressed
2002
Ed. 10
Spitbite, sugarlift, line etching
6⅞ x 21 in.
PLATE 120

Universe
2002
Ed. 10; 2 artist's proofs
Drypoint, spitbite
15½ x 17 in.
PLATE 130

Black Arc
2003
Ed. 12; 4 artist's proofs
Sugarlift, spitbite
7½ x 17⅞ in.
PLATE 131

Evidence of Night
Poems by Jennifer Boyden, prints and drawings by Frank Boyden
2003
Published by Crab Quill Press, Walla Walla, Washington
Ed. 15
Handmade book
15⅜ x 9 x 1 in.
Collection of Frank and Jane Boyden, Otis, Oregon
PLATES 132–133

The Transfiguration of Uncle Skulky, from *The Irreverences, Provocations, & Connivances of Uncle Skulky*
2003
Ed. 10; 6 artist's proofs; 2-color trial proofs
Drypoint, spitbite, hand-colored; 2 copper plates
7 x 4⅞ in.
PLATE 134

The Possession of Uncle Skulky, from *The Irreverences, Provocations, & Connivances of Uncle Skulky*
2003
Ed. 16; 4 artist's proofs
Drypoint, aquatint; 2 copper plates, one wiped "à la poupée"
8 x 7⅜ in.
PLATE 135

Uncle Skulky bekons the artist from his mirror of illusions, from *The Irreverences, Provocations, & Connivances of Uncle Skulky*
2003
Ed. 16; 5 artist's proofs
Drypoint, aquatint, spitbite
5 x 7 in.
PLATE 136

Uncle Skulky appears to James Ensor and mocks him with a fake nose, from *The Irreverences, Provocations, & Connivances of Uncle Skulky*
2003
Ed. 15; 4 artist's proofs
Line etching, drypoint, spitbite; 2 copper plates
5 x 4 in.
PLATE 137

Uncle Skulky examines some fluff, from *The Irreverences, Provocations, and Connivances of Uncle Skulky*
2003
Ed. 12; 6 artist's proofs
Drypoint; 1 copper plate
4½ x 5 in.
PLATE 138

The betrothal of Uncle Skulky, from *The Irreverences, Provocations, & Connivances of Uncle Skulky*
2003
Ed. 17; 3 artist's proofs
Drypoint
9 x 4¾ in.
PLATE 139

The pompous, arrogant, copycat Uncle Skulky sells out another exhibition, from *The Irreverences, Provocations, & Connivances of Uncle Skulky*
2003
Ed. 15; 5 artist's proofs
Drypoint, spitbite; 1 copper plate
5 x 7 in.
PLATE 140

The resplendent Uncle Skulky leers from behind his curtain of stars as his dolled-up and pompous detractors, like fetid bits of odium, gather to mock him, from *The Irreverences, Provocations, & Connivances of Uncle Skulky*
2003
Ed. 15; 3 artist's proofs
Drypoint, aquatint, spitbite, hand-colored with watercolor and colored pencils; 3 copper plates
7⅞ x 7¼ in.
PLATE 141

Uncle Skulky is accosted by a few of his Demons, from *The Irreverences, Provocations, & Connivances of Uncle Skulky*
2003
Ed. 15; 3 artist's proofs
Drypoint, spitbite, hand-colored; 2 copper plates
9 x 7 in.
PLATE 142

The Transcendence of Uncle Skulky, from *The Irreverences, Provocations, & Connivances of Uncle Skulky*
2003
Ed. 15; 2 artist's proofs
Drypoint, spitbite; 3 copper plates
7⅛ x 5 in.
PLATE 143

The Field of Aki: A Translation of a Poem by Kakinomoto no Asomi Hitomaro
Translation by Edward Morris, prints by Frank Boyden
2004
Published by Crab Quill Press, Walla Walla, Washington
Ed. 6
Handmade book
10¾ x 29 x 1½ in.
Collection of Frank and Jane Boyden, Otis, Oregon
PLATE 146

Uncle Skulky
2004
Published by Crab Quill Press, Walla Walla, Washington
Ed. 6
Handmade book with lacquer cover
14⅜ x 11⅝ x 1⅞ in.
Collection of Frank and Jane Boyden, Otis, Oregon
PLATES 144–145

Empathies 1
2005
Ed. 5; 2 artist's proofs
Drypoint
29 x 29 in.
PLATE 147

Empathies 2
2005
Ed. 5; 2 artist's proofs
Drypoint
29 x 29 in.
PLATE 148

Empathies 3
2005
Ed. 5; 2 artist's proofs
Drypoint
29 x 29 in.
PLATE 149

Empathies 4
2005
Ed. 5; 2 artist's proofs
Drypoint
29 x 29 in.
PLATE 150

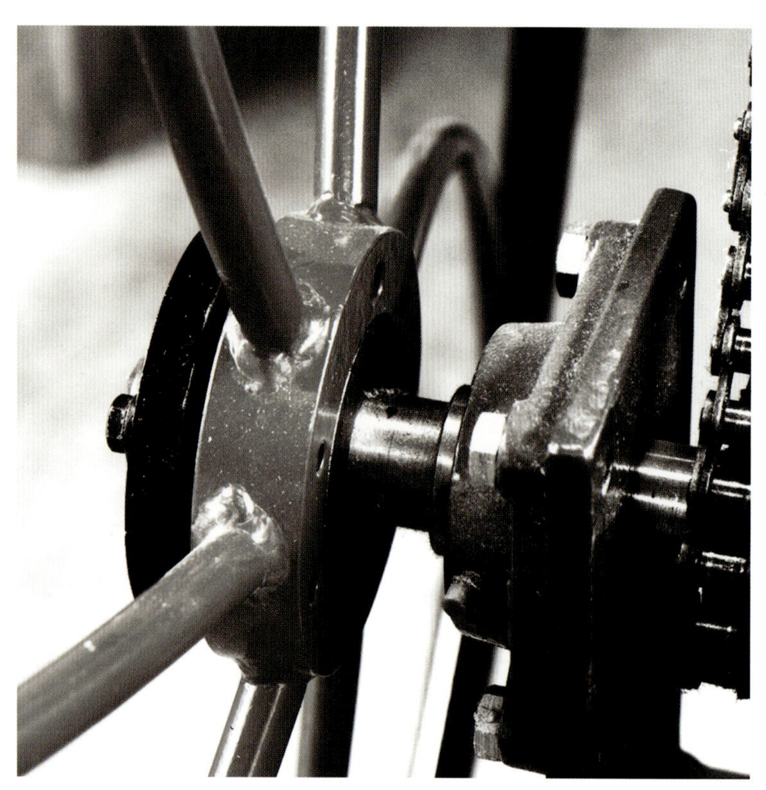